SUBSTANCE
USE AND ABUSE

HEALTH AND DISEASE IN SOCIETY

SUBSTANCE
USE AND ABUSE

EDITED BY KARA ROGERS, SENIOR EDITOR, BIOMEDICAL SCIENCES

Britannica
Educational Publishing

IN ASSOCIATION WITH

ROSEN
EDUCATIONAL SERVICES

Published in 2011 by Britannica Educational Publishing
(a trademark of Encyclopædia Britannica, Inc.)
in association with Rosen Educational Services, LLC
29 East 21st Street, New York, NY 10010.

First Edition

Britannica Educational Publishing
Michael I. Levy: Executive Editor
J.E. Luebering: Senior Manager
Marilyn L. Barton: Senior Coordinator, Production Control
Steven Bosco: Director, Editorial Technologies
Lisa S. Braucher: Senior Producer and Data Editor
Yvette Charboneau: Senior Copy Editor
Kathy Nakamura: Manager, Media Acquisition
Kara Rogers: Senior Editor, Biomedical Sciences

Rosen Educational Services
Jeanne Nagle: Senior Editor
Nelson Sá: Art Director
Cindy Reiman: Photography Manager
Nicole Russo: Designer
Matthew Cauli: Cover Design
Introduction by Stephanie Watson

Library of Congress Cataloging-in-Publication Data

Substance use and abuse/edited by Kara Rogers.
    p. cm. — (Health and disease in society)
"In association with Britannica Educational Publishing, Rosen Educational Services."
Includes bibliographical references and index.
ISBN 978-1-61530-338-0 (library binding)
1. Substance abuse. I. Rogers, Kara.
HV4998.S836 2011
616.86—dc22

2010032761

Manufactured in the United States of America

On the cover: © www.istockphoto.com/Nicholas Monu

On pages 1, 26, 45, 71, 92, 106, 129, 145, 164: *An Afghani man smoking crystal
methamphetamine. Behrouz Mehri/AFP/Getty Images*

CONTENTS

7

31

52

CHAPTER 4: NONNARCOTIC DRUGS, CANNABIS, AND PERFORMANCE-ENHANCING DRUGS   71

CHAPTER 5: ALCOHOL CONSUMPTION AND HEALTH   92

109

117

138

167

171

175

INTRODUCTION

Films and television shows often portray substance abuse as an issue confined to secret back rooms and dark alleys, the purview of the weak and vile. The truth is that the use and misuse of drugs, legal or otherwise, doesn't discriminate by race, gender, age, or socioeconomic status. Alcohol and tobacco are similarly addictive, prone to abuse, and damaging to human health.

In this volume, readers will discover many of the issues related to substance use and abuse. Included are a discussion of substances that have a high propensity for abuse, the properties that make them so addictive, and the physiological factors that lead to dependence. Also covered in these chapters are the historical factors that have contributed to alcohol, tobacco, and drug use throughout the centuries, as well as the moral, ethical, and legislative arguments that have been at the heart of the debate over the use of addictive substances.

Substance use is widespread. So is abuse. Studies and surveys have indicated that every year, the United States spends more than half a trillion dollars to pay for the costs of substance abuse. One of the most significant reasons for these high costs is the damaging health effects of alcohol, tobacco, and drugs. Cigarette smoking is responsible for 87 percent of deaths from lung cancer and 20 percent of heart disease deaths each year. About one-third of AIDS cases and the majority of hepatitis C cases can be traced to intravenous drug use.

Health care isn't the only cost involved in substance abuse. Also significant are the consequences of people's actions while they are involved with drugs and alcohol use. In the United States, drug use is implicated in about half of all major crimes, and drug-related offenses often land adults in federal prisons.

The use of drugs and alcohol is certainly nothing new. These substances have been around for thousands of years. Centuries ago, drugs that are now considered recreational were used for medicinal purposes. In the Andean region of South America, chewing coca (cocaine) leaves helped relieve both hunger and altitude sickness. Narcotics such as opium were prescribed by ancient physicians as a curative. Combined with camphor, opium was transformed into paregoric, which was used to calm the digestive tract and treat diarrhea. In 1898 heroin—which is now known to be the most addictive opiate—was sold on the commercial market as a pain reliever. Because of cocaine's potent abilities to dry up the nasal passages, it was recommended for sinus problems and hay fever in the early 20th century. This led to the nasal use of cocaine that continues today.

In other cases, certain civilizations have incorporated hallucinogens and other drugs into ritualistic ceremonies. For example, eating peyote—a species of

Alcohol and tobacco use have been around for ages, as this image of gentlemen in a tavern, dated to the 1820s, shows. Hulton Archive/Getty Images

cactus with hallucinogenic properties—had been and remains an important part of the religious rituals of some North American Indians. Peyote was a way for shamans and participants to reach a higher state of being. Native Americans also smoke tobacco in pipes during rituals meant to convey community and peaceful interactions among nations. References to drunkenness date back to ancient Egypt and Mesopotamia.

The way in which people take drugs has changed over time. New delivery methods and formulations made drugs more potent and easier to use. When native peoples used substances for ritual purposes, they ingested them often by simply chewing them or drinking them in a tea. In some cases, such as through specially crafted pipes, they burned plant material and inhaled the smoke. The ability to purify drugs from plants made it possible for drugs to be formulated as pills or injectable fluids. The latter was facilitated by the invention of the hypodermic needle in the 1800s. The hypodermic needle quickly found widespread use in medicine. Soldiers injured during the Civil War were treated with morphine injections. Injecting drugs directly into the bloodstream in this fashion increased the speed of the drug's effect. Upon their return home, many of these men found themselves face-to-face with a new adversary—morphine addiction. The problem was so rampant, addiction to this substance came to be known as the "soldier's disease."

As time went by, new drugs were introduced that were also habit-forming. Scientists experimented in laboratories until they found new ways to stimulate the brain's reward centres, creating drugs such as PCP, barbiturates, and amphetamines. In the 1960s, psychedelic drugs like LSD became popularized in American culture thanks to the efforts of drug gurus like Timothy Leary, a psychologist who advocated drug experimentation for "therapeutic" purposes.

In addition to changes in the development of drugs themselves, the transition of drug use from medicinal and spiritual purposes to recreational ones was due, in part, to changes within communities. The Industrial Revolution also gave rise to another factor that spurred the growth of drug, alcohol, and tobacco use: wealth. With more money—and leisure time—at their disposal, people were able to indulge in a wide variety of pursuits, including drinking and drug use. By the latter part of the 20th century, these pursuits had become firmly ingrained in American culture, and addictive substances had become easily accessible to people of every socioeconomic status.

As drugs and alcohol became more widespread, their use naturally came under greater scrutiny. Calls for controls on the use and abuse of illicit substances poured forth, particularly at the instigation of social reformers and religious groups. Alcohol has been a frequent target of reform. In the late 19th and early 20th centuries, the temperance movement in the United States combined religious and secular objections to alcohol use, with great success. In 1846, Maine became the first state to pass a law prohibiting the sale and use of alcohol. By 1920, it was illegal to drink in the United States due to the Volstead Act, which ushered in the age of Prohibition.

While religious and reform groups have objected to alcohol and drugs for reasons tied to morality, various governments have had mixed responses to legislating substance use. Some leaders sought to protect their citizens against what they saw as the scourge of substance use by enacting laws that were strict to the point of being Draconian. Upon ascending the throne of the Ottoman Empire in the 17th century, Sultan Murad IV forbade the use of tobacco, alcohol, and even coffee. The punishment for imbibing in any of these substances was death. Russians of the same era were either beaten or exiled to the Siberian hinterlands upon their first offense of smoking, which had been outlawed. Those who didn't learn their lesson and continued with their tobacco habit could be executed.

The response to substance use in the United States was less drastic. In the 1860s Chinese labourers were brought in to help build railroads in the American West. A number of these workers were addicted to opium. Fervent anti-Chinese sentiment at the time led to the passage of several laws in the West that prohibited opium smoking and importation. The outlook for Chinese opium users was

even more dire in their home country. In response to the growing problem of opium smuggling and abuse, the country established a law that called for anyone who "clandestinely opens an opium smoking shop" to be "strangled after his term of imprisonment."

Early in the 20th century the focus of substance use control and legislation shifted, as doctors began to realize the addictive and health-damaging potential of drugs and alcohol. In response to health concerns, the United States government enacted the Pure Food and Drug Act of 1906, which required medicine manufacturers to specify on their packaging the amount of opium, heroin, and other habit-forming drugs their products contained. This was followed by the Harrison Narcotics Act of 1914, which regulated the supply of opiates.

After Prohibition was repealed in 1933, people were once again allowed to drink alcohol freely. Yet anti-drug laws grew increasingly more restrictive throughout the 20th century. The Comprehensive Drug Abuse Prevention and Control Act of 1970 led to more severe punishment for drug crimes. In 1971, U.S. Pres. Richard Nixon called drug abuse "public enemy No. 1," and declared a "war" on drugs—a war that Pres. Ronald Reagan escalated in the 1980s. The punishments for drug violations grew more severe.

The tobacco industry, by contrast, enjoyed little regulation in its early years. Instead of viewing tobacco use as a public nuisance, the U.S. government initially saw it as a way to earn significant revenues through taxation. With virtually no restrictions on the sale of tobacco, its use flourished. By the 1950s, tobacco had reached its golden age. People smoked everywhere—in restaurants, airplanes, and offices. It wasn't until the latter part of the 20th century, when reports emerged highlighting the addictiveness of tobacco and linking smoking to cancer and other deadly diseases, that the government began efforts to regulate the tobacco industry. Eventually manufacturers were required to include on their cigarette packages dire warnings about the consequences of smoking. When researchers uncovered the dangerous effects of secondhand smoke, cities worldwide began banning smoking in public places, including restaurants.

As increasingly stricter legislation to regulate substance use was enacted, efforts were under way in the scientific community to better understand the causes of addiction. Scientists learned how drugs target the brain's reward centres and interfere with the way the brain sends, receives, and processes information. They also began to understand that some people are more susceptible to drug and alcohol abuse than others because of their genes, gender, ethnicity, or family background. What researchers have learned about the physiologic processes involved in substance abuse has transformed how society views addiction. Experts now realize that it is a chronic disease that causes changes in the brain's structure and function, rather than simply a moral weakness.

Understanding the processes that underlie addiction is also helping doctors find new ways to treat this disorder. They are developing therapies that prevent withdrawal symptoms and cravings to help addicts more easily transition off drugs, alcohol, and tobacco. One day, doctors might even be able to target the genes that make people susceptible to addition. Until then, the use and abuse of addictive substances will continue to be a point of discussion and debate.

CHAPTER 1

DRUG USE AND ABUSE

Substances that affect the mind and alter mood, emotion, and behaviour have long been used in human societies. Their relationship with and place in society, however, is exceedingly complex. Many substances that have acquired reputations for their abuse actually have legitimate applications and thus can have benefits for a society. For example, in many instances, the ways in which a substance came to be used for purposes of enjoyment or abuse originated from its use for medical purposes. Nicotine, the active ingredient in tobacco, historically was used to treat a variety of human ailments, including headache. This function, however, was superseded by tobacco use for pleasure and by the popularization of practices such as snuffing and smoking.

In other instances, a substance has been used for so long within a society that today many consider it simply a social norm—an element of social culture. The use of alcohol as a social beverage in pubs and taverns, a practice that extends back centuries, illustrates this phenomenon. But alcohol and tobacco, which can be classified as drugs, present difficult problems for societies, in part because of their potentially negative effects on human health. Nicotine, for example, is highly addictive, and tobacco consumption is associated with the development of certain types of cancer.

The use of substances such as alcohol and tobacco is widespread throughout the world, and as a result the number of people affected by their physical and psychological side effects is very high. In comparison, other substances of abuse—namely the mind-altering, or psychotropic, drugs, such as cocaine and opium—are used and abused on a much smaller scale. This is largely because their use is often not condoned by societies, and in fact they are often illegal to possess in the first place. Thus, rather than being popular across a society, these substances are abused sporadically, often within small geographical pockets, such as in certain regions of countries or in large cities or small towns. The geographical and social patterns of abuse of such drugs are influenced significantly by socioeconomic factors.

The powerful effects on the mind and the severely addictive properties of psychotropic drugs are a major source of drug-related problems in societies worldwide. Likewise, alcohol and tobacco cause hundreds of thousands of preventable deaths globally each year. Because these drugs can have such severe physiological, psychological, and social effects, many governments regulate their use. Yet, substance use and abuse continues on an enormous scale today, for reasons that are sometimes difficult to understand. Indeed, at the root of all substance use and abuse lies the extraordinarily complex element of human behaviour,

A Japanese man, with an alcoholic drink and burning cigarette in hand. Substance use and abuse knows no boundaries with regard to geography, race, gender, or economic status. Asaki Koshikawa/Aflo/Getty Images

influenced heavily by motivation and perception.

DEFINING DRUG ABUSE

Drug abuse is the excessive, maladaptive, or addictive use of drugs for nonmedical purposes despite social, psychological, and physical problems that may arise from such use. Abused substances include agents such as anabolic steroids, which are used by some athletes to accelerate muscular development and increase strength and which can cause heart disease, liver damage, and other physical problems. Abused drugs also include psychotropic agents, substances that affect the user's mental state and are used to produce changes in mood, feeling, and perception. The latter category, which has a much longer history of abuse than anabolic steroids, includes opium (and its derivatives, such as heroin), hallucinogens, barbiturates, cocaine, amphetamines, tranquilizers, the several forms of cannabis, and alcohol.

The history of nonmedical drug consumption is ancient. The discovery of the mood-altering qualities of fermented fruits and substances such as opium has led to their use and, often, acceptance into society. Just as alcohol has a recognized social place in the West, so many other psychotropics have been accepted in different societies.

The major problem that arises from the consumption of psychotropic drugs is dependence, the compulsion to use the drug despite any deterioration in health, work, or social activities. Dependence varies from drug to drug in its extent and effect. It can be physical or psychological or both. Physical dependence becomes apparent only when the drug intake is decreased or stopped and an involuntary illness called the withdrawal (or abstinence) syndrome occurs. Drugs known to produce physical dependence are the opiates (i.e., opium and its derivatives) and central-nervous-system depressants such as barbiturates and alcohol. Psychological dependence is indicated when the user relies on a drug to produce a feeling of well-being. This type of dependence varies widely with both substance and user. In its most intense form the user becomes obsessed with the drug and focuses virtually all his or her interest and activity on obtaining and using it.

Another related phenomenon is tolerance, a gradual decrease in the effect of a certain dose as the drug is repeatedly taken, with the result that increasingly larger doses are needed to produce the desired effect. Tolerance does not always develop. It is most marked with habitual opiate users. The term *addiction* is often used synonymously with *dependence* but should probably be reserved for drugs known to cause physical dependence.

Other hazards of drug abuse include general risks, such as the danger of diseases that can be communicated by use of nonsterile needles or syringes when drugs are taken by injection. An example of one such disease is AIDS (acquired immune deficiency syndrome), which is caused by HIV (human immunodeficiency virus), an agent that can be readily transmitted through needle sharing with an infected individual. Some hazards are associated with the specific effects of the particular drug—paranoia with high doses of stimulants, for example. In addition, adverse social effects stemming from drug abuse are numerous.

Heroin, an opiate that is not used medically in the United States, is one of the drugs most associated with abuse and addiction in the eyes of the public. In general, opiates are called narcotics because they are used medically to relieve pain and produce sleep. Other opiates that have been abused are opium, morphine, pethidine, codeine, dipipanone, and methadone. Methadone is often used in substitution therapy as a less-addictive opiate that, theoretically at least, can be used to wean the user off heroin and eventually off opiates altogether.

Drugs that either depress or stimulate the central nervous system have long been used for nonmedical reasons. Depressants include all sedatives and hypnotics such as barbiturates and benzodiazepines (minor tranquilizers). These are usually taken by mouth but can be injected. The main stimulants are amphetamines or their derivatives and cocaine, a natural component of the leaves of the coca plant. Amphetamines can be taken by mouth or injected. Cocaine is either injected or inhaled through the nose. One form of cocaine (freebase, or crack) is generally smoked. Other drugs that are frequently abused include cannabis (marijuana, hashish, etc., from the

hemp plant *Cannabis sativa*), PCP, and hallucinogens, or psychedelics, such as LSD and mescaline.

The purchase, sale, and nonmedical consumption of all the aforementioned drugs are illegal, and these psychotropic drugs can be obtained only on the black market. However, this is not the only route to drug abuse. Alcohol, for instance, can be legally purchased throughout much of the world, despite its high potential for abuse. Also, dependence on prescribed drugs is not uncommon, especially with tranquilizers and hypnotics. What was once a serious social problem of dependence on prescribed barbiturates has been overtaken largely by the widespread use of benzodiazepine tranquilizers such as diazepam (Valium) and chlordiazepoxide (Librium). Millions of legal prescriptions for these drugs are issued every year.

Problems relating to drug abuse can also occur with substances not normally thought of as drugs. Solvent abuse, commonly known as "glue-sniffing," was a growing problem in the late 20th century, especially among teenagers and even younger children. The inhalation of volatile solvents produces temporary euphoria but can lead to death by respiratory depression, asphyxiation, or other causes.

CHARACTERISTICS OF DRUG USE AND ABUSE

Drug use and abuse and how these practices are defined varies significantly worldwide. Despite differences in cultural and societal perspectives, however, there are several fundamental characteristics that transcend the use and abuse of substances in all societies. Drug use serves many different functions, from medicinal to ritual to aesthetic. Thus, it can be said that all drugs are used with a specific purpose in mind. Among perhaps the most important characteristics separating the functions of drugs in terms of use and abuse, however, are addiction and dependence. Regardless of a drug's function and how it is used or abused, addiction and dependence are at the root of most social concerns arising from drug abuse.

Variations in social acceptance of the use and abuse of certain drugs is largely a reflection of differences in how drugs affect the human body and human behaviour. For example, caffeine is addictive, yet millions of people consume caffeine in coffee and soft drinks every day. Most people do not perceive caffeine consumption as a social ill. In fact, the substance is widely viewed as beneficial to human health. In contrast, LSD is not considered to be an addictive drug, but its use is rejected in many societies because it causes extreme and unpredictable deviations in mood and behaviour, sometimes resulting in long-lasting psychological damage.

THE FUNCTIONS OF PSYCHOTROPIC DRUGS

To consider drugs only as medicinal agents or to insist that drugs be confined to prescribed medical practice is to fail to understand human nature. The remarks of the American sociologist Bernard Barber are poignant in this regard:

> *Not only can nearly anything be called a "drug," but things so called turn out to have an enormous variety of psychological and social functions—not only religious and therapeutic and "addictive," but political and aesthetic and ideological and aphrodisiac and so on. Indeed, this has been the case since the beginning of human society. It seems that always and everywhere drugs have been involved in just about every psychological and social function there is, just as they are involved in every physiological function.*

The enhancement of aesthetic experience is regarded by many as a noble pursuit of humans. Although there is no general agreement on either the nature or the substance of aesthetics, certain kinds of experience have been highly valued for their aesthetic quality. To German philosopher Arthur Schopenhauer (*The World as Will and Representation*), contemplation was the one requisite of aesthetic experience. A kind of contemplation that enables one to become so absorbed in the quality of what is being presented to the senses that the "Will" becomes still and all needs of the body silent. Drugs reportedly foster this kind of nirvana and are so used by many today. For German scholar and philosopher Friedrich Nietzsche (*Birth of Tragedy*), humans are able to lose their futile individuality in the mystic ecstasy of universal life under the Dionysiac spell of music, rhythm, and dance.

Love is a highly valued human emotion. Thus, not surprisingly, there has been a great deal of preoccupation with the feeling of love and with those conditions believed to enhance the attainment of love. Little is known concerning the aphrodisiac action of certain foods and drugs, but both have been associated in people's minds with the increased capacity for love. Though the physiological effects may be doubtful, the ultimate effect in terms of one's feeling of love is probably a potent incentive for the repetition of the experience and for those conditions believed to have produced the experience. Hallucinogenic substances such as LSD are said by many to induce a feeling of lovingness. But what the drug user regards as love and what persons around him or her regard as love in terms of the customary visible signs and proofs often do not coincide. Even so, it is plausible that the dissipation of tensions, the blurring of the sense of competition, the subsidence of hostility and overt acts of aggression—all have their concomitant effect on the balance between the positive and negative forces within the individual, and, if nothing else, the ability of drugs to remove some of the hindrances to loving is valued by the user.

Native societies of the Western Hemisphere have utilized, for thousands of years, plants containing hallucinogenic substances. The sacred mushrooms of Mexico were called "God's flesh" by the Aztecs. During the 19th century, the Mescalero Apaches of the southwestern United States practiced a peyote rite that was adopted by many of the Plains tribes. Psychedelic drugs have the unusual ability to evoke at least one kind of a mystical-religious experience, and positive change in religious feeling is a common finding in studies of the use of these drugs. Whether they are also capable of producing religious lives is an open question. Their supporters argue that the drugs appear to enhance personal security and that from self-trust may spring trust of others and that this may be the psychological soil for trust in God. In the words of English novelist Aldous Huxley (*The Doors of Perception*): "When, for whatever reason, men and women fail to transcend themselves by means of worship, good works and spiritual exercise, they are apt to resort to religion's chemical surrogates."

American philosopher and psychologist William James (*The Varieties of Religious Experience*) observed at the beginning of the 20th century that "Our normal waking consciousness, rational consciousness as we call it, is but one special type of consciousness, whilst all about it, parted from it by the filmiest of screens, there lie potential forms of consciousness entirely different." Some

Navajos participating in a peyote ceremony in the 1950s. Peyote, a known hallucinogen, has been used by several Native American tribes as a spiritual and religious aid. Carl Iwasaki/Time& Life Images/Getty Images

people deliberately seek this other consciousness through the use of drugs, whereas others come upon them by accident while on drugs. Only certain people ever have such a consciousness-expanding (psychedelic) experience in its fullest meaning, and the question of its value to the individual must be entirely subjective. For many people, the search for the psychedelic experience is less a noble aim and more the simple need of a psychic jolt or lift.

Human conduct is a paradox of sorts. Although people go to great lengths to produce order and stability in their lives, they also go to great lengths to disrupt their sense of equanimity, sometimes briefly, sometimes for extended periods of time. It has been asserted that there are moments in everyone's life when uncertainty and a lack of structure are a source of threat and discomfort, and moments when things are so structured and certain that unexpectedness can be a welcome relief. Whatever the reason, people everywhere and throughout history have deliberately disrupted their own consciousness, the functioning of their own ego. Alcohol is and has been a favourite tool for this purpose. With the rediscovery of some old drugs and the discovery of some new ones, people now have a wider variety of means for achieving this end.

Many persons face situations with which, for one reason or another, they cannot cope successfully, and in the pressure of which they cannot function effectively. Either the stresses are greater than usual or the individual's adaptive abilities are less than sufficient. In either instance, there are a variety of tranquilizing and energizing drugs that can provide psychological support. This is not chemotherapy in its more ideal sense, but it does enable large numbers of persons to face problems that they might not have otherwise been able to face. Some situations or stresses are beyond the control of the individual, and some individuals simply find themselves far more human and productive with drugs than without drugs. An enormous amount of drug support goes on by way of familiar home remedies, such as aspirin, a luncheon cocktail, and a customary evening drink. Few people, however, refer to these practices as "drug support." There is no clear dividing line between drug support and drug therapy. It is all therapy of sorts, but deliberate drug manipulation is a cut different from drug buffering, and much of the psychological support function is just that—taking the "raw edge" off of stress and stabilizing responses.

The therapeutic use of drugs is so obvious as to require little explanation. Many of the chemical agents that affect living cells are not capable of acting on the brain, but some of those that do are important in medical therapeutics. Examples are alcohol, general anesthetics, analgesic (pain-killing) opiates, and hypnotics, which produce sleep—all classified as central-nervous-system depressants. Certain other drugs, such as strychnine, nicotine, picrotoxin, caffeine, cocaine, and amphetamines, stimulate the nervous system. Most drugs truly useful in the treatment of mental illness, however, were unknown to science until the middle of the 20th century. With the discovery of reserpine and chlorpromazine, some of the major forms of mental illness, especially the schizophrenias, became amenable to pharmacological treatment. These tranquillizing drugs seem to reduce the incidence of certain kinds of behaviour, particularly hyperactivity and agitation. A second group of drugs has achieved popularity in the management of milder psychiatric conditions, particularly those in which patients manifest anxiety. This group includes drugs that have a mild calming or sedative effect and that are also useful in inducing sleep. Not all drugs in psychiatric use have a tranquillizing action. The management of depression requires a different pharmacological effect, and the drugs of choice have been described as being euphorizing, mood-elevating, or antidepressant, depending on their particular pharmacological properties. There are also drugs useful in overactive states such as epilepsy and Parkinsonism. The so-called psychedelic drugs also may have therapeutic uses.

Drugs have other functions that are not so intimately related to individual use. Several important early studies in physiology were directed toward understanding the site and mode of action of some of these agents. Such studies have proved indispensable to the understanding of basic physiology, and drugs continue to be a powerful research tool

of the physiologist. The ability of drugs to alter mental processes and behaviour affords the scientist the unique opportunity to manipulate mental states or behaviour in a controlled fashion. The use of LSD to investigate psychosis and the use of scopolamine to study the retention of learning are examples. The use of drugs as potential instruments of chemical and biological warfare has been studied and pursued by many countries and clandestine operations.

THE NATURE OF DRUG ADDICTION AND DEPENDENCE

If opium were the only drug of abuse, and the only kind of abuse were one of habitual, compulsive use, discussion of addiction might be a simple matter. But opium is not the only drug of abuse, and there are probably as many kinds of abuse as there are drugs to abuse, or, indeed, as maybe there are persons who abuse. Various substances are used in so many different ways by so many different people for so many different purposes that no one view or one definition could possibly embrace all the medical, psychiatric, psychological, sociological, cultural, economic, religious, ethical, and legal considerations that have an important bearing on addiction. Prejudice and ignorance have led to the labelling of all use of nonsanctioned drugs as addiction and of all drugs, when misused, as narcotics. The continued practice of treating addiction as a single entity is dictated by custom and law, not by the facts of addiction.

The tradition of equating drug abuse with narcotic addiction originally had some basis in fact. Historically, questions of addiction centred on the misuse of opiates, the various concoctions prepared from powdered opium. Then various alkaloids of opium, such as morphine and heroin, were isolated and introduced into use. Being the more active principles of opium, their addictions were simply more severe. Later, drugs such as methadone and Demerol were synthesized, but their effects were still sufficiently similar to those of opium and its derivatives to be included in the older concept of addiction. With the introduction of various barbiturates in the form of sedatives and sleeping pills, the homogeneity of addictions began to break down. Then came various tranquilizers, stimulants, new and old hallucinogens, and the various combinations of each. At this point, the unitary consideration of addiction became untenable. Legal attempts at control often forced the inclusion of some nonaddicting drugs into old, established categories—such as the practice of calling marijuana a narcotic. Problems also arose in attempting to broaden addiction to include habituation and, finally, drug dependence. Unitary conceptions cannot embrace the diverse and heterogeneous drugs currently in use.

Popular Misconceptions

Common misconceptions concerning drug addiction have traditionally caused bewilderment whenever serious attempts are made to differentiate states of addiction or degrees of abuse. For many years, a popular misconception was the stereotype that a drug user is a socially unacceptable criminal. The carry-over of this conception from decades past is easy to understand but not very easy to accept today. A second misconception involves the ways in which drugs of abuse are defined. Many substances are capable of acting on a biological system, and whether a particular substance comes to be considered a drug of abuse depends, in large measure, upon whether it is capable of eliciting a "druglike" effect that is valued by the user. Hence, a substance's attribute as a drug is imparted to it by use.

Caffeine, nicotine, and alcohol are clearly drugs, and the habitual, excessive use of coffee, tobacco, or an alcoholic drink is clearly drug dependence if not addiction. The same could be extended to cover tea, chocolates, or powdered sugar, if society wished to use and consider them that way. The task of defining addiction, then, is the task of being able to distinguish between opium and powdered sugar while at the same time being able to embrace the fact that both can be subject to abuse. This requires a frame of reference that recognizes that almost any substance can be considered a drug, that almost any drug is capable of abuse, that one kind of abuse may differ appreciably from another kind of abuse, and that the effect valued by the user will differ from one individual to the next for a particular drug, or from one drug to the next drug for a particular individual. This kind of reference would still leave unanswered various questions of availability, public sanction, and other considerations that lead people to value and abuse one kind of effect rather than another at a particular moment in history, but it does at least acknowledge that drug addiction is not a unitary condition.

PHYSIOLOGICAL EFFECTS OF ADDICTION

Certain physiological effects are so closely associated with the heavy use of opium and its derivatives that they have come to be considered characteristic of addictions in general. Some understanding of these physiological effects is necessary in order to appreciate the difficulties that are encountered in trying to include all drugs under a single definition that takes as its model opium.

Tolerance is a physiological phenomenon that requires the individual to use more and more of the drug in repeated efforts to achieve the same effect. At a cellular level this is characterized by a diminishing response to a foreign substance (drug) as a result of adaptation. Although opiates are the prototype, a wide variety of drugs elicit the phenomenon of tolerance, and drugs vary greatly in their ability to develop tolerance. Opium derivatives rapidly produce a high level of tolerance, whereas alcohol and the barbiturates produce a very low level of tolerance. Tolerance is characteristic for morphine and heroin and, consequently,

is considered a cardinal characteristic of narcotic addiction.

In the first stage of tolerance, the duration of the effects shrinks, requiring the individual to take the drug either more often or in greater amounts to achieve the effect desired. This stage is soon followed by a loss of effects, both desired and undesired. Each new level quickly reduces effects until the individual arrives at a very high level of drug with a correspondingly high level of tolerance. Humans can become almost completely tolerant to 5,000 mg of morphine per day, even though a "normal," clinically effective dosage for the relief of pain would fall in the 5 to 20 mg range. An addict can achieve a daily level that is nearly 200 times the dose that would be dangerous for a normal, pain-free adult.

Tolerance for a drug may be completely independent of the drug's ability to produce physical dependence. There is no wholly acceptable explanation for physical dependence. It is thought to be associated with central-nervous-system depressants, although the distinction between depressants and stimulants is not as clear as it was once thought to be.

Physical dependence manifests itself by the signs and symptoms of abstinence when the drug is withdrawn. All levels of the central nervous system appear to be involved, but a classic feature of physical dependence is the "abstinence" or "withdrawal" syndrome. If the addict is abruptly deprived of a drug upon which the body has physical dependence, there will ensue a set of reactions, the intensity of which will depend on the amount and length of time that the drug has been used. If the addiction is to morphine or heroin, the reaction will begin within a few hours of the last dose and will reach its peak in one to two days.

Initially, there is yawning, tears, a running nose, and perspiration. The addict lapses into a restless, fitful sleep and, upon awakening, experiences a contraction of pupils, gooseflesh, hot and cold flashes, severe leg pains, generalized body aches and constant movement. The addict then experiences severe insomnia, nausea, vomiting, and diarrhea. At this time the individual has a fever, mild high blood pressure, loss of appetite, dehydration, and a considerable loss of body weight. These symptoms continue through the third day and then decline over the period of the next week.

There are variations in the withdrawal reaction for other drugs. In the case of the barbiturates, minor tranquilizers, and alcohol, withdrawal may be more dangerous and severe. During withdrawal, drug tolerance is lost rapidly. The withdrawal syndrome may be terminated at any time by an appropriate dose of the addicting drug.

Chemical Dependency

Chemical dependency is the body's physical and psychological addiction to a psychoactive substance, such as narcotics, alcohol, or nicotine. The two most common forms of chemical dependency are alcoholism and addiction to nonnarcotic central-nervous-system drugs. The latter include short- and intermediate-acting barbiturates, such as secobarbital, pentobarbital, and amabarbital; tranquilizers, such as chlordiazepoxide, diazepam, meprobamate and methaqualone; and amphetamines, such as methamphetamine and dextroamphetamine. Characteristics of dependency on these drugs include a strong desire or need to continue taking the drug, a periodic tendency to increase the dosage, and a psychological and physical need to rely on the drug's effects for the maintenance of homeostasis (physical balance). Individuals who develop a dependency for one drug may also consume other types of mind-altering drugs to affect feelings and perceptions. Polydrug users may swing between ingesting barbiturates ("downers") and amphetamines ("uppers").

Excess of both barbiturates and alcohol may result in a form of intoxication with the similar symptoms of impaired mental and psychomotor skills. Taken together, barbiturates and alcohol, potentiate each other—the effects of the two drugs taken together is greater than the sum of their effects when taken separately.

Treatment for chemical dependency, known as detoxification, should only be conducted under close medical supervision, usually in a hospital. Detoxification programs may be either self-contained or part of broader psychiatric-treatment programs and normally involve both medical and psychological personnel.

Individual and group psychotherapy are critical elements in aiding the patient to adjust to the physical symptoms of withdrawal and the pressures which underlay the addiction. Support groups, mainly Alcoholics Anonymous, have been very successful in treating alcoholics. It is generally agreed, however, that a person with a vulnerability to a certain kind of chemical substance abuse can never be totally cured in a medical sense. He or she must remain vigilant and committed to avoiding similar problems in the future. In fact, the ability to admit addiction and the will to change are necessary first steps to any successful detoxification program.

The individual dependent on opiate drugs such as heroin or morphine may be permanently dependent. Opiate-addicted individuals are often treated by maintaining them with the synthetic narcotic methadone in a manner comparable to the way that a diabetic needs insulin to correct a physiologic deficiency.

RELATIONSHIPS BETWEEN ADDICTION, HABITUATION, AND DEPENDENCE

The traditional distinction between "addiction" and "habituation" centres on the ability of a drug to produce tolerance and physical dependence. The opiates clearly possess the potential to massively challenge the body's resources, and, if so challenged, the body will make the corresponding biochemical, physiological, and psychological readjustment to the stress. At this point, the cellular response has so altered itself as to require the continued presence of the drug to maintain normal function. When the substance is abruptly withdrawn or blocked, the cellular response becomes abnormal for a time until a new readjustment is made.

The key to this kind of conception is the massive challenge that requires radical adaptation. Some drugs challenge easily, but it is not so much whether a drug can challenge easily as it is whether the drug was actually taken in such a way as to present the challenge. Drugs such as caffeine, nicotine, bromide, the salicylates, cocaine, amphetamine and other stimulants, and certain tranquilizers and sedatives are normally not taken in sufficient amounts to present the challenge. They typically but not necessarily induce a strong need or craving emotionally or psychologically without producing the physical dependence that is associated with "hard" addiction. Consequently, their propensity for potential danger is judged to be less, so that continued use would lead one to expect habituation but not addiction. The key word here is *expect*.

These drugs, in fact, are used excessively on occasion and, when so used, do produce tolerance and withdrawal signs. Morphine, heroin, other synthetic opiates, and to a lesser extent codeine, alcohol, and the barbiturates, all carry a high propensity for potential danger in that all are easily capable of presenting a bodily challenge. Consequently, they are judged to be addicting under continued use. The ultimate effect of a particular drug, in any event, depends as much or more on the setting, the expectation of the user, the user's personality, and the social forces that play upon the user, as it does on the pharmacological properties of the drug itself.

Enormous difficulties were encountered in trying to apply these definitions of addiction and habituation because of the wide variations in the pattern of use. (The one common denominator in drug use is variability.) As a result, in 1964 the World Health Organization recommended a new standard that replaces both the term *drug addiction* and the term *drug habituation* with the term *drug dependence*, which in subsequent decades became more and more commonplace in describing the need to use a substance to function or survive. Drug dependence is defined as a state arising from the repeated administration of a drug on a periodic or continual basis. Its characteristics will vary with the agent involved, and this must be made clear by designating drug dependence as being of a particular type—that is, drug dependence of morphine type, of cannabis type, of barbiturate type, and so forth. As an example, drug dependence of a cannabis (marijuana) type is described as a state involving repeated administration, either periodic or continual. Its characteristics include (1) a desire or need for repetition of the drug for its subjective effects and the feeling of enhancement of one's capabilities that it effects, (2) little or no tendency to increase the dose since there is little or no tolerance development, (3) a psychological dependence on the effects of the drug related to subjective and individual appreciation of those effects, and (4) absence of physical dependence so that there is no definite and characteristic abstinence syndrome when the drug is discontinued.

Considerations of tolerance and physical dependence are not prominent in this definition, although they are still conspicuously present. Instead, the emphasis tends to be shifted in the direction of the psychological or psychiatric makeup of the individual and the pattern of use of the individual and his or her subculture. Several considerations are involved here. There is the concept of psychological reliance in terms of both a sense of well-being and a permanent or semipermanent pattern of behaviour. There is also the concept of gratification by chemical means that has been substituted for other means of gratification. In brief, the drug has been substituted for adaptive behaviour. Descriptions such as hunger, need, craving, emotional dependence, habituation, or psychological dependence tend to connote a reliance on a drug as a substitute gratification in the place of adaptive behaviour.

PSYCHOLOGICAL DEPENDENCE

Several explanations have been advanced to account for the psychological dependence on drugs, but as there is no one entity called addiction, so there is no one picture of the drug user. The great majority of addicts display "defects" in personality. Several legitimate motives of humans can be fulfilled by the use of drugs. There is the relief of anxiety, the seeking of elation, the avoidance of depression, and the relief of pain. For these purposes, the several potent drugs are equivalent, but they do differ in the complications that ensue. Should the user develop physical dependence, euphoric effects become difficult to attain, and the continued use of the drug is apt to be aimed primarily at preventing withdrawal symptoms.

It has been suggested that drug use can represent a primitive search for euphoria, an expression of prohibited infantile cravings, or the release of hostility and of contempt. The measure of self-destruction that follows can constitute punishment and the act of expiation. This type of psychodynamic explanation assumes that the individual is predisposed to this type of psychological adjustment prior to any actual experience with drugs. It has also been suggested that the type of drug used will be strongly influenced by the individual's characteristic way of relating to the world. The detached type of person might be expected to choose the "hard" narcotics to facilitate indifference and withdrawal from the world. Passive and ambivalent types might be expected to select sedatives to assure a serene dependency. Passive types of persons who value independence might be expected to enlarge their world without social involvement through the use of hallucinogenic drugs, whereas the dependent type of person who is geared to activity might seek stimulants. Various types of persons might experiment with drugs simply in order to play along with the group that uses drugs. Such group identification may be joined with youthful rebellion against society as a whole.

Obviously, these descriptions are highly speculative because of the paucity of controlled clinical studies. The quest of the addict may be the quest to feel full, sexually satisfied, without aggressive strivings, and free of pain and anxiety. Utopia would be to feel "normal," and this is about the best that the narcotic addict can achieve by way of drugs.

Although many societies associate addiction with criminality, most countries regard addiction as a medical problem to be dealt with in appropriate therapeutic ways. Furthermore, narcotics fulfill several socially useful functions in those countries that do not prohibit or necessarily censure the possession of narcotics. In addition to relieving mental or physical pain, opiates have been used medicinally in tropical countries where large segments of the population suffer from dysentery and fever.

HISTORY OF DRUG CONTROL

The first major national efforts to control the distribution of narcotic and other dangerous drugs were the efforts of the Chinese in the 19th century. Commerce in opium poppy and coca leaf (cocaine) developed on an organized basis during the 1700s. The Qing rulers of China attempted to discourage opium importation and use, but the English East India Company, which maintained an official monopoly over British trade in China, was engaged in the profitable export of opium from India to China. This monopoly of the China trade was eventually abolished in 1839–42, and friction increased between the British and the Chinese over the importation of opium. Foreign merchants, including those from France and the United States, were bringing in ever-increasing quantities of opium.

Finally, the Qing government required all foreign merchants to surrender their stocks of opium for destruction. The British objected, and the Opium War (1839–42) between the Chinese and the British followed. The Chinese lost and were forced into a series of treaties with England and other countries that took advantage of the British victory. In 1858 the importation of opium into China was legalized by the Treaty of Tianjin, which fixed a tariff rate for opium importation. Further difficulties followed. An illegal opium trade carried on by smugglers in south China encouraged gangsterism and piracy, and the activity eventually

OPIUM TRADE IN CHINA IN THE 18TH AND 19TH CENTURIES

An important era in the history of opium concerned its trafficking in China in the 18th and 19th centuries. Opium trafficking emerged in China when Western nations, mostly Great Britain, exported opium grown in India and sold it to China. The British used the profits from the sale of opium to purchase Chinese luxury goods, such as porcelain, silk, and tea, which were in great demand in the West.

Opium was first introduced to China by Turkish and Arab traders in the late 6th or early 7th century. Taken orally to relieve tension and pain, the drug was used in limited quantities until the 17th century, when the practice of smoking tobacco spread from North America to China. The smoking of opium soon became popular throughout China. Opium addiction increased, and opium importations grew rapidly. By 1729 it had become such a problem that Yongzheng, the third emperor of China's Qing dynasty, prohibited the sale and smoking of opium. This failed to hamper the trade, and in 1796 Jiaqing, the fifth emperor of the Qing dynasty, outlawed opium importation and cultivation. In spite of such decrees, however, the opium trade continued to flourish.

Early in the 18th century the Portuguese found that they could import opium from India and sell it in China at a considerable profit. By 1773 the British had discovered the trade, and that year they became the leading suppliers of the Chinese market. The British East India Company established a monopoly on opium cultivation in the Indian province of Bengal, where they developed a method of growing opium poppies cheaply and abundantly. Other Western nations also joined in the trade, including the United States, which dealt in Turkish as well as Indian opium.

Britain and other European nations undertook the opium trade because of their chronic trade imbalance with China. There was tremendous demand in Europe for Chinese tea, silks, and porcelain pottery, but there was correspondingly little demand in China for Europe's

manufactured goods and other trade items. Consequently, Europeans had to pay for Chinese products with gold or silver. The opium trade, which created a steady demand among Chinese addicts for opium imported by the West, solved this chronic trade imbalance.

The East India Company did not carry the opium itself but, because of the Chinese ban, farmed it out to "country traders"—private traders licensed by the company to take goods from India to China. The country traders sold the opium to smugglers along the Chinese coast. The gold and silver the traders received from these sales were then turned over to the East India Company. In China the company used the gold and silver it received to purchase goods that could be sold profitably in England.

The amount of opium imported into China increased from around 200 chests a year in 1729 to about 1,000 chests in 1767 and to around 10,000 a year between 1820 and 1830. By 1838 the amount had grown to some 40,000 chests imported into China annually. The balance of payments for the first time began to run against China and in favour of Britain.

Meanwhile, a network of opium distribution had formed throughout China, often with the connivance of corrupt officials. Levels of opium addiction grew so high that it began to affect the imperial troops and the official classes. The efforts of the Qing dynasty to enforce the opium restrictions resulted in the trading conflict between Britain and China known as the first Opium War (1839–42). This war did not legalize the trade, but it did halt Chinese efforts to stop it. In the second Opium War (1856–60), the Chinese government was forced to legalize the trade, though it did levy a small import tax on opium. By that time opium imports to China had reached 50,000 to 60,000 chests a year, and they continued to increase for the next 30 years.

By 1906, however, the importance of opium in the West's trade with China had declined, and the Qing government was able to begin to regulate the importation and consumption of the drug. In 1907 China signed the Ten Years' Agreement with India, whereby China agreed to forbid native cultivation and consumption of opium on the understanding that the export of Indian opium would decline in proportion and cease completely in 10 years. The trade was thus almost completely stopped by 1917.

Opium smoking and addiction remained a problem in China in subsequent decades, however, since the weakened central government could not wipe out the native cultivation of opium. Opium smoking was finally suppressed by the Chinese Communists after they came to power in 1949.

became linked with powerful secret societies in the south of China.

INTERNATIONAL CONTROLS

Throughout the 1800s, the Chinese government considered opium an important moral and economic question, but obviously China needed international help. In 1909, U.S. President Theodore Roosevelt proposed an international investigation of the opium problem. A meeting of 13 nations held in Shanghai in the same year resulted in recommendations that formed the basis of the first opium convention held at The Hague in 1912. Ratification of the Hague Convention occurred during the meetings of 1913 and 1914. Although further regulatory activity was suspended during the course of World War I, ratification of the Versailles peace treaties of 1919–20 also constituted a ratification of the Hague Convention of 1912. The League of Nations was then given responsibility to supervise agreements with regard to the traffic in opium and other dangerous drugs.

A further important development in drug control was the convention of 1925, which placed further restrictions on the production and manufacture of narcotics. Six more international conventions and agreements were concluded between 1912 and 1936. Under a Protocol on Narcotic Drugs of December 1946 the functions of the League of Nations and of the Office International d'Hygiène Publique were transferred to the United Nations and to the World Health Organization. In 1948 a protocol extended the control system to synthetic and natural drugs outside the scope of the earlier conventions. In 1953 a further protocol was adopted to limit and regulate the cultivation of the poppy plant and the production of, or international and wholesale trade in, and use of opium.

Before the protocol became operative in 1963 the international control organs found a need for codifying and strengthening the existing treaties, and a Single Convention on Narcotic Drugs was drawn up in New York in 1961. This convention drew into one comprehensive control regime all the earlier agreements, limited the use of coca leaves and cannabis to medical and scientific needs, and paved the way for the International Narcotics Control Board. The convention came into force in 1964, and the new board began duty in 1968. Later, two other treaties, the Convention on Psychotropic Substances of 1971 and the United Nations Convention against Illicit Traffic in Narcotic Drugs and Psychotropic Substances of 1988, came into existence. While a major function of the 1961 and 1971 treaties is to codify drug control measures on an international level, all three serve to prevent drug trafficking and drug abuse.

NATIONAL CONTROLS

The United States is perhaps the country most preoccupied with drug control, and it is largely the countries that have mimicked the United States' approach that have made narcotics regulation a matter of public policy with the consequent network of laws, criminal detection agencies, and derived social effects. Principal U.S. legislation during the 20th century included the Harrison Narcotics Act of 1914, the Opium Poppy Control Act of 1942, and the Narcotic Drug Control Act of 1956. The Drug Abuse Control Amendment of 1965 added controls over depressant, stimulant, and hallucinogenic drugs not covered under the other narcotic control acts. In 1970 the Comprehensive Drug Abuse and Control Act, which introduced the Controlled Substances Act (CSA), replaced the earlier laws overseeing the use of narcotics and other dangerous drugs in the United States. The CSA was implemented to control the prescription and dispensation of psychoactive drugs and hallucinogens. Under the CSA, a classification system with five schedules was created to identify drugs based on their potential for abuse, their applications in medicine, and their likelihood of producing dependence. According to this system, Schedule I drugs are substances with no legitimate medical use. These substances include LSD, heroin, and cannabis. Schedule II drugs, which include cocaine, opium, and morphine, have legitimate medical uses but are considered to have a high abuse potential. Schedule III, IV, and V drugs all have legitimate medical uses but with decreasing potential for abuse. Many barbiturates, tranquilizers, and performance-enhancing drugs are Schedule III or higher. Some Schedule V drugs are sold over-the-counter.

Federal agents confiscating special lights used for growing marijuana in San Francisco, California. The Drug Enforcement Administration (DEA) is charged with enforcing drug laws in the United States. Justin Sullivan/Getty Images

The Comprehensive Act of 1970 enabled the United States to fulfill the obligations set forth by the international drug-control treaties. The CSA continues to serve as the primary legislation for drug control in the United States. Alcohol and tobacco, which are not included in the CSA schedule system, are regulated by the Bureau of Alcohol, Tobacco, Firearms, and Explosives and the Alcohol and Tobacco Tax and Trade Bureau.

Another major step in drug control in the United States was the creation of the Drug Enforcement Administration (DEA) in 1973. The DEA was a consolidation of the Bureau of Drug Abuse Control and the Bureau of Narcotics, both of which were involved in enforcing drug control in the 1960s. The increase in drug use during that decade, however, prompted U.S. Pres. Richard Nixon to combine the existing agencies into a single entity, thereby centralizing funds and efforts to control drug abuse. The DEA continues to serve a vital role in law enforcement and drug control in the United States.

In 1988 the Anti-Drug Abuse Act led to the creation of the Office of National Drug Control Policy (ONDCP). The ONDCP plays a central role in establishing drug control policy and in setting national goals for reducing the illicit use and trafficking of drugs. It also is responsible for producing the National Drug Control Strategy (NDCS). The NDCS is designed to facilitate effective drug control measures at local levels by providing information on drugs and drug abuse for community members and by making available to local officials various resources for drug control.

In Great Britain, legislation controlling the manufacture, distribution, and sale of narcotics has experienced substantial change and revision since the late 19th century. In 1971 the Misuse of Drugs Act (MDA), which has been amended multiple times but remains the country's primary means of drug control, replaced the Dangerous Drugs Act of 1965, which itself had replaced earlier legislation stemming from the 1912 Hague Convention. Similar to the CSA in the United States, the MDA uses a classification system to categorize the different drugs of abuse. The MDA, however, recognizes only three categories, Class A, Class B, and Class C, with substances such as heroin and LSD placed in Class A and substances such as tranquilizers and anabolic steroids placed in Class C. Similar to the CSA, the MDA does not list alcohol or tobacco as controlled substances.

EXTENT OF CONTEMPORARY DRUG ABUSE

Complete and reliable data on the extent of drug abuse for most countries is sparse. To specify the size and extent of the drug problem, accurate information as to manufacture, distribution, and sale of drugs is needed. Complete evaluation also requires knowledge of the incidence of habituation and addiction in the general population, the number of persons admitted to hospitals because of drug

MEXICO'S RAGING DRUG WARS

Though drug trafficking flourished in Mexico throughout much of the 20th century, the ever-increasing brutal violence associated with the production and trafficking of illicit drugs had by 2009 sparked the dispersal of 45,000 Mexican soldiers and 5,000 policemen across the country and attracted worldwide attention as images of beheaded corpses were featured in the international media. From December 2006 (when Felipe Calderón succeeded Vicente Fox as president of Mexico) to October 2009, some 14,000 people in the country were executed by drug traffickers, and more than 3,000 of those deaths occurred during the first half of 2009 alone. These statistics underscored the enormity of the situation and the fact that the Mexican government was at war with a very powerful enemy.

During the 20th century Mexico was a primary source of marijuana and heroin for the U.S. market, and since the 1980s the country had served as an important transit point for South American cocaine destined for the United States. The marked escalation in drug-related violence in the 21st century could be partly attributed to the rise to power of younger cartel leaders, more prone to violence, who took the place of their bosses when vast numbers of them were arrested in a crackdown during the Fox administration (2000–06). Another factor was the dramatic increase since the late 1990s in the consumption of illegal drugs in Mexico. As domestic consumption grew, fights between drug cartels erupted over new territories. As part of their preparations for war against other cartels, many drug-trafficking organizations hired trained mercenaries. The Gulf cartel based in the border city of Matamoros, for example, recruited a group of former Mexican army commandos called the Zetas, who became known for their efficient use of violence. Other cartels recruited members of Central American street gangs, or maras, as well as former Guatemalan elite troops known as the Kaibiles.

Most of the recent killings resulted from confrontations between the cartels. Approximately 90 percent of those murdered were linked to the drug trade. The remainder were policemen and soldiers—some of them probably involved in drug trafficking—and a small number of civilians. One of the most egregious incidents took place in December 2009. Arturo Beltran Leyva, the "boss of bosses" whose family-led cartel had close links to the Zetas, was shot dead with four alleged associates by state security forces during a massive assault on a location in Cuernavaca. One elite soldier was also killed, and within hours of the soldier's funeral, four members of his family were brutally murdered in their home in an apparent retaliation by the cartel.

The spike in violence between the cartels was one sign of the accelerating fragmentation of these organizations. The big cartels that appeared in the mid-1990s in Mexico—such as the Tijuana, Juárez, Sinaloa, and Gulf cartels—by 2009 did not exist in the same configuration. Splits occurred in all of them, with new groups emerging to challenge for control over the drug trade. This fragmentation along with the growth in the domestic market for illegal drugs led not only to more executions but also to the increasing brutality with which killings were carried out. The purpose of this cruelty was twofold: it was used to intimidate other cartels, and it created an image of extreme violence in the country that might lead to public pressure on the Mexican government to modify its antidrug strategy. Many bodies of those executed had been found with messages intended for other drug-trafficking organizations as well as for the Mexican authorities. The cartels also posted messages in public places accusing the government of having engaged in corruption or of having favoured one cartel over the others. They also were said to sponsor popular protests against the presence of the army in some parts of the country. In response, the Calderón administration argued that organized crime was waging a propaganda war in an effort to intimidate the government into backing down from its fight against drug trafficking.

Since 2006 criticism of the extreme violence and the government's use of the military in combating drug trafficking increased. Some of Calderón's critics suggested openly or implicitly that the government should return to the policy of tolerance of—or even complicity with—drug trafficking that was for the most part adhered to by the Institutional Revolutionary Party (PRI), which ruled Mexico from 1929 to 2000. This argument was based on the fact that during those years there were lower levels of drug-related violence. It was tolerance, however, that allowed the cartels to grow to the point that they became a serious national security threat. This policy was possible in an authoritarian system in which the rule of law did not exist. A negotiation or even a simple indifference to the activities of drug traffickers would be impossible in a truly democratic system. Clearly, tolerance was not an option for the Calderón administration. Consequently, the Mexican government in the short term decided to combat drug trafficking with the few resources it had. Unfortunately, the Mexican state historically had very poor law-enforcement tools—institutions were weak, corruption was rampant, legal culture was virtually nonexistent, and human and material resources were insufficient. The Mexican government was forced to fight this war handicapped. It was precisely the weakness of the Mexican state that precipitated the high levels of violence seen during recent years. If the cost of tolerance is corruption and the aggravation of the problem, the cost of confrontation is violence.

Calderón made the fight against drug trafficking a priority of his government. Some argued that this was an easy way to secure domestic legitimacy, given his close and contested victory in the presidential elections of 2006. When he became president, however, drug traffickers controlled significant parts of the country, and there was a clear demand from the public for a harder stance against this phenomenon. Several polls confirmed popular support for Calderón's efforts. In a poll conducted at the end of 2008, 72 percent of Mexicans considered the government's attempts to combat drug trafficking to be adequate. Another poll taken in July 2009, after the country's midterm elections, revealed that 51 percent of Mexicans believed that the government was going to win the war in the long run. Only 31 percent thought that the drug traffickers would win. This high level of domestic support allowed Calderón to promote significant reforms of the police force and judicial system—reforms that were supported by all political parties. The proposed changes, which included the establishment of oral trials (rather than those conducted secretively through written briefs) and the strengthening of the federal police force in the hope that it could replace the army in the war on drug trafficking, promised to give the government more resources to fight organized crime.

If the approved security reforms are successful, the Mexican government may be able to control the pervasive effects of drug trafficking. The goal is to transform the problem of *drug trafficking into a public security issue rather than a national security threat. The final result, however, is uncertain. The main obstacle that the Mexican government faces is corruption. If the government is unable to control corruption, the Mexican war on drugs will be lost, and the temptation to go back to the policy of tolerance—despite the fact that it will likely worsen the problem—will be tremendous. If that happens, at some point Mexico and the international community will have to think of alternatives "outside the box," such as legalizing or decriminalizing some drugs. Although in August 2009 Mexico decriminalized small-scale drug possession, this move only suggested that the government considers it pointless to prosecute small-time users. It does not mean that the legalization of drugs is imminent—a still very distant scenario.*

intoxication, and the number of arrests for drug sales that do not conform to the law. For countries lacking adequate drug-tracking organizations and technologies, this kind of determination is extraordinarily difficult.

Furthermore, in most cases of contemporary drug abuse, drug traffic is from uncontrolled, illicit sources, about which there is very little reliable information. Black market diversion of drugs may occur at any point from the manufacture of basic chemicals used to synthesize the drugs, through the process of actually preparing the drug, to the distribution of the final drug form to the retail drugstore or even the physician. This is a complex chain involving chemical brokers, exporters, and dealers in addition to those more directly involved in drug production. Thus, anticipating which drugs will emerge and become problematic in any given year is nearly impossible for drug enforcement agencies.

The extent of drug use in societies is generally monitored by a government-run organization. The National Institute on Drug Abuse (NIDA), which is part of the U.S. National Institutes of Health, is tasked with conducting research on drug use in the United States. NIDA monitors trends in drug abuse primarily through the National Survey on Drug Use and Health (NSDUH) and the Monitoring the Future (MTF) survey. The MTF tracks drug use and attitudes toward drugs among students in the 8th, 10th, and 12th grades. The NSDUH tracks the prevalence of drug use among persons ages 12 and older across the country. These surveys distinguish patterns in use of substances ranging from alcohol to cannabis to designer drugs such as PCP. This information is shared with the Drug Enforcement Administration (DEA), assisting the agency in monitoring drug supplies, trafficking, and diversion. In Europe, data on the extent of drug use in individual countries is organized and maintained by the European Monitoring Centre for Drugs and Drug Addiction (EMCDDA). The information provided by the EMCDDA is used by the European Union and its member states to assess the

Designer Drugs

Designer drugs are illegal synthetic, laboratory-made chemicals. Although the term is not precisely defined, it is understood to refer to commonly abused drugs such as fentanyl, ketamine, LSD, PCP, quaaludes, methcathinone, and GHB (gammahydroxy butyrate), as well as to amphetamine derivatives such as Ecstasy (3,4, Methylenedioxymethamphetamine; MDMA) and methamphetamine. Designer drugs constitute a substantial proportion of the illegal drug market.

Designer drugs usually are synthesized for the first time in an attempt to create an analogue of some better-known chemical. Analogues of certain legal drugs have been produced by pharmaceutical companies in order to make the drugs safer, more effective, or more readily available to a mass public, and indeed the term designer drug *originally referred to legal pharmaceuticals. It began to be applied to illegal substances in the 1980s, when authorities in the United States became concerned about the use of synthetic heroins such as fentanyl. In either usage, the term echoed advertisements for designer jeans and carried connotations of the faddishness and the elite cachet of expensive consumer goods.*

Illegal designer drugs aroused alarm because their production in clandestine laboratories thwarted efforts to control them by more usual means, such as import restrictions, and because they were thought to pose grave physical and psychological dangers to users. Some designer drugs were far stronger than the drugs for which they served as popular substitutes, which thus increased the likelihood of overdose. Also, minor errors in the synthetic process could result in substances very different from—and far more deadly than—the desired product.

The possibility of creating different designer versions of the same drug sometimes made regulation of designer drugs difficult. Legislators would sometimes pass laws prohibiting a substance used in a designer drug only to see a marginally different version appear, using substances not covered in the original law. In the United States this problem was addressed in the Anti-Drug Abuse Act of 1986, which contained a Controlled Substance Analogue Enforcement Act (commonly called the Designer Drug Act), which prohibited the manufacture of "substantially similar" analogues of banned chemicals.

In the United States, concern about designer drugs subsided in the mid-1980s, when crack cocaine was perceived to be a major problem. In the 1990s there were renewed fears regarding various synthetic drugs, especially Ecstasy and methamphetamine. Ecstasy, which was consumed by young people at dances known as "raves," became a major component of youth subcultures. In the late 1990s, a new wave of concern focused on the so-called "date-rape drugs," synthetic chemicals such as GHB (gamma hydroxybutyrate) and Rohypnol, which were used to render potential victims unconscious.

extent of drug use across the region and to identify patterns of drug flow between countries.

Drug abuse patterns change over a relatively short time. For example, in the 1960s the designer drug LSD became popular in the hippie subculture, being used to increase the level of consciousness. In contrast, it had been only a short time earlier that youthful drug abuse involved only the hypnotics and alcohol, which depress consciousness and blunt experience. Because of the work of organizations such as NIDA and EMCDDA, researchers investigating patterns of drug abuse have been able to quickly identify shifts in drug-abuse trends, similar to the sudden rise in popularity of LSD in the 1960s. This information is used to improve drug prevention programs and to inform drug policy.

CHAPTER 2

SOCIAL AND ETHICAL ISSUES OF DRUG USE AND ABUSE

There are many social and ethical issues surrounding the use and abuse of drugs. These issues are made complex particularly because of conflicting values concerning drug use within modern societies. Values may be influenced by multiple factors—including social, religious, and personal views—and within a single society, values and opinions can diverge substantially, resulting in conflicts over various issues involving drug abuse.

Since the 1960s, drug abuse has occupied a significant place in the public consciousness. This heightened awareness of drugs and their consequences has been influenced largely by campaigns and programs oriented toward educating the public about the dangers of drug abuse and about how individuals and societies can overcome drug-related problems. One of the most hotly contested issues concerning contemporary drug abuse centres on whether currently illicit drugs should be legalized. Another major area of concern involves the abuse of drugs in sports, which can send conflicting messages to young generations whose idols are professional athletes.

CONFLICTING VALUES IN DRUG USE

Modern industrialized societies are certainly not neutral with regard to the voluntary nonmedical use of psychotropic drugs. Whether one takes the position of American psychologist Erich Fromm, that people are brought up to desire and value the kinds of behaviour required by their economic and social system, or speaks of the Protestant ethic in the sense that German sociologist Max Weber used it to delineate the industrialist's quest for salvation through worldly work alone, it is simply judged not "right," "good," or "proper" for people to achieve pleasure or salvation chemically. It is accepted that the only legitimate earthly rewards are those that have been "earned" through striving, hard work, personal sacrifice, and an overriding sense of duty to one's country, the existing social order, and family. This orientation is believed to be fairly coincident with the requirements of industrialization.

But the social and economic requirements of many modern societies have undergone radical change in the last few decades, even though the inertia of the existing social character, its desires and its values, are still felt. In some places, current drug controversies are a reflection of cultural lag, with all of the consequent conflict of values being a reflection of the absence of correspondence between traditional teachings and the view of the world as it is now being perceived by large numbers within society. Thus, modern societies in a state of rapid transition often experience periods of instability with regard to prevailing views on drugs and drug use.

Cultural transitions notwithstanding, the dominant social order has strong negative feelings about any nonsanctioned use of drugs that contradicts its existing value system. Can society succeed if individuals are allowed unrestrained self-indulgence? Is it right to dwell in one's inner experience and glorify it at the expense of the necessary ordinary daily pursuits? Is it bad to rely on something so much that one cannot exist without it? Is it legitimate to take drugs if one is not sick? Does one have the right to decide for oneself what one needs? Does society have the right to punish someone if he or she has done no harm to himself or herself or to others? These are difficult questions that do not admit to ready answers. One can guess what the answers would be to the nonsanctioned use of drugs.

The traditional ethic dictates harsh responses to conduct that is "self-indulgent" or "abusive of pleasure." But how does one account for the quantities of the drugs being manufactured and consumed today by the general public? It is one thing to talk of the "hard" narcotic users who are principally addicted to the opiates. One might still feel comfortable in disparaging the widespread illicit use of hallucinogenic substances. But the sedatives, tranquilizers, sleeping remedies, stimulants, alcohol, coffee, tea, and tobacco are complications that trap the advocate in some glaring inconsistencies. It may be asked by partisans whether the cosmetic use of stimulants for weight control is any more legitimate than the use of stimulants to "get with it?"; whether the conflict-ridden adult is any more entitled to relax chemically (alcohol, tranquilizers, sleeping aids, sedatives) than the conflict-ridden adolescent?; whether physical pain is any less bearable than mental pain or anguish? Billions of pills and capsules of a nonnarcotic type are manufactured and consumed yearly.

Sedatives and tranquilizers account for somewhere around 12 percent to 20 percent of all doctor's prescriptions. In addition, there are many different sleeping aids that are available for sale without a prescription. The alcoholic beverage industry produces countless millions of gallons of wine and spirits and countless millions of barrels of beer each year. One might conclude that there is a whole drug culture; that the problem is not confined to the young, the poor, the disadvantaged, or even to the criminal; and that existing attitudes are at least inconsistent, possibly hypocritical. One always justifies one's own drug use, but one tends to view the other fellow who uses the same drugs as an abuser who is weak and undesirable. It must be recognized that the social consensus in regard to drug use and abuse

ERICH FROMM

(b. March 23, 1900, Frankfurt am Main, Ger.—d. March 18, 1980, Muralto, Switz.)

German-born American psychoanalyst and social philosopher Erich Fromm explored the interaction between psychology and society. By applying psychoanalytic principles to the remedy of cultural ills, Fromm believed, humankind could develop a psychologically balanced "sane society."

After receiving his Ph.D. from the University of Heidelberg in 1922, Fromm trained in psychoanalysis at the University of Munich and at the Berlin Psychoanalytic Institute. He began practicing psychoanalysis as a disciple of Sigmund Freud but soon took issue with Freud's preoccupation with unconscious drives and consequent neglect of the role of societal factors in human psychology. For Fromm an individual's personality was the product of culture as well as biology. He had already attained a distinguished reputation as a psychoanalyst when he left Nazi Germany in 1933 for the United States. There he came into conflict with orthodox Freudian psychoanalytic circles. From 1934 to 1941 Fromm was on the faculty of Columbia University in New York City, where his views became increasingly controversial. In 1941 he joined the faculty at Bennington College in Vermont, and in 1951 he was appointed professor of psychoanalysis at the National Autonomous University of Mexico, Mexico City. From 1957 to 1961 he held a concurrent professorship at Michigan State University, and he returned to New York City in 1962 as professor of psychiatry at New York University.

In several books and essays, Fromm presented the view that an understanding of basic human needs is essential to the understanding of society and humankind itself. Fromm argued that social systems make it difficult or impossible to satisfy the different needs at one time, thus creating both individual psychological and wider societal conflicts.

In Fromm's first major work, *Escape from Freedom* (1941), he charted the growth of freedom and self-awareness from the Middle Ages to modern times and, using psychoanalytic techniques, analyzed the tendency, brought on by modernization, to take refuge from contemporary insecurities by turning to totalitarian movements such as Nazism. In *The Sane Society* (1955), Fromm presented his argument that modern humans have become alienated and estranged from themselves within consumer-oriented industrial society. Known also for his popular works on human nature, ethics, and love, Fromm additionally wrote books of criticism and analysis of Freudian and Marxist thought, psychoanalysis, and religion. Among his other books are *Man for Himself* (1947), *Psychoanalysis and Religion* (1950), *The Art of Loving* (1956), *May Man Prevail?* (1961, with D.T. Suzuki and R. De Martino), *Beyond the Chains of Illusion* (1962), *The Revolution of Hope* (1968), and *The Crisis of Psychoanalysis* (1970).

Philosopher and psychologist Erich Fromm, enjoying a smoke, in 1948. Leonard McCombe/Time & Life Pictures/Getty Images

is limited, conflict ridden, and often glaringly inconsistent. The problem is not one of insufficient facts but one of multiple objectives that at the present moment appear unreconcilable.

YOUTH AND DRUGS

Young people seem to find great solace in the fact that the "establishment" is a drug user. One cannot deny that many countries today are drug-oriented societies, but the implications of drug use are not necessarily the same for adults as they are for adolescents. The adult has already acquired some sense of identity and purpose in life. He or she has come to grips with the problems of love and sex, has some degree of economic and social skill, and has been integrated or at least assimilated into some dominant social order. Whereas the adult may turn to drugs and alcohol for many of the same reasons as the adolescent, drug use does not necessarily prevent the adult from remaining productive, discharging obligations, maintaining emotional and occupational ties, acknowledging the rights and authority of others, accepting restrictions, and planning for the future. The adolescent, in contrast, is apt to become ethnocentric and egocentric with drug usage. The individual withdraws within a narrow drug culture and within himself or herself. Drug usage for many adolescents becomes a preposterous "cop-out" at a time when more important developmental experiences are required.

It would appear that the "establishment" is a drug user, and this has important implications in terms of the expectations, roles, values, and rewards of the social order. But the "establishment" does not "cop-out" on drugs, and this is a fact of fundamental importance in terms of youth. Drugs may be physiologically "safe," but the drug experience can be very nonproductive and costly in terms of the individual's chances of becoming a fully participating adult.

NARCOTICS IN THE PUBLIC CONSCIOUSNESS

The narcotics problem came into public consciousness in the late 1960s as the "drug culture," an aspect of the youth movement, or the "counter-culture," as it was frequently called. The use of the hallucinatory drug LSD, promoted by Harvard University psychologist Timothy Leary, and other narcotics soon was widely practiced in so-called hippie communities, notably in the Haight-Ashbury neighborhood of San Francisco. By the end of the decade drug abuse was described by government officials as an epidemic, and the smoking of marijuana spread far beyond the youth culture.

The use of LSD fell off rapidly by 1970, but other "hard" drugs such as "speed" and heroin persisted, education campaigns and stricter laws notwithstanding. One byproduct of growing drug use was an increase in crime, particularly in urban areas. Drug abuse by soldiers in Vietnam was also reported to be very extensive, and many veterans returned home as addicts. In October 1970 Congress passed the toughest drug control law in history, but no great hope was entertained that laws alone could stem the situation. One of the best known spokesmen in the campaign against drugs was television entertainer Art Linkletter, whose daughter had died after using LSD.

Narcotics have held an important place in the public consciousness because of outreach efforts such as Linkletter's. Since the 1970s, many other prominent figures have spoken out on the detrimental impacts of drug abuse as well. Their stories, which are often filled with regret and loss, serve as vital reminders of the tragic ways in which drug abuse can affect individuals, families, and societies. Heightened public awareness of the detrimental impacts of high-risk, drug-related behaviours, such as drunk driving and needle sharing, has played a fundamental role in guiding social and ethical values on drug use.

ISSUES OF LEGALIZATION

Perhaps no 20th-century social problem posed a more vexing challenge than that of drug abuse. In the 1960s drug use dramatically escalated in the United States, bringing with it severe social consequences. Addiction rates soared, crime rates rose, and a sense of public alarm took hold. Despite the grave nature of illicit drug use, the federal government seemed unable to respond effectively to stem its spread, though not from a lack of action. In the 1970s and 1980s the government "declared war" on drugs, imposed increasingly strict prison sentences for drug possession, gave the U.S. Drug Enforcement Administration wide powers to stop the flow of narcotics into the United States, and established the office of "drug czar" to manage the government's antidrug policy.

Despite these expensive measures, the drug problem continued to plague American society. Dismayed by the government's inability to curb drug use, some observers declared that the war on drugs had failed and that the government should reverse its policies and try decriminalization as a solution. This proposal to legalize drugs received strong criticism from both policymakers and the general public.

In May of 2002, hundreds of protestors marched in the streets of New York and other cities around the world to advocate for the legalization of marijuana. Spencer Platt/ Getty Images

SPEAKING OUT ON DRUG DECRIMINALIZATION

Excerpted in the following sections is testimony that Barry McCaffrey, director of the White House Office of National Drug Control Policy (ONDCP), gave in June 1999 before a Congressional committee on the issue of decriminalizing drugs.

1. Proponents of Legalization

Proponents of legalization know that the policy choices they advocate are unacceptable to the American public. Because of this, many advocates of this approach have resorted to concealing their real intentions and seeking to sell the American public legalization by normalizing drugs through a process designed to erode societal disapproval.

For example, ONDCP has expressed reservations about the legalization of hemp as an agricultural product because of the potential for increasing marijuana growth and use. While legitimate hardworking farmers may want to grow the crop to support their families, many of the other proponents of hemp legalization have not been as honest about their goals. A leading hemp activist is quoted in the *San Francisco Examiner* and on the Media Awareness Project's homepage (a group advocating drug policy reforms) as saying he "can't support a movement or law that would lift restrictions from industrial hemp and keep them for marijuana." If legalizing hemp is solely about

developing a new crop and not about eroding marijuana restrictions, why does this individual only support hemp deregulation if it is linked to the legalization of marijuana?

Similarly, when Ethan Nadelmann, Director of the Lindesmith Center (a drug research institute), speaks to the mainstream media, he talks mainly about issues of compassion, like medical marijuana and the need to help patients dying of cancer. However, Mr. Nadelmann's own words in other fora reveal his underlying agenda: legalizing drugs. Here is what he advocates:

> *Personally, when I talk about legalization, I mean three things: the first is to make drugs such as marijuana, cocaine, and heroin legal....*

> *I propose a mail order distribution system based on a right of access....*

> *Any good non-prohibitionist drug policy has to contain three central ingredients. First, possession of small amounts of any drug for personal use has to be legal. Second, there have to be legal means by which adults can obtain drugs of certified quality, purity, and quantity. These can vary from state to state and town to town, with the Food and Drug Administration playing a supervisory role in*

controlling quality, providing information, and assuring truth in advertising. And third, citizens have to be empowered in their decisions about drugs. Doctors have a role in all this, but let's not give them all the power.

We can begin by testing low potency cocaine products—coca-based chewing gum or lozenges, for example, or products like Mariani's wine and the Coca-Cola of the late 19th century—which by all accounts were as safe as beer and probably not much worse than coffee. If some people want to distill those products into something more potent, let them.....

International financier George Soros, who funds the Lindesmith Center, has advocated: "If it were up to me, I would establish a strictly controlled distributor network through which I would make most drugs, excluding the most dangerous ones like crack, legally available." William F. Buckley, Jr. has also called for the "legalization of the sale of most drugs, except to minors."

Similarly, when the legalization community explains their theory of harm reduction—the belief that illegal drug use cannot be controlled and, instead, that government should focus on reducing drug-related harms, such as overdoses—the underlying goal of legalization is still present. For example,

in a 1998 article in *Foreign Affairs,* Mr. Nadelmann expressed that the following were legitimate "harm reduction" policies: allowing doctors to prescribe heroin for addicts; employing drug analysis units at large dance parties, known as raves, to test the quality of drugs; and "decriminalizing" possession and retail sale of cannabis and, in some cases, possession of "hard drugs."

Legalization, whether it goes by the name harm reduction or some other trumped-up moniker, is still legalization. For those who at heart believe in legalization, harm reduction is too often a linguistic ploy to confuse the public, cover their intentions, and thereby quell legitimate public inquiry and debate. Changing the name of the plan doesn't constitute a new solution or alter the nature of the problem....

Proponents argue that legalization is a cure-all for our nation's drug problem. However, the facts show that legalization is not a panacea but a poison. In reality, legalization would dramatically expand America's drug dependence, significantly increase the social costs of drug abuse, and put countless more innocent lives at risk....

During the 1970s, our nation engaged in a serious debate over the shape of our drug control policies. (For example, within the context of this debate, between 1973 and 1979, 11 states "decriminalized" marijuana). During this timeframe, the number of Americans supporting marijuana legalization hit a modern-day high.

While it is difficult to show causal links, it is clear that during this same period, from 1972 to 1979, marijuana use rose from 14 percent to 31 percent among adolescents, 48 percent to 68 percent among young adults, and 7 percent to 20 percent among adults over 26. This period marked one of the largest drug use escalations in American history.

A similar dynamic played out nationally in the late 1800s and early 1900s. Until the 1890s, today's controlled substances—such as marijuana, opium, and cocaine—were almost completely unregulated. It was not until the last decades of the 1800s that several states passed narcotics control laws. Federal regulation of narcotics control did not come into play until the Harrison Act of 1914.

Prior to the enactment of these laws, narcotics were legal and widely available across the United States. In fact, narcotics use and its impacts were commonplace in American society. Cocaine was found not only in early Coca-Cola (until 1903) but also in wine, cigarettes, liqueur-like alcohols, hypodermic needles, ointments, and sprays. Cocaine was falsely marketed as a cure for hay fever, sinusitis, and even opium and alcohol abuse. Opium abuse was also widespread. One year before Bayer introduced aspirin to the market, the company also began marketing heroin as a "nonaddictive," no prescription necessary, over-the-counter cure-all.

During this period, drug use and addiction increased sharply. While there are no comprehensive studies of drug abuse for this period that are on par with our current *National Household Survey on Drug Abuse* and *Monitoring the Future* studies, we can, for example, extrapolate increases in opium use from opium imports, which were tracked. Yale University's Dr. David Musto, one of the leading experts on the patterns of drug use in the United States, writes: "The numbers of those overusing opiates must have increased during the nineteenth century as the per capita importation of crude opium increased from less than 12 grains annually in the 1840s to more than 52 grains in the 1890s." Only in the 1890s when societal concerns over and disapproval of drug use began to become widespread and triggered legal responses did these rates level off. Until this change in attitudes began to denormalize drug use, the United States experienced over a 400 percent increase in opium use alone. This jump is even more staggering if one considers that during this period other serious drugs, such as cocaine, were also widely available in every-day products.

Moreover, while we do not believe that the period of prohibition on alcohol is directly analogous to current efforts against drugs, our experiences with alcohol prohibition also raise parallel concerns. While Prohibition was not without its flaws, during this period alcohol usage fell to between 30 to 50 percent of its pre-Prohibition levels. From 1916 to 1919 (just prior to [when]

Prohibition went into effect in 1920), U.S. alcohol consumption averaged 1.96 gallons per person per year. During prohibition, alcohol use fell to a low of .90 gallons per person per year. In the decade that followed Prohibition's repeal, alcohol use increased to a per capita annual average of 1.54 gallons and has since steadily risen to 2.43 gallons in 1989. Prohibition also substantially reduced the rates of alcohol-related illnesses.

The United States has tried drug legalization and rejected it several times now because of the suffering it brings. The philosopher Santayana was right in his admonition that "those who cannot remember the past are condemned to repeat it." Let us not now be so foolish as to once again consider this well worn, dead-end path.

2. The Impact on Youth

Most importantly the legalization of drugs in the United States would lead to a disproportionate increase in drug use among young people. In 1975, the Alaskan Supreme Court invalidated certain sections of the state's criminal code pertaining to the possession of marijuana. Based on this finding, from 1975 to 1991, possession of up to 4 ounces of the drug by an adult who was lawfully in the state of Alaska became legal. Even though marijuana remained illegal for children, marijuana use rates among Alaskan youth increased

significantly. In response, concerned Alaskans, in particular the National Federation of Parents for Drug-Free Youth, sponsored an anti-drug referendum that was approved by the voters in 1990, once again rendering marijuana illegal.

In addition to the impact of expanded availability, legalization would have a devastating effect on how our children see drug use. Youth drug use is driven by attitudes. When young people perceive drugs as risky and socially unacceptable youth drug use drops. Conversely, when children perceive less risk and greater acceptability in using drugs, their use increases. If nothing else, legalization would send a strong message that taking drugs is a safe and socially accepted behavior that is to be tolerated among our peers, loved ones, and children. Such a normalization would play a major role in softening youth attitudes and, ultimately, increasing drug use.

The significant increases in youth drug use that would accompany legalization are particularly troubling because their effects would be felt over the course of a generation or longer. Without help, addictions last a lifetime. Every additional young person we allow to become addicted to drugs will impose tremendous human and fiscal burdens on our society. Legalization would be a usurious debt upon our society's future—the costs of such an approach would mount exponentially with each new addict, and over each new day.

3. The Impact of Drug Prices

If drugs were legalized, we can also expect the attendant drop in drug prices to cause drug use rates to grow as drugs become increasingly affordable to buy. Currently 1 gram of cocaine sells for between $150 and $200 on U.S. streets. The cost of cocaine production is as low as $3 per gram. In order to justify legalization, the market cost for legalized cocaine would have to be set so low as to make the black market, or bootleg cocaine, economically unappealing. Assume, for argument sake, that the market price was set at $10 per gram, a 300 percent plus markup over cost, each of the 50 hits of cocaine in that gram could retail for as little as 10 cents.

With the cost of "getting high" as low as a dime (10 cents)—about the cost of a cigarette—the price of admission to drug use would be no obstacle to anyone even considering it. However, each of these "dime" users risks a life-long drug dependence problem that will cost them, their families, and our society tens of thousands of dollars.

In addition to the impact on youth, we would also expect to see falling drug prices drive increasing drug use among the less affluent. Among these individuals the price of drug use—even at today's levels—remains a barrier to entry into use and addiction. The impact of growing use within these populations could be severe. Many of these communities are already suffering the harms of drug use—children who see no other future turning to drugs as an escape, drug dealers driving what remains of legitimate business out of their communities, and families being shattered by a loved one hooked on drugs. Increased drug use would set back years of individual, local, state, and federal efforts to sweep these areas clean of drugs and build new opportunities.

Critics argue that the harm to our society from drugs, such as the costs of crime, could be reduced if drugs were legalized. The logic is flawed. By increasing the availability of drugs, legalization would dramatically increase the harm to innocent people. With more drugs and drug use in our society, there would be more drug-related child abuse, more drugged driving fatalities, and more drug-related workplace accidents. None of these harms are caused by law or law enforcement but by illegal drugs.

Even with respect to the crime-related impact of drugs, drug-related crimes are driven far more by addiction than by the illegality of drugs. Law enforcement doesn't cause people to steal to support their habits; they steal because they need money to fuel an addiction—a drug habit that often precludes them from earning an honest living. Even if drugs were legal, people would still steal and prostitute themselves to pay for addictive drugs and support their addicted lifestyles. Dealers don't deal to children because the law makes it illegal; dealers deal to kids to build their market by hooking them on a life-long habit at an early age, when drugs can be marketed as cool and appealing to young people who have not matured enough to consider the risks. Make no mistake: legalizing drugs won't stop pushers from selling heroin and other drugs to kids. Legalization will, however, increase drug availability and normalize drug-taking behavior, which will increase the rates of youth drug abuse.

For example, although the Dutch adopted a more tolerant approach to illegal drugs, crime is in many cases increasing rapidly in Holland. The most recent international police data (1995) shows that Dutch per capita rates for breaking and entering, a crime closely associated with drug abuse, are three times the rate of those in Switzerland and the United States, four times the French rate, and 50 percent greater than the German rate. "A 1997 report on hard-drug use in the Netherlands by the government-financed Trimbos Institute acknowledged that 'drug use is considered the primary motivation behind crimes against property'—23 years after the Dutch [drug] policy was supposed to put a brake on that." Moreover, *Foreign Affairs* recently noted that in areas of Holland where youth cannabis smokers are most prevalent, such as Amsterdam, Utrecht, and Rotterdam, the rates of juvenile crime have "witnessed skyrocketing growth" over the last three to four years. Statistics from the Dutch Central Bureau of Statistics indicate that between 1978 and 1992, there was a gradual, steady increase in violence of more than 160 percent.

In contrast, crime rates in the United States are rapidly dropping. For example, the rate of drug-related murders in the United States has hit a ten-year low. In 1989, there were 1,402 drug-related murders. By 1997 that number fell to 786. In 1995, there were 581,000 robberies in the United States. By 1997, that number fell to roughly 498,000.

America's criminal justice system is not the root cause of drug-related crime. It is the producers, traffickers, pushers, gangs, and enforcers who are to blame, as are all the people who use drugs and never think about the web of criminality and suffering their drug money supports.

DRUG ABUSE IN SPORTS

Humans have long used substances to enhance their physical performance. Athletes in ancient Greece reportedly consumed various potions and herbal concoctions to help them defeat their opponents. Substances such as wine, morphine, strychnine, and cocaine were used by 19th-century athletes to augment strength and stamina. In the 20th century, the struggle to control drug abuse in sports emerged as a significant problem, primarily because of the increased number of performance-enhancing substances that became available. Some of the most widely abused substances in sports are anabolic steroids, which were made infamous in the late 20th and early 21st century in the United States, largely as a result of their abuse in professional baseball.

Steroid Use in Major League Baseball

In 1991 it became illegal to possess or sell anabolic steroids in the United States without a valid prescription, yet the continued easy availability of these drugs and their widespread use to enhance athletic performance prompted President George W. Bush to address the matter in his 2004 State of the Union message. Football players, swimmers, weight lifters, and track athletes had been at the center of scandals involving performance-enhancing drugs, but it was Major League Baseball (MLB), which had no formal policy on steroid use until 2002, that was most intensely scrutinized.

In the mid-1990s rumors circulated of the spreading use of steroids (which

José Canseco promotes his book Juiced, *in which he alleged that steroid use had become rampant in Major League Baseball.* Tim Boyle/Getty Images

increase muscle mass) among Major Leaguers as records began to fall: before 1994 a player hit 50 or more home runs in a season just 18 times; from 1995 to 2002 there were 15 50-homer seasons. Some argued that better bats, smaller ballparks, and pitching diluted by expansion were responsible, but many pointed to steroid use. In May 2002 Ken Caminiti admitted to having used steroids while winning the 1996 Most Valuable Player award. In 2003 it was alleged that several players had obtained an illegal steroidal cream from the Bay Area Laboratory Co-Operative, including Barry Bonds, whose 73 home runs in 2001 broke baseball's single season record. Finally, in February 2005 former all-star José Canseco published a tell-all book, *Juiced*, in which he alleged that several of baseball's biggest stars had used steroids.

In response to these events, the House of Representatives Committee on Oversight and Government Reform conducted hearings in March 2005. Among the players to testify were sluggers Mark McGwire (who refused to answer direct questions about his alleged steroid use during his testimony but who in 2010 admitted to having used steroids intermittently from 1989 through the '90s, including during his record-setting 1998 season), Sammy Sosa, Frank Thomas, and Rafael Palmeiro (who testified, "I have never used steroids. Period"—though he later received a 10-day suspension for steroid use under MLB's new zero tolerance policy).

STATEMENTS BEFORE CONGRESS

The following are excerpts from statements to the House Committee on Oversight and Government Reform by José Canseco Jr. and pitcher Curt Schilling, a prominent opponent of steroid use.

JOSÉ CANSECO

Mr. Chairman, members of the Committee, distinguished guests; I am humbled by this opportunity to appear before you today. Never in my wildest dreams could I have imagined that my athletic ability and love for America's game would lead me to this place and the subject that has brought me before the Committee. When I decided to write my life's story, I was aware that what I revealed about myself and the game I played for a majority of my life would create a stir in the athletic world. I did not know that my revelations would reverberate in the halls of this chamber and in the hearts of so many.

I had hoped that what I experienced firsthand, when revealed, would give insight into a darker side of a game that I loved. That maybe it would force baseball to acknowledge it condoned this activity for the sole purpose of increasing revenue at the gate. Unfortunately, by our presence here today, it is clear the MLB is not interested in admitting the truth. It is also clear that although others have tried to come out in support of my revelations, fear of repercussions from MLB haunts their conscience.

The book that I wrote was meant to convey one message. The preface makes my position very clear. I do not condone or encourage the use of any particular drugs, medicine, or illegal substances in any aspect of life. My book was informational and intended to enlighten the world about a problem that until my book was released had only been spoken of in whispers. I did not write my book to single out any one individual or player. I am saddened that the media and others have chosen to focus on the names in the book and not on the real culprit behind the issue. That the focus of my life and those involved in it may have inadvertently damaged players was not my intent. I hoped rather that finally the media and the world would try and dig beyond the easy answer and not fix blame but fix the problem. A problem that would continue unabated if I did not call attention to it.

Because of my truthful revelations I have had to endure attacks on my credibility. I have had to relive parts of my life that I thought had been long since buried and gone. All of these attacks have been spurred on by an organization that holds itself above the law. An organization that chose to exploit its players for the increased revenue that lines its pockets and then sacrifice those same players to protect the web of secrecy that was hidden for so many years. The time has come to end this secrecy and to confront those who refuse to acknowledge their role in encouraging the behavior we are gathered to discuss.

I love the sport of baseball. I love it in its purest and simplest form. I still long for the time when I could pick up a bat and ball and hit one over the fence for the game-winning run. I am appreciative of the opportunities that the sport of baseball has given to me along with the quality of life it has provided. It permitted me to take care of my family and provide a better life for myself and others close to me. However, had I known that this opportunity would cost me so much, I would have refused the offer so many years ago.

The pressure associated with winning games, pleasing fans, and getting the big contract, led me, and others, to engage in behavior that would produce immediate results. This is the same pressure that leads the youth of today, other athletes and professionals, to engage in that same behavior. The time has come to address this issue and set the record straight about what risks are involved in that behavior. To send a message to America, especially the youth that these actions, while attractive at first, may tarnish and harm you later. That sometimes there are things more important than simply money.

Why did I take steroids? The answer is simple. Because, myself and others had no choice if we wanted to continue playing. Because MLB did nothing to take it out of the sport. As a result, no one truly knew who was on muscle-enhancing drugs. As a result, a player who wanted to continue to play, to perform as a star, was forced to put into their bodies whatever they could just to compete at the same level as those around them.

However, why we are before Congress today is only part of a much larger problem. The American public continues to place athletes in a position above everyone else. "Some people are born to greatness and others have greatness thrust upon them." A successful athlete is viewed as the voice of a city, state, and country. He or she, in playing their sport, often represents the very spirit of a nation and its people. We rarely see riots and the gut-wrenching emotion so apparent in sports in any other forum. When the Boston Red Sox failed to get to the World Series two years ago, the pain echoed throughout the fans as a personal attack on the city and on the individual residents there. When a Chicago Cubs fan got caught up in the moment and interfered with the game, he was attacked, vilified, and forced to move and change his life.

Such emotional investment is felt by the players daily. We want only to please those who hold us in such high esteem. We feel deeply the obligation that we each have to perform and win. It is a burden that we take on willingly and without hesitation or regret. However, perhaps, in addition to addressing this pressing issue we should take the opportunity to look at the priority that we place on athletes and athletics and change our focus.

Baseball owners and the players union have been very much aware of the undeniable fact that as a nation we will do anything to win. They turned a blind eye to the clear evidence of steroid use in baseball. Why? Because it sold tickets and resurrected a game that had recently suffered a black eye from a player strike. The result was an intentional act by baseball to promote, condone, and encourage the players to do whatever they had to do to win games, bring back the fans, and answer the bottom line. Salaries went up, revenue increased and owners got richer. But this comes with a cost.

MLB issued press releases years ago stating clearly the position that banned substances that enhanced performance were not a part of MLB. MLB set forth "for cause testing" to support this position. However, during my entire career no player was ever tested for performance-enhancing substances. "For cause" became a hollow threat that was never used by anyone involved with MLB. It was again made clear that press releases were the only thing MLB was going to do to "clean up" MLB's image. The duplicity present throughout my career continues today.

Many have said that my motivation for revealing this problem is myriad; revenge, monetary gain, vindication. The truth is that I would have played baseball for free. I even offered to play for free some years ago and to donate my salary to charity just to be a part of the game. This offer was rejected and MLB turned its back on me just as it had turned a blind eye to the drugs that were running rampant through the sport. My motivation is nothing more than a clearing of conscience and an effort to resurrect a sport that has given joy to so many.

I am moved by the efforts Congress is taking to address this problem. I am humbled that my book may have played a small part in setting forth this juggernaut. I am hopeful that it will yield a positive result.

As I sit here today I would be remiss if I did not again stress that I do not condone the use of any drugs or illegal substances. I urge parents to become more active and involved in the lives of their children. I hope that my message will be received as it is intended, that we, as professional athletes, are no better than anyone else. We just have a special ability that permits us to play ball. We should not be held up to any higher standard of behavior than any other mother or father. Our children's heroes should not be solely the athletes they watch, but more importantly the parents who are with them each day.

Thank you for this opportunity to appear before you. I hope that my statements and answers to those questions posed to me will help find a solution to this problem. That the intentional failure of MLB to address this issue will finally be put to rest, and that those who follow me into this sport will have the opportunity to do so free of the pressure to compromise themselves simply for increased revenue.

To those players who have been thrust into this debate I simply ask them to tell the truth as I have told the truth. To join with me and help resurrect the sport we love from where the owners and union have let it go.

Curt Schilling

My hope is that this hearing results in an increased awareness of steroids and their inherent danger to America's youth. I understand from the invitation I received to appear before this Committee that my presence has been requested because I have been outspoken on this issue. I am honored to be a co-chairman on an advisory committee tasked with putting together recommendations on how to prevent steroid usage among young people. I recognize that professional athletes are role models for many of the youth of this country. Most athletes take that role very seriously and I hope through my appearance here that I am conveying my seriousness and understanding of this issue. While I don't profess to have the medical expertise to adequately describe the dangers of steroid use, I do believe that I have the expertise to comment on whether steroids are necessary to excel in athletics. I think it is critical to convey to the youth who desire to excel in sports that steroids are not the answer, that steroids are not necessary in order to excel in any athletic event and that success is achieved through hard work, dedication and perseverance.

I also hope that by being here, I can raise a level of awareness on several other fronts. First, I hope the Committee recognizes the danger of possibly glorifying the so-called author scheduled to testify today or by indirectly assisting him to sell more books through his claim that what he is doing is somehow good for this country or the game of baseball. A book which devotes hundreds of pages to glorifying steroid usage and which contends that steroid usage is justified and will be the norm in this country in several years is a disgrace, was written irresponsibly, and sends exactly the opposite message that needs to be sent to kids. The allegations made in that book, the attempts to smear the names of players, both past and present, having been made by one who for years vehemently denied steroid use, should be seen for what they are, an attempt to make money at the expense of others. I hope we come out of this proceeding aware of what we are dealing with when we talk about that so-called author and that we not create a buzz that results in young athletes buying the book and being misled on the issues and dangers of steroids.

I must also tell you, members of the Committee, that I hope that a result of this hearing there is a better awareness of the steroid program recently implemented by Major League Baseball and its Players Association. That program, though certainly not perfect, and I dare say there is no such thing as a perfect testing program, is a substantial step in the right direction that appears, from initial statistics, to be having the desired effect—that is removing steroids from baseball. Statistics have shown that from 2003 to 2004 the number of players using steroids in the major leagues has gone from 5-7% to 1.7%. In fact, in yesterday's *New York Times* it was reported that there were 96 positive tests during the 2003 testing period, and in 2004 that number saw a dramatic decrease as only 12 players tested positive. I see that as progress, I see that as a positive. It troubles me when I hear the program being identified as a joke, a travesty and a program not designed to rid baseball of steroids. I think those numbers show this to be a meaningful program, one that is working, and steroid usage is dropping.

I find solace in the fact that a man who I hold in the highest regard, Senator John McCain, an American war hero, a man of the highest moral standards and integrity, indicated his satisfaction that the league and its players had made a meaningful step in dealing with the steroid problem. Senator McCain had a problem with baseball and its earlier steroid program. He voiced that problem and both the league and the Players Association listened and took action. The Players Association, in an unprecedented move, reopened the collective bargaining agreement for the sole purpose of strengthening the drug-testing procedures and its penalties. You may view the reopening of the agreement as a nonissue, or as one of minimal consequences, we don't.

It appears that the main complaint about the current program revolves around the current penalties for being caught, or failing a test. It is my view as a 19-year veteran of professional baseball that there will be no system of suspensions or discipline that can be implemented that will stand up to, or match, the agreement made by the players that positive test results will be made public, subjecting the player to public humiliation and labeling as a steroid user or cheater. Given the intense media coverage that now permeates professional sports, there is no doubt in my mind that any player who is caught after this program has been implemented, will for all intents and purposes have his career blacklisted, forever. When a player's suspension is over, he may be able to lose the label of a player who is under suspension, but I am convinced he will never lose the label of a steroid user.

Members of the Committee, do I believe steroids are being used by Major League Baseball players? Yes. Past and present testing says as much. Do I believe we should continue to test and monitor steroid usage in Major League Baseball? Absolutely. In fact in that regard I believe the message has been heard by players, and that serious, positive, forward thinking steps have been taken on this issue. I urge the Committee to focus its efforts in that direction as well and not to dwell on what may have occurred in the past.

I also urge the Committee to not make this process just about baseball. Steroids and supplement usage appears to be not a "baseball" problem, but a society problem. Everywhere you look, we are bombarded by advertising of supplements and feel-good medications. I urge you to evaluate the way in which these products are manufactured, and more importantly, the way in which they are marketed. If we are going to send a message to the young athlete that steroid use is bad, and that steroids are not necessary to achieve success, you cannot allow that message to be drowned out by the manufacturer's advertising to the contrary. If the Government thought enough of the youth of this country to rally against the tobacco industry and its advertising to our youth, why should the supplement industry be any different?

I cannot conclude my statement without expressing my admiration to the Hootons and the Garibaldis for appearing here today and I extend my deepest sympathy to each of them for their loss. As a father of four children, I cannot begin to imagine the pain they must be suffering. Maybe their loss will result in an awareness of the tragedy that follows steroid use.

CHAPTER 3

PSYCHOTROPIC AND HALLUCINOGENIC DRUGS

Psychotropic and hallucinogenic drugs include any of the so-called mind-expanding drugs that are able to induce states of altered perception and thought. These substances frequently induce a heightened awareness of sensory input but with diminished control over what is being experienced. Psychoactive drugs include the opiates (opium and its derivatives), as well as the hallucinogens, such as LSD (lysergic acid diethylamide) and PCP (phencyclidine). Opiates are known for their ability to suppress pain and for their powerfully addictive properties. Hallucinogens, on the other hand, have extraordinarily potent psychological effects and usually are not addictive. Chronic use of substances such as LSD, however, may lead to psychoses or difficulties with memory or abstract thinking.

OPIUM AND ITS DERIVATIVES

The opiates are unrivalled in their ability to relieve pain. Opium is the dried milky exudate obtained from the unripe seed pods of the opium poppy plant (*Papaver somniferum*), which grows naturally throughout most of Turkey. Of the 20 or more alkaloids found in opium, only a few are pharmacologically active. The important constituents of opium are morphine (10 percent), papaverine (1 percent), codeine (0.5 percent), and thebaine (0.2 percent). (Papaverine is pharmacologically distinct from the narcotic agents and is essentially devoid of effects on the central nervous system.)

In about 1804 a young German apothecary's assistant named F.W.A. Sertürner isolated crystalline morphine as the active analgesic principle of opium. Codeine is considerably less potent and is obtained from morphine. Diacetylmorphine—or heroin—was developed from morphine by the Bayer Company of Germany in 1898 and is five to 10 times as potent as morphine itself. Opiates are not medically ideal. Tolerance is developed quite rapidly and completely in the more important members of the group, morphine and heroin, and they are highly addictive. In addition, they produce respiratory depression and frequently cause nausea and emesis.

As a result, there has been a constant search for synthetic substitutes. Meperidine (Demerol), first synthesized in Germany in 1939, is a significant addition to the group of analgesics, being $1/10$ as potent as morphine. Alphaprodine (Nisentil) is one-fifth as potent as morphine but is rapid-acting. Methadone,

synthesized in Germany during World War II, is comparable to morphine in potency, and levorphanol (Levo-Dromoran) is an important synthetic with five times the potency of morphine. These synthetics exhibit a more favourable tolerance factor than the more potent of the opiates, but in being addictive they fall short of an ideal analgesic. Of this entire series, codeine has the least addiction potential and heroin has the greatest.

Opium is obtained by slightly incising the seed capsules of the opium poppy after the plant's flower petals have fallen. The slit seedpods exude a milky latex that coagulates and changes colour, turning into a gumlike brown mass upon exposure to air. This raw opium may be ground into a powder, sold as lumps, cakes, or bricks, or treated further to obtain such derivatives as morphine, codeine, and heroin.

Opium Alkaloids

The pharmacologically active principles of opium reside in its alkaloids, the most

Opium Poppy

Opium poppy (Papaver somniferum) is a flowering plant of the family Papaveraceae and is native to Turkey. Opium, morphine, codeine, and heroin are all derived from the milky fluid found in its unripe seed capsule. A common garden annual in the United States, the opium poppy bears blue-purple or white flowers 5 inches (13 cm) wide on plants about 3–16 feet (1–5 metres) tall, with lobed or toothed silver-green foliage. It is also grown for its tiny nonnarcotic ripe seeds, which are kidney-shaped and grayish blue to dark blue. The seeds are used in bakery products and for seasoning, oil, and birdseed.

important of which is morphine. Opium alkaloids are of two types, depending on chemical structure and action. Morphine, codeine, and thebaine, which represent one type, act upon the central nervous system and are analgesic, narcotic, and potentially addicting compounds. Papaverine, noscapine (formerly called narcotine), and most of the other opium alkaloids act only to relax involuntary (smooth) muscles.

MORPHINE

Morphine is used in medicine in the form of its hydrochloride, sulfate, acetate, and tartrate salts. In its power to reduce the level of physical distress, morphine is among the most important naturally occurring compounds, being of use in the treatment of pain caused by cancer and in cases where other analgesics have failed. It also has a calming effect that protects the system against exhaustion in traumatic shock, internal hemorrhage, congestive heart failure, and debilitated conditions (as certain forms of typhoid fever). It is most frequently administered by injection to ensure rapid action, but it is also effective when given orally.

Morphine produces a relaxed, drowsy state and many side effects that result from the depression of the respiratory, circulatory, and gastrointestinal systems. It also is an emetic and a general depressant. The most serious drawback to the drug is its addictiveness.

The structure of morphine proposed in the 1920s by J.M. Gulland and R. Robinson was confirmed in 1952 by its total synthesis, accomplished by M. Gates and G. Tschudi. Synthetic organic chemistry also has provided a number of compounds (as meperidine, methadone, and pentazocine) that have in part supplanted morphine in medical use. Following its extraction from the dried milky exudate of the unripe seed capsule of the opium poppy, morphine appears as colourless crystals or a white crystalline powder.

HEROIN

Heroin, which is also called diacetylmorphine, is a highly addictive morphine derivative that makes up a large portion of the illicit traffic in narcotics. Heroin is made by treating morphine with acetic anhydride. Heroin was originally used as a narcotic analgesic, but its undesirable side effects were found to far outweigh its value as a pain-killing drug, and there are now strict prohibitions on its use in many countries.

Heroin constricts the user's pupils, slows respiration, heartbeat, and gastrointestinal activity, and induces sleep. Among those addicted to it, however, heroin's most valued effect is the ecstatic reaction that it gives after being intravenously injected. Within seconds a warm, glowing sensation spreads over the body. This brief but intense rush is then followed by a deep, drowsy state of relaxation and contentment that is marked by a clouding of consciousness and by poor concentration and attention. This state lasts two to four hours and then gradually wears off. Some individuals do react negatively to heroin, experiencing only anxiety, nausea, and depression.

Heroin in powder form can be sniffed, or inhaled. When dissolved in water, it can be injected subcutaneously (skin-popping) or intravenously (mainlining). But heroin addicts, as opposed to novice users of the drug, almost invariably inject it intravenously, because this produces the most rapid and intense euphoric effects.

Heroin is a highly addictive drug, and an addict must usually inject heroin about twice a day in order to avoid the discomfort of withdrawal symptoms, which include restlessness, body aches, insomnia, nausea, vomiting, and diarrhea. An addict trying to break the body's dependence on heroin must undergo an intense withdrawal period lasting three or four days, with symptoms lessening markedly thereafter. Heroin addicts also develop a high tolerance to the drug. Thus an addict must use the drug more often or in greater amounts to achieve the desired euphoric effects. Nevertheless, these effects tend to disappear completely in the case of very heavy use, although the physical addiction remains.

A heroin addiction is expensive to maintain, and such addicts, when not gainfully employed, often must engage in prostitution, procuring, burglary, robbery, or small-time narcotics peddling to supply their habit. Heroin addicts commit a disproportionately large share of property crimes in Western countries where use of the drug is a problem.

Heroin illegally available on the street has been diluted to a purity of only 2 to 5 percent, being mixed with baking soda, quinine, milk sugar, or other substances. The unwitting injection of relatively pure heroin is a major cause of heroin overdose, the main symptoms of which are extreme respiratory depression deepening into coma and then into death. Aside from this danger, heroin addicts are prone to hepatitis and other infections stemming from their use of dirty or contaminated syringes. Scarring of the surfaces of the arms or legs is another common injury, because of repeated needle injections and subsequent inflammations of the surface veins.

The private use and possession of heroin is illegal in most countries of the world, although the drug may be used as a painkiller for terminal cancer patients and others who suffer severe pain. Most illegally distributed heroin comes from opium produced in the Middle East, Southeast Asia, and Mexico. At the start of the 21st century, the leading opium-producing countries included Afghanistan, Myanmar (Burma), and Laos. Heroin addiction first appeared in the early 20th century, and for several decades thereafter it was customarily confined to the marginal or criminal elements in Western societies. But from the 1960s on its use spread somewhat to youths in middle- and upper-income families and to Third World populations.

Heroin use and trafficking are worldwide problems, and both national and international law enforcement and regulatory agencies seek to control and suppress those activities.

OXYCODONE

Oxycodone is a semisynthetic drug with potent pain-relieving effects that is derived from thebaine. Oxycodone was synthesized from thebaine in 1916 and was first used clinically the following year. Today it is prescribed for moderate to severe pain and is sold under various brand names, including OxyContin, Percolone, and Oxyfast. A widely prescribed drug known as Percocet contains oxycodone in combination with acetaminophen.

Oxycodone produces pain-relieving effects by binding to and stimulating opioid receptors in the central nervous system. This action, which inhibits the neural relay of pain signals from affected parts of the body to the brain, mimics the behaviour of endorphins, which are pain-suppressing compounds that occur naturally in the human body. In addition to effecting pain relief, stimulation of opioid receptors by oxycodone also elicits psychological responses such as euphoria and activates reward pathways in the brain. These activities render the drug highly addictive and are responsible for producing withdrawal symptoms in patients who have been taking oxycodone for prolonged periods of time.

Prolonged use also desensitizes opioid receptors, resulting in tolerance to oxycodone and necessitating increasing doses of the drug to achieve pain relief. Excessive doses, however, can produce respiratory depression, convulsion, and loss of consciousness.

Oxycodone has a high risk of abuse because of its addictive nature. In many countries its manufacture, prescription, and distribution are regulated on a federal level. For example, in the United States the drug is listed as a Schedule II substance under the Controlled Substances Act, and it is regulated and monitored by the Drug Enforcement Administration. In addition, trafficking of oxycodone is punishable by law in many states and countries, including Australia, Canada, Germany, the United Kingdom, and the United States.

In the 1990s abuse of oxycodone in the United States increased dramatically, particularly in rural, economically depressed areas. Controlled-release tablets, which contain high amounts of oxycodone but dissolve slowly as they pass through the gastrointestinal tract, resulting in gradual and sustained drug release, became the most widely abused form of the drug. The tablets were designed with the intention of lowering the risk of severe side effects and reducing the frequency of administration for patients prescribed oral oxycodone. However, when crushed, the tablets yielded potent quantities of drug that could be snorted, injected, or swallowed to produce a powerful high.

In some areas, oxycodone abuse superseded heroin abuse.

Physiological Actions of Opiates

Opium was for many centuries the principal painkiller known to medicine and was used in various forms and under various names. Laudanum, for example, was an alcoholic tincture (dilute solution) of opium that was used in European medical practice as an analgesic and sedative. Physicians relied on paregoric, a camphorated solution of opium, to treat diarrhea by relaxing the gastrointestinal tract.

Opiates exert their main pain-relieving effects by acting on the brain and spinal cord. They achieve their effect on the brain because, as explained previously for oxycodone, their structure closely resembles that of the body's naturally occurring endorphins. Opiate alkaloids are able to occupy the same receptor sites as endorphins, thereby mimicking the effects of endorphins in suppressing the transmission of pain impulses within the nervous system.

In addition to pain relief, all opiates are also capable of alleviating anxiety, inducing relaxation, drowsiness, and sedation, and imparting a state of euphoria or other enhanced mood. Opiates also have important physiological effects; they slow respiration and heartbeat, suppress the cough reflex, and relax the smooth muscles of the gastrointestinal tract.

All opiates are addictive drugs, and their chronic use leads to tolerance. The higher opiates—heroin and morphine—are more addictive than opium or codeine. Opiates are classified as narcotics because they relieve pain, induce stupor and sleep, and produce addiction. The habitual use of opium produces physical and mental deterioration and shortens life. An acute overdose of opium causes respiratory depression which can be fatal.

History of Opium

The opium poppy was native to what is now Turkey. Ancient Assyrian herb lists and medical texts refer to both the opium poppy plant and opium, and in the 1st century CE the Greek physician Dioscorides described opium in his treatise *De materia medica*, which was the leading Western text on pharmacology for centuries. The growth of poppies for their opium content spread slowly eastward from Mesopotamia and Greece. Apparently, opium was unknown in either India or China in ancient times, and knowledge of the opium poppy first reached China about the 7th century. At first, opium was taken in the form of pills or was added to beverages. The oral intake of raw opium as a medicine does not appear to have produced widespread addictions in ancient Asian societies.

Opium smoking began only after the early Europeans in North America discovered the Indian practice of smoking tobacco in pipes. Some smokers began to mix opium with tobacco in their pipes, and smoking gradually became the preferred method of taking opium. Opium smoking was introduced into China from Java in the 17th century and spread rapidly. The Chinese authorities reacted by prohibiting the sale of opium, but these edicts were largely ignored. During the 18th century European traders found in China an expanding and profitable market for the drug, and the opium trade enabled them to acquire Chinese goods such as silk and tea without having to spend precious gold and silver. Opium addiction became widespread in China, and the Chinese government's attempts to prohibit the import of opium from British-ruled India brought it into direct conflict with the British government. As a result of their defeat in the Opium Wars, the Chinese were compelled to legalize the importation of opium in 1858. Opium addiction remained a problem in Chinese society until the Communists came to power in 1949.

In the West, opium came into wide use as a painkiller in the 18th century, and opium, laudanum, and paregoric were active ingredients in many patent medicines. These drugs were freely available without legal or medical restrictions, and the many cases of addiction they caused did not arouse undue social concern. Morphine was used on hundreds of thousands of sick or wounded American soldiers in the Civil War. The result of this, however, was unprecedented numbers of addicts. By the early decades of the 20th century the legal use of opiates of any kind had been curtailed. The traffic in such drugs then went underground, leading to a vast illicit trade in heroin.

Although opium trade routes extending from the southeastern and southwestern regions of Asia closed temporarily during World War II, cultivation of the plant continued and even prospered in areas of China. In 1948 Burma (Myanmar), located along the southwestern border of China, gained independence and soon after emerged as a major producer of the drug, paralleling the suppression of opium cultivation in China. Throughout the 1960s and '70s, Southeast Asia experienced substantial growth in illicit opium trade. The border area shared by Myanmar, Laos, and Thailand eventually became known as the Golden Triangle, a region that by the mid-1990s was the world's leader in opium cultivation.

Smoking of opium declined in the 20th century, partly because it had been supplanted by more potent derivatives and partly because of determined efforts in China and other developing countries to eradicate it. In the late 1990s, drug-control programs headed by the United Nations and by individual governments contributed to a reduction in opium poppy cultivation in the Golden Triangle. However, the region subsequently became a major producer of other illicit substances, including methamphetamines.

Also in the late 1990s, opium poppy cultivation increased in Afghanistan, and that country became a leading producer of heroin. As cultivation of the plant continued to soar there in the early 2000s, drug trade in the region became associated with terrorism and lawlessness. Near the end of the decade, however, increased law-enforcement efforts and the outbreak of a poppy fungal disease caused poppy cultivation and opium production in Afghanistan to drop significantly. As a result, opium prices increased across the region, threatening to undermine the country's illegal opium and heroin trade. The declines were seen as an opportunity to persuade local farmers to cultivate legal crops. Because of Internet pharmacies that sold the drug illegally, however, global opium trafficking remained high.

The legitimate use of certain opiate alkaloids in medicine has compounded issues surrounding the cultivation of opium poppies. Today *P. somniferum* is legally grown in Australia, Turkey, and India for the production of medicinal alkaloids. However, unlicensed cultivation of opium plants remains a serious legal offense in many countries, including the United States, since the substance is the starting product for heroin, which has millions of addicts worldwide.

A young boy helps cultivate poppies in Kandahar, Afghanistan. Poppy fields are a common sight in Afghanistan, which has become a chief producer of opium. John D. McHugh/AFP/ Getty Images

OPIATE USERS

There is no single narcotic addict personality type: addiction is not a unitary phenomenon occurring in a single type. The great variation in addiction rates and classes of addicts in various countries caution against placing too great an emphasis on personality variables as major causative factors. Even within the United States, there is great danger in generalizing from the cases of the patients found at the public health service hospitals. Such individuals are a highly select group of adults who have spent previous time in correctional institutions. They are not representative of the adolescent addict or the adult addict who has not had continual difficulty with the law.

Another type of user is the addict who is a member of a closely knit adolescent gang. This subculture is highly tolerant of drug abuse, and the members have ready access to narcotic drugs. They do not actively seek the opportunity to try heroin. Neither are they deliberately "hooked" on heroin by adult drug peddlers. They are initiated to narcotic use by friends, gang members, or neighbourhood acquaintances, and the opportunity for such use is almost always casual but ever present. This "kicks" user is apt to abandon narcotics when gang membership is abandoned. The chronic user is more likely to be the immature adolescent at the periphery of gang activities who uses narcotics for their adjustive value in terms of deep-seated personality problems. Such individuals do not abandon drug use for the more conventional pursuits when entering adulthood. Instead, old ties are severed; interest in previous friendships is withdrawn; athletic and scholastic strivings are abandoned; competitive, sexual, and aggressive behaviour becomes markedly reduced, and the individual retreats further into a drug-induced

THOMAS DE QUINCEY

(b. Aug. 15, 1785, Manchester, Lancashire, Eng.—d. Dec. 8, 1859, Edinburgh, Scot.)

English essayist and critic Thomas De Quincey was best known for his Confessions of an English Opium-Eater.

As a child De Quincey was alienated from his solid, prosperous mercantile family by his sensitivity and precocity. At age 17 he ran away to Wales and then lived incognito in London (1802–03). There he formed a friendship with a young prostitute named Ann, who made a lasting impression on him. Reconciled to his family in 1803, he entered Worcester College, Oxford, where he conceived the ambition of becoming "the intellectual benefactor of mankind." He became widely read in many subjects and eventually would write essays on such subjects as history, biography, economics, psychology, and German metaphysics. While still at college in

1804, he took his first opium to relieve the pain of facial neuralgia. By 1813 he had become "a regular and confirmed opium-eater" (i.e., an opium addict), keeping a decanter of laudanum (tincture of opium) by his elbow and steadily increasing the dose. He remained an addict for the rest of his life.

De Quincey was an early admirer of the revolutionary Lyrical Ballads *(1798), and in 1807 he became a close associate of its authors, William Wordsworth and Samuel Taylor Coleridge. He rented Wordsworth's former home, Dove Cottage at Grasmere, on and off from 1809 to 1833. In 1817 De Quincey married Margaret Simpson, who had already borne him a son. Though he wrote voluminously, he published almost nothing. His financial position as head of a large family went from bad to worse until the appearance of* Confessions *(1821) in* London Magazine *made him famous. It was reprinted as a book in 1822.*

The avowed purpose of the first version of the Confessions *is to warn the reader of the dangers of opium, and it combines the interest of a journalistic exposé of a social evil, told from an insider's point of view, with a somewhat contradictory picture of the subjective pleasures of drug addiction. The book begins with an autobiographical account of the author's addiction, describes in detail the euphoric and highly symbolic reveries that he experienced under the drug's influence, and recounts the horrible nightmares that continued use of the drug eventually produced. The highly poetic and imaginative prose of the* Confessions *makes it one of the enduring stylistic masterpieces of English literature.*

In 1856 he seized the opportunity provided by the publication of his collected works to rewrite the book that had made him famous. He added some descriptions of opium-inspired dreams that had appeared about 1845 in Blackwood's Magazine *under the title "Suspiria de Profundis" ("Sighs from the Depths"). But by this time he had lost most of the accounts he had kept of his early opium visions, so he expanded the rather short original version of the* Confessions *in other ways, adding much autobiographical material on his childhood and his experiences as a youth in London. His literary style in the revised version of the* Confessions, *however, tends to be difficult, involved, and even verbose.*

De Quincey became increasingly solitary and eccentric, especially after his wife's death in 1837, and he often retreated for long periods into opium dreams. Of the more than 14 volumes of his work, only the original Confessions *is a definitive literary expression.*

state. Identification is now with the addict group: a special culture with a special language. The addict's world revolves around obtaining drugs.

Means of Administration

Most persistent users follow a classic progression from sniffing (similar to the oral route), to "skin popping" (subcutaneous route), to "mainlining" (intravenous route)—each step bringing more intense experience, a higher addiction liability. With mainlining, the initial "thrill" is more immediate. Within seconds, a warm, glowing sensation spreads over the body, most intense in the stomach and intestines, comparable to sexual release. This intense "rush" is then followed by a deep sense of relaxation and contentment. The user is "high" and momentarily free. It is this initial state of intense pleasure that presumably brings the novice to repeat the experience, and it is this mode of administration that hastens a user on the way to drug tolerance and physical dependence. Soon the user finds that the effects are not quite there. Instead, his or her body is beginning to experience new miseries. At this juncture, the user "shoots" to avoid discomfort. The euphoria is gone. The individual now spends every waking moment in obtaining further supplies to prevent the inevitable withdrawal symptoms should supplies run out.

Habits are expensive. If indigent, the addict must spend all his or her time "hustling" for drugs—which means that the person must steal or raise money by other means such as prostitution, procuring, or small-time narcotics peddling. An addict is judged by his or her success in supporting the habit. The addict always faces the danger of withdrawal, the danger of arrest, the danger of loss of available supply, the danger of infection, of collapsed veins, or of death from overdosage. Very few individuals are still addicted by age 40. They have either died, somehow freed themselves from their addiction, or sought treatment.

THERAPY FOR OPIATE DEPENDENCE

Drug dependence can be viewed as an ethical problem: Is it right and permissible to need a narcotic agent? How one answers this question dictates the position one will take in regard to addiction therapy. In general, the addict can be given the drug, can be placed on a substitute drug, or drugs can be barred altogether. Narcotic maintenance, which gives the addict the drug, is the system employed in the management of opiate dependence in some institutions. Methadone treatment is a drug substitution therapy that replaces opiate addiction with methadone addiction in order that the addict might become a socially useful citizen. Some drug therapy groups involve an intensive program of familylike resocialization, with total abstinence as the goal. Psychological approaches to total abstinence through reeducation involve psychotherapy, hypnosis, and various conditioning techniques that attempt to attach unpleasant or aversive associations to the thoughts and actions accompanying drug use. Each of these approaches has had successes and has limitations.

Great Britain began to control the use of narcotics in 1950, embracing the principle of drug maintenance. Supporters of the approach insisted that narcotic addiction in Great Britain remained a very minor problem because addiction was considered an illness rather than a crime. (In recent years, however, addiction has become more widespread.) The British physician was earlier allowed to prescribe maintenance doses of a narcotic if, in his or her professional judgment, the addict was unable to lead a useful life without the drug. But in 1967 the British government took the right to prescribe for maintenance addiction away from the general practitioner and placed it in the hands of drug-treatment clinics. Although some addicts must obtain legal supplies from the clinic, others are allowed to obtain supplies from a neighbourhood pharmacy and medicate themselves. These clinics also provide social and re-educative services such as psychotherapy for the addict. The general experience among these clinics has been that a large proportion of the addicts are becoming productive, socially useful members of the community.

There are two major drawbacks to the maintenance use of narcotic drugs. Both the physical and the social health of the user remains unsatisfactory. A high incidence of hepatitis, bacterial endocarditis, abcesses, and, on occasion, fatal overdosage accompanies the self-administration of opiates. Socially, the addict on self-administration also tends to remain less productive than his or her peers—the reason apparently being that the individual on narcotic maintenance is still very preoccupied with certain aspects of narcotic use. Narcotic addiction is a two-faceted problem: the yearning for the "high" and the felt sense of not being physiologically normal. The addict on narcotic maintenance often attempts to obtain or retain both drug effects: frequent intravenous use prevents the feeling of drug hunger and maximizes his or her attempt to experience euphoria.

Methadone therapy aims to block the abnormal reactions associated with narcotic addiction while permitting the addict to live a normal, useful life as a fully participating member of the community. Methadone provides a "narcotic blockade" in that it is possible to increase methadone medication to a point at which large oral doses will induce a state of cross-tolerance in which the euphoric effects of other narcotics cannot be felt even in very high doses. Additionally methadone has the ability to allay the feeling of not being right physically, which the addict finds he or she can correct only by repeated narcotic use. Methadone treatment, then, rests on these two pharmacological actions: the blockade of euphoric effects and the relief of "narcotic hunger." Methadone is not successful in every case, but results have been dramatic in some cases. In various studies conducted on addicts who entered a methadone treatment program, most remained in the program, and virtually none returned to daily use of heroin. The majority either accepted employment or started school, and previous patterns of antisocial behaviour were either eliminated or significantly reduced. Methadone is a drug of addiction in its own right, but it does not have some of the more serious undesirable consequences associated with heroin.

There are various types of drug counseling units that advocate complete abstinence from drug dependency. Such drug therapy, usually involving a

VINCENT PAUL DOLE

(b. May 18, 1913, Chicago, Ill., U.S.—d. Aug. 1, 2006, New York, N.Y.)

American physician Vincent Paul Dole conducted important studies in nephrology (the effect of salt in the diet of kidney patients) and metabolic medicine (research in obesity) but was best remembered for his groundbreaking treatment for heroin addicts—using methadone as a maintenance drug. Together with his second wife, psychiatrist Marie Nyswander, Dole began dispensing methadone in 1964 to hard-core addicts at a New York City storefront clinic. Though much controversy resulted—the addict was still reliant on a drug—Dole found that methadone, unlike heroin, would not create a high, produce violent mood swings, or induce a passive state of withdrawal, a state in which addicts would spend their days contemplating their next fix. For his work he was awarded the 1988 Albert Lasker Award for Clinical Medical Research.

group of addicts, tries to promote personal growth and teach self-reliance. Individual counseling and psychotherapy may or may not be provided for the members of the group, but generally it is believed that moral support is derived from the experiences of fellow addicts and former addicts who have or are trying to become chemically independent. Success rates for various drug therapy groups vary widely.

In countries where the addict is treated as a criminal, physicians may be prevented from administering opiates for the maintenance of addiction. Acceptable treatment includes enforced institutionalization for several months, strict regulation against ambulatory care until the person is drug free, and the total prohibition of self-administration of drugs even under a physician's care. Estimates of cures based upon decades of such government-regulated procedures range from 1 to 15 percent.

HALLUCINOGENIC DRUGS AND HALLUCINATION

It is difficult to find a suitable generic name for a class of drugs having as many diverse effects as have been reported for "hallucinogens." Abnormal behaviour as profound as the swings in mood, disturbances in thinking, perceptual distortions, delusions, and feelings of strangeness that sometimes occur with these drugs is usually indicative of a major mental disorder. Consequently these substances are often called psychotomimetic to indicate that their effects mimic the symptoms of a naturally occurring psychosis. There are indeed points of similarity between the drug states and the natural psychoses, but there are also many dissimilarities—so many as to make the resemblance quite superficial. Substances such as the bromides, heavy metals, belladonna alkaloids, and intoxicants can, however, cause abnormal behaviour to a degree sometimes described as psychotic, and if the list is extended to include the drugs being discussed here, then the objection—that the term *psychotomimetic* should refer only to the mimicking of a natural psychosis—is no longer valid. Taking this point of view, some investigators prefer the term *psychotogenic* ("psychosis causing"). One of the most conspicuous features of this kind of drug experience is the occurrence of the distinctive change in perception called hallucination. For this reason the term *hallucinogenic* is sometimes used. Most people are aware, however, even while under the influence

Ergot, the main source of LSD, attacks rye and can cause disease in humans. Walter Dawn

of the drug, that their unusual perceptions have no basis in reality, so this is not a very accurate use of the term. Strictly speaking, very few people truly hallucinate as a result of taking a hallucinogen.

All these terms are borrowed from medicine and are closely identified with pathology. In this sense, all are negative. It has been suggested that these drugs be called psychedelic ("mind manifesting"). This term shifts the emphasis to that aspect of the drug experience that involves an increased awareness of one's surroundings and also of one's own bodily processes—in brief, an expansion of consciousness. The term also shifts emphasis from the medical or therapeutic aspect to the educational or mystical-religious aspect of drug experience. Only certain people, however, ever have a psychedelic experience in its fullest meaning, and the question of its value to the individual is entirely subjective. The possibility of dangerous consequences, too, may be masked by such a benign term. None of these terms, then, is entirely satisfactory, and one or two are distinctly misleading.

TYPES OF HALLUCINOGENS

Widespread interest and bitter controversy have surrounded drugs that produce marked aberrations of behaviour. Among the most important of these drugs are LSD, which originally was derived from ergot (*Claviceps purpurea*), a fungus on rye and wheat; mescaline, the active principle of the peyote cactus (*Lophophora* williamsii), which grows in the southwestern United States and Mexico; and psilocybin and psilocin, which come from Mexican mushrooms (notably *Psilocybe mexicana* and *Stropharia cubensis*).

Other notable mind-altering substances include ketamine, PCP, and bufotenine, which is related to LSD and was originally isolated from the skin of toads. Bufotenine has also been isolated in the plant *Piptadenia peregrina* and the mushroom *Amanita muscaria* and is thought to be the active principle of the hallucinogenic snuff called cohoba and yopo and used by the Indians of Trinidad and by the Otamac Indians of the Orinoco valley. Harmine is an alkaloid found in the seed coats of a plant (*Peganum harmala*) of the Mediterranean region and the Middle East and also in a South American vine (*Banisteriopsis caapi*).

There are some amides of lysergic acid contained in the seeds of two species of morning glory (*Rivea corymbosa*, also called *Turbina corymbosa*, and *Ipomoea tricolor*, also called *I. rubrocaerulea* or *I. violacea*). Synthetic compounds of interest are DMT (dimethyltryptamine) and STP (dimethoxyphenylethylamine; DOM).

LSD

LSD is a potent synthetic hallucinogenic drug that can be derived from the ergot alkaloids (as ergotamine and ergonovine, principal constituents of ergot). LSD usually is prepared by chemical synthesis in a laboratory. Its basic chemical structure is similar to that of the ergot alkaloids, and it is structurally related to several other drugs (e.g., bufotenine, psilocybin, harmine, and ibogaine), which can all block the action of serotonin (the indole amine transmitter of nerve impulses) in brain tissue.

LSD produces marked deviations from normal behaviour, probably the consequence of its ability to inhibit the action of serotonin, though the mechanism of the drug remains uncertain. LSD was used experimentally in medicine as a psychotomimetic agent to induce mental states that were believed to resemble those of actual psychotic diseases (primarily the schizophrenias). After administration, LSD can be absorbed readily from any mucosal surface—even the ear—and acts within 30 to 60 minutes. Its effects usually last for 8 to 10 hours, and occasionally some effects persist for several days. Two serious side effects are the prolongation and transient reappearance of the psychotic reaction.

Since LSD is not an approved drug, its therapeutic applications are regarded as experimental. In the 1960s LSD was proposed for use in the treatment of neuroses, especially for patients who were recalcitrant to more conventional psychotherapeutic procedures. LSD also was tried as a treatment for alcoholism and to reduce the suffering of terminally ill cancer patients. It was studied as an adjunct in the treatment of narcotic addiction, of children with autism, and of the so-called psychopathic personality. None of these uses were successful by the early 1990s, and most researchers concluded that there was no clinical value in the use of LSD. In the early 21st century, however, research into the treatment of alcoholism with LSD was revived, some researchers concluding that it might provide benefits.

The use of LSD outside a clinical setting can be dangerous. Mood shifts, time and space distortions, and impulsive behaviour are especially hazardous complications to an individual who takes the drug. The individual may become increasingly suspicious of the intentions and motives of others and may act aggressively against them.

Legitimate use of LSD declined markedly in the mid-1960s. In the United States, manufacture, possession, sale, transfer, and use of LSD came under the restrictions of the Drug Abuse Control Amendment of 1965. The following year the only authorized manufacturer of LSD in the United States withdrew the drug from the market and transferred its supplies to the federal government. Research projects have continued under the supervision of the National Institute of Mental Health, a governmental agency.

During the 1960s LSD was popular within the hippie subculture that emerged in the United States and western Europe. One critical pioneer in this movement was Augustus Owsley Stanley III, a California-based underground chemist who manufactured several million doses of the drug. Owsley's efforts supplied the drug to several figures who would become advocates for LSD, including novelist Ken Kesey and Harvard psychologist Timothy Leary (Owsley also was a personal supplier of LSD to the Grateful Dead). During the mid-1960s, LSD ("acid") spread widely in the emerging counterculture, and the shapes and colours characteristic of LSD-induced trips appear frequently in the visual art of the period. The drug also powerfully shaped the popular music of the 1960s and encouraged the mystical experimentation of these years. LSD retained a youth following into the mid-1970s, when publicity about the drug's psychiatric ill effects slowed usage. Nevertheless, a revival of LSD use occurred in the United States and elsewhere in the 1990s.

PCP

PCP, or "angel dust," is a hallucinogenic drug with anesthetic properties, having the chemical name 1–(1–phencyclohexyl) piperidine. It was first developed in 1956 by Parke Davis Laboratories of Detroit for use as an anesthetic in veterinary medicine, though it is no longer used in this capacity. Used for a brief time as a general anesthetic in humans, its side effects range from distorted self-perception to severe disorientation and unpredictable, psychotic behaviour, which quickly discouraged its legal use.

As with other hallucinogens, PCP does not cause physical dependence. In low doses it produces effects similar

ALBERT HOFMANN

(b. Jan. 11, 1906, Baden, Switz.—d. April 29, 2008, Burg, Switz.)

Swiss chemist Albert Hofmann discovered the psychedelic drug LSD (lysergic acid diethyl-amide), which he first synthesized in 1938 by isolating compounds found in ergot (Claviceps purpurea), a fungus affecting rye.

Hofmann attended the University of Zürich, graduating in 1929 with a doctorate in medicinal chemistry. Upon graduation he was hired by Sandoz Laboratories in Basel, where he was assigned to a program developing methods for synthesizing compounds found in medicinal plants. It was there, while testing the analeptic (stimulant) properties of ergot derivatives, that Hofmann stumbled upon LSD-25 (the 25th such derivative tested) in 1938.

Hofmann's initial discovery was set aside for five years until April 1943, when he returned to his earlier therapeutic research on the compound. After accidentally absorbing a small amount of the synthesized drug, he experienced dreamlike hallucinations. Following his initial experience, Hoffman purposely ingested the drug numerous times, concluding that it could be of significant use in psychiatric treatment. He spent years investigating LSD's hallucinogenic properties in the belief that the drug would one day be useful in the therapeutic treatment of schizophrenics and other psychiatric patients. While disapproving of the casual recreational use that came to define the drug in the 1960s, Hofmann maintained that the drug, when taken under controlled circumstances and with full knowledge of the possible effects, could prove useful in both psychiatric and spiritual contexts, an argument that he conveyed in his 1979 book LSD, mein Sorgenkind (LSD: My Problem Child, 1980).

Hofmann also isolated methergine, a drug used to treat postpartum hemorrhaging, from ergot. However, most of his later research focused on the psychotropic qualities of various plants and fungi. In 1958 he synthesized psilocybin and psilocin, the hallucinogenic compounds in the mushroom Psilocybe mexicana, having been sent samples by an amateur mycologist intrigued by his work with LSD. In 1960 he discovered a compound similar to LSD in a species of morning glory (Rivea corymbosa), and in 1962 he traveled to Mexico to research the plant Salvia divinorum, though he

Albert Hofmann, the father of LSD. Keystone/Hulton Archive/Getty Images

was ultimately unable to discern its actively hallucinogenic components. While in Mexico, he was able to convince a curandera (female shaman) to preside over a ritual that employed the compounds he had isolated from the Psilocybe mushrooms, which grew naturally in the area. Hofmann also investigated the pharmacological properties of a number of other plants as well, including peyote, from which mescaline is derived.

Hofmann, who had become director of natural products at Sandoz Laboratories in 1956, retired in 1971. In 1988 the Albert Hofmann Foundation, an organization advocating the responsible use of hallucinogens, was established in his honour. He contributed to several books, including The Road to Eleusis: Unveiling the Secret of the Mysteries (1978), which speculates that the Eleusinian Mysteries, a series of ancient Greek religious rites, were catalyzed by consumption of hallucinogenic mushrooms; The Botany and Chemistry of Hallucinogens (1973); and Plants of the Gods: Origins of Hallucinogenic Use (1979). Hofmann independently wrote Insight/Outlook (1989), concerning the perception of reality, and the posthumously published Hofmann's Elixir: LSD and the New Eleusis (2008).

to those of LSD, though violent and psychotic behaviour seem to be more characteristic of PCP. Although most users do not have psychotic episodes, the effects of the drug are extremely unpredictable. A PCP user is often impervious to pain and generally exhibits emotional instability, excited intoxication, a lack of coordination, high blood pressure, and increased deep-tendon muscle reflexes. At high doses, PCP is highly toxic and can cause convulsions and coma. PCP's effects vary by user and are influenced by mood, dosage, and setting. Effects are evident one to two hours after ingestion and generally last four to six hours. Among chronic users, visual, memory, and speech disorders have been noted. In an illegal setting, the drug is typically mixed in powdered form with a leafy substance such as parsley, mint, tobacco, or marijuana and is smoked. It may also be dissolved in a liquid and sprayed onto the leaves. In addition, it can be injected or inhaled.

Because PCP is relatively easy and inexpensive to manufacture, it became a major illegal drug in North America, though its popularity never really spread further. In the United States an illicit trade in PCP sprang up during the mid-1960s, and violence related to the use of PCP—including suicide, homicide, and self-mutilation—grew to alarming proportions in the 1970s and '80s. It was estimated that at least seven million Americans used PCP on at least one occasion between 1975 and 1983. By the mid-1980s, PCP use declined, largely as a result of the increased popularity of crack cocaine.

KETAMINE

Ketamine, known chemically as 2-(2-chlorophenyl)-2-(methylamino)-cyclohexanone (or CI581), is a general anesthetic agent related structurally to PCP. Ketamine was first synthesized in 1962 at Parke Davis Laboratories by American scientist Calvin Stevens, who was searching for a new anesthetic to replace PCP. Ketamine was originally patented in Belgium in 1963 and was approved for use in humans by the U.S. Food and Drug Administration in 1970. Soon after, it was put to use to treat American soldiers fighting in the Vietnam War.

Today, since ketamine can produce minor hallucinogenic side effects in humans, it is used most often as a veterinary anesthetic. However, the drug does have valuable applications in human medicine, especially as an anesthetic for children and for individuals undergoing minor surgery.

Unlike inhalation anesthetics or sedative anesthetics (e.g., narcotics and benzodiazepines), ketamine does not depress respiration or other basic functions of the central nervous system. Thus, ketamine has a relatively wide margin of safety. In addition, it is distinct from other anesthetics because it has three major effects: analgesia (pain relief), hypnosis (sedation), and amnesia. The drug is known particularly for its ability to induce a dissociative (cataleptic) state, which is characterized by a lack of pain sensation, unconsciousness, and increased muscle tone. These characteristics are often accompanied by open eyes, jumping eye movements (nystagmus), and involuntary limb movements.

Ketamine works by altering the activity of neurons in the brain. This is accomplished through the drug's inhibition of neuronal uptake of various neurotransmitters, including serotonin, glutamate, and dopamine. The net effect is a depression of neural communication between the thalamus and the cerebral cortex, resulting in an uncoupling of brain activity associated with memory, motor function, sensory experience, and emotion. Ketamine also stimulates activity in the limbic system, a region of the brain involved in controlling certain autonomic functions and in integrating various brain activities, including those associated with motivation and emotion.

In clinical use ketamine is administered intramuscularly or intravenously. Minor side effects of the drug include tearing (lacrimation) when emerging from the dissociative anesthetic state. Patients can sometimes experience severe and troubling hallucinogenic effects, such as intense dreams and delirium, upon waking. These effects are more common in adults than in children. Hallucinations are directly related to dose. Thus, higher doses produce more pronounced delirium and other symptoms of hallucination than do lower doses.

Ketamine's ability to produce hallucinogenic effects within minutes after administration has led to its abuse as a recreational drug. The dissociative effect of ketamine that is produced by high doses is often described by recreational users as the "K hole"—a separation of the mind and body, or a hallucinatory "out of body" experience. Ketamine is known by various street names, including K, special K, jet, super acid, and cat valium. It may be snorted, injected, or taken orally, and its effects may last from 30 minutes to more than an hour. However, for one or more days after taking the drug, users may display symptoms of amnesia, schizophrenia, impaired judgment, and lack of coordination. In addition, long-term abuse can lead to paranoia, depression, and other evidence of cognitive dysfunction. Many individuals appear to be in a stupor when the drug has been taken in low doses. However, high doses can cause unconsciousness, cardiovascular depression, and death.

MESCALINE

Mescaline, also known as β-3,4,5-trimethoxyphenethylamine, is a naturally occurring alkaloid, the active principle contained in the flowering heads of the peyote cactus (species *Lophophora williamsii*) of Mexico and the southwestern United States. It is best known for its use as a drug to induce hallucination. The mescaline molecule is related structurally

PEYOTE

Peyote, or mescal-button, is either of the two species of the cactus genus Lophophora, family Cactaceae. The plants are native to North America, almost exclusively to Mexico.

Peyote is well-known for its hallucinogenic effects. The plant contains at least 28 alkaloids, the principal one of which is mescaline. Peyote figures prominently in the traditional religious rituals of certain North American Indian peoples, as well as in the current rituals (many adapted from traditional rituals) of the Native American Church. The sale, use, or possession of dried mescal buttons or live plants is prohibited by law in many places, although a number of areas also provide exemptions for use in formal religious rites. The American Indian

Peyote (Lophophora williamsii). Dennis E. Anderson

Religious Freedom Act (1978) is the primary legislation governing the religious uses of peyote in the United States.

Peyote is found only on limestone soils of the Chihuahuan Desert of southern Texas and northern Mexico. Averaging about 8 cm (3 inches) wide and 5 cm (2 inches) tall, the body of the peyote cactus is spineless, soft, and in most cases, blue green in colour.

The more common species, L. williamsii, has pink to white flowers in summer, the fruit ripening the following year. L. diffusa, more primitive, grows in a small area in central Mexico. Its flowers are white to yellow, and the body is yellow green.

to two hormones secreted by the adrenal glands, adrenaline and noradrenaline. Both are catecholamine compounds that take part in the transmission of nerve impulses. Mescaline was isolated as the active principle of peyote in 1896, and its structural resemblance to adrenaline was recognized by 1919.

In experiments mescaline requires two to three hours for onset of action, and its effects sometimes last for more than 12 hours. The hallucinatory effects vary greatly among individuals and even for a particular individual from one drug session to the next. Hallucinations are usually visual, less often auditory. Side effects include nausea and vomiting. Mescaline is prepared from the peyote cactus by extraction and purification, but it can be synthesized.

PSILOCIN AND PSILOCYBIN

Psilocin and psilocybin are hallucinogenic principles contained in certain mushrooms (notably two Mexican species, *Psilocybe mexicana* and *Stropharia cubensis*). Hallucinogenic mushrooms used in religious ceremonies by the Indians of Mexico were considered sacred and were called "god's flesh" by the Aztecs. In the 1950s the active principles psilocin and psilocybin were isolated from the Mexican mushrooms. They are not used in modern medicine.

Chemically, psilocin and psilocybin are indole hallucinogens that block the action of serotonin (the indole amine transmitter of nerve impulses) in brain tissue. Psilocybin differs from psilocin in having a phosphate group attached to the molecule at the oxygen atom. Psilocin and psilocybin produce experiences similar to those produced by mescaline and LSD. They act within 20 to 30 minutes, and the duration of action is about four hours.

HISTORY OF HALLUCINOGENS

Native societies of the Western Hemisphere have for 2,000 years utilized various naturally occurring materials such as the "sacred" mushroom of Mexico and the peyote cactus. Scientific interest in the hallucinogenic drugs developed slowly. A neurologist wrote about his experience with peyote before the turn of the 20th century, and his account attracted the serious attention of two distinguished psychologists, Havelock Ellis and William James. Following the isolation of mescaline in 1896 and the subsequent discoveries concerning its structure, there emerged some interest in model psychoses (drug-induced simulations of abnormal behaviour patterns). In 1943 Swiss chemist Albert Hofmann accidentally ingested a synthetic preparation of LSD and experienced its psychedelic effects. This discovery attracted significant attention, leading many to believe that the psychedelic effects of LSD triggered a chemical schizophrenia. The model psychosis stage of LSD investigations was convenient for enabling experimentation with the drug. It also took place in an era when little was understood about the biochemical abnormalities involved in psychological disorders such as schizophrenia, and thus there appeared to be legitimate reasons to believe that the drug could produce a model psychosis. Today, however, the model psychosis theory of LSD's actions has been largely rejected. The drug does not induce a chemical schizophrenia. It instead induces an altered psychological state very different from that caused by organic psychological disease.

Physiological and Psychological Effects

The psychedelics are capable of producing a wide range of subjective and objective effects. However, there is apparently no reaction that is distinctive for a particular drug. Subjects are unable to distinguish among LSD, mescaline, and psilocybin when they have no prior knowledge of the identity of the drug ingested. These drugs induce a physiological response that is consistent with the type of effect expected of a central-nervous-system stimulant. Usually there is elevation of the systolic blood pressure, dilatation of the pupils, some facilitation of the spinal reflexes, and excitation of the sympathetic nervous system and the brain.

There is considerable difference in the potency of these drugs. A grown man requires about 500 mg of mescaline or 20 mg of psilocybin or only 0.1 mg of LSD for full clinical effects when the substances are ingested orally. The active principle in the seeds of the morning glory is about $1/10$ as potent as LSD. There are also differences in the time of onset and the duration of effects. Psilocybin acts within 20 to 30 minutes, and the effects last about five to six hours. LSD acts within 30 to 60 minutes, and the effects usually last eight to 10 hours, although occasionally some effects persist for several days. Mescaline requires two to three hours for onset, but the effects last more than 12 hours. All psychedelics presumably are lethal if taken in quantities large enough, but the effective dose is so low compared with the lethal dose that death has not been a factor in experimental studies. Physiological tolerance for these drugs develops quite rapidly—fastest for LSD, somewhat more slowly and less completely for psilocybin and mescaline. The effects for a particular dose level of LSD are lost within three days of repeated administration, but the original sensitivity is quickly regained if several days are allowed to intervene. Cross-tolerance has been demonstrated for LSD, mescaline, psilocybin, and certain of the lysergic acid derivatives. Tolerance to one of the drugs reduces the effectiveness of an equivalent dose of a second drug, thus suggesting a common mode of action for the group.

Most persons regard the experience with one of these drugs as totally removed from anything ever encountered in normal everyday life. The subjective effects vary greatly among individuals and, for a particular person, even from one drug session to the next. The variations seem to reflect such factors as the mood and personality of the subject, the setting in which the drug is administered, the user's expectation of a certain kind of experience, the meaning for the individual of the act of taking the drug, and the user's interpretation of the motives of the person administering the drug. Nevertheless, certain invariant reactions experienced by hallucinogen users stand out. The one most easily described by users is the effect of being "flooded" with visual experience, as much when the eyes are closed as when they are open. Light is greatly intensified; colours are vivid and seem to glow; images are numerous and persistent, yielding a wide range of illusions and hallucinations; details are sharp; perception of space is enhanced; and music may evoke visual impressions, or light may give the impression of sounds.

A second important aspect, which people have more difficulty describing, involves a change in the feelings and the awareness of the self. The sense of personal identity is altered. There may be a fusion of subject and object; legs may seem to shrink or become extended, and the body to float; space may become boundless and the passage of time very slow; and the person may feel completely empty inside or may believe that he is the universe. This type of reaction has been called depersonalization, detachment, or dissociation. Increased suspiciousness of the intentions and motives of others may also become a factor. At times the mood shifts. Descriptions of rapture, ecstasy, and an enhanced sense of beauty are readily elicited; but there can also be a "hellish" terror, gloom, and the feeling of complete isolation. For some people the experience is so disturbing that psychiatric hospitalization is required. Studies of performance on standardized tests show some reduction in reasoning and memory, but the motivation of the subject probably accounts for much of the performance decrement, since many people are uncooperative in this type of structured setting while under the influence of a drug.

Interest in these drugs was routinely scientific for the first few years following the discovery of LSD, but in the 1950s some professional groups began to explore the use of the psychedelics as adjuncts to psychotherapy and also for certain purposes of creativity. It was at this juncture, when the drugs were employed to "change" people, that they became a centre of controversy. LSD is not an approved drug in most countries. Consequently its therapeutic applications can only be regarded as experimental. In the 1960s, LSD was proposed as an aid in the treatment of neurosis with special interest in cases recalcitrant to the more conventional psychotherapeutic procedures. LSD also was being given serious trial in the treatment of alcoholism, particularly in Canada, where experimentation was not heavily restricted. LSD has also been employed to reduce the suffering of terminally ill cancer patients. The drug was also under study as an adjunct in the treatment of narcotic addiction, of autistic children, and of the so-called psychopathic personality. The use of various hallucinogens was advocated in the experimental study of abnormal behaviour because of the degree of control that they offer.

LSD can be dangerous when used improperly. Swings of mood, time and space distortion, "hallucinations," and impulsive behavior are complications especially hazardous to the individual when he is alone. Driving while under the influence of one of these drugs is particularly dangerous. Acts of aggression are rare but do occur. The recorded suicide rate was not high in the various investigational (legal use) groups, but the rate of serious untoward psychological effects requiring psychiatric attention climbed steadily. These drugs do induce psychotic reactions that may last several months or longer. Negative reactions, sometimes called bad trips, are most apt to occur in unstable persons or in other persons taking very large amounts of a drug or taking it under strange conditions or in unfamiliar settings. So far as is known, these drugs are nontoxic, and there are no permanent physical effects associated with their use. There is no physical dependence or withdrawal symptom associated with long-term use, but certain individuals may become psychologically dependent on the drug, become deeply preoccupied with its use, and radically change their lifestyle with continued use.

Hallucinogen Users

Prior to the mid-1960s, LSD-type drugs were taken by several different types of persons including many who were respected, successful, and well established socially. Intellectuals, educators, medical and mental health professionals, volunteer research subjects, psychiatric patients, theological students, and participants in special drug-centre communities were some of the first users of these hallucinogenic substances.

Beginning in 1966, experimentation in most countries was severely restricted, and subsequent use was almost entirely of a black market type.

LSD use has declined substantially, since the drug was replaced by cannabis and the amphetamines. Most users tend to be of the middle class—either young,

TIMOTHY LEARY

(b. Oct. 22, 1920, Springfield, Mass., U.S.—d. May 31, 1996, Beverly Hills, Calif.)

American psychologist and author Timothy Leary was a leading advocate for the use of LSD and other psychoactive drugs.

Leary, the son of a U.S. Army officer, was raised in a Catholic household and attended Holy Cross College, the U.S. Military Academy at West Point, and the University of Alabama (B.A., 1943). In 1950 he received a doctorate in psychology from the University of California at Berkeley, where he was an assistant professor until 1955. During the 1950s Leary developed an egalitarian model for interaction between the psychotherapist and the patient, promoted new techniques of group therapy, and published a system for classifying interpersonal behaviour. He acquired a reputation as a promising young scholar and was appointed to the position of lecturer at Harvard University in 1959.

At Harvard, Leary began experimenting with psilocybin, a synthesized form of the hallucinogenic agent found in certain mushrooms. He concluded that psychedelic drugs could be effective in transforming personality and expanding human consciousness. Along with a colleague, he formed the Harvard Psychedelic Drug Research Program and began administering psilocybin to graduate students; he also shared the drug with several prominent artists, writers, and musicians. Leary explored the cultural and philosophical implications of psychedelic drugs; in contrast to those within the psychedelic research community who argued that the drugs should be used only by a small elite, Leary came to believe that the experience should be introduced to the general public, particularly to young people.

Leary's experiments were highly controversial, and he was dismissed from Harvard in 1963 after colleagues protested. During the mid-1960s Leary lived in a mansion in Millbrook, New York, where he formed the centre of a small hedonistic community and began to intensively explore LSD, a more powerful psychedelic drug. His research, which initially had emphasized careful control over the "set and setting" of the psychedelic experience, became increasingly undisciplined and unstructured. He traveled widely and gave many public lectures, especially on college campuses, and because of his high public profile, he became a focus of the emerging public debate over LSD. His phrase "turn on, tune in, drop out" became a popular counterculture slogan. Cultural conservatives saw Leary as a corrosive influence on society—President Richard Nixon called him "the most dangerous man in America"—while many researchers felt that Leary delegitimized the serious study of psychedelic drugs.

After arrests in 1965 and 1968 for possession of marijuana and a prolonged legal battle, Leary was incarcerated in 1970. He soon escaped and became a fugitive, living outside the United States for more than two years until being recaptured in Afghanistan. He was freed in 1976 and settled in southern California. During the 1980s and '90s Leary continued to appear publicly in lectures and debates, although he never regained the stature he had enjoyed during the 1960s. He also designed computer software and was an early advocate of the potential of new technologies such as virtual reality and the Internet.

college-educated persons or those who have drifted to the fringe of society. Drug initiation is typically by way of a personal friend or acquaintance. Employers or teachers also have a powerful influence over subordinates and students in terms of drug acceptance. The user of LSD seems often to have an almost fanatic need to proselytize others to drug use. Those who have taken a hallucinogenic substance generally have had experience with other drugs prior to the LSD experience, and there is also a tendency on the part of those who take these drugs to repeat the drug experience and to experiment with other drugs. The special language, method of proselytizing, and psychological dependence surrounding the use of psychedelics bear striking resemblance to the context of narcotics addiction. The chronic LSD user tends to be introverted and passive. Motives for LSD use are many: psychological insight; expansion of consciousness; the desire to become more loving, more creative, open, religious; a desire for new experience, profound personality change, and simple "kicks."

CHAPTER 4

NONNARCOTIC DRUGS, CANNABIS, AND PERFORMANCE-ENHANCING DRUGS

There are many sanctioned uses for drugs that exert an effect on the central nervous system. Consequently, there are several classes of nonnarcotic drugs that have come into extensive use as sleeping aids, sedatives, hypnotics, energizers, mood elevators, stimulants, and tranquilizers. Examples of such nonnarcotic substances include alcohol, caffeine, nicotine, cocaine, Ecstasy, and methamphetamine. Cannabis (marijuana), although it has legitimate medicinal applications, is tightly controlled. Indeed, its use medicinally in the United States is legal only in several states, and the substance's illegal use and trafficking have severely complicated issues surrounding its legalization and medical application. Other nonnarcotic drugs whose medical uses have become closely monitored and regulated as a result of illicit trafficking and abuse include the performance-enhancing drugs, such as anabolic steroids and blood-oxygen enhancers.

BARBITURATES, STIMULANTS, AND TRANQUILIZERS

Sedatives and hypnotics differ from general anesthetics only in degree. All are capable of producing central-nervous-system depression, loss of consciousness, and death. The barbiturates, bromides, chloral hydrate, and paraldehyde are well-known drugs—with the barbiturates being of greatest interest because of the increasing number of middle and upper class individuals who have come to rely on them for immediate relaxation, mild euphoria, and an improved sense of well-being. But alcohol has been and continues to be the drug of choice for these same effects.

Of the drugs that excite the nervous system, nicotine, caffeine, the amphetamines, and the potentially addicting cocaine are well known. The use of stimulants to facilitate attention, sustain wakefulness, and mask fatigue has made the amphetamines an increasingly popular drug by students and those who engage in mental work. Originally the drug of truck drivers, amphetamine is now a common cause of arrest among teenagers and young adults who commit drug offenses. Cocaine has always been a potentially dangerous drug, and it has become especially popular among the middle and upper classes. Stimulants do not create energy, and the energy mobilized by these drugs is eventually depleted with serious consequences.

The tranquilizers are a heterogeneous group, as are the behaviours that they are employed to alter. In general, tranquilizing drugs reduce hyperactivity, agitation, and anxiety, which tend to cause a loss of behavioral control. Tranquilizing drugs do not characteristically produce general anesthesia, no matter what the dose. This attribute tends to distinguish tranquilizing drugs from the barbiturates.

All the barbiturates, stimulants, and tranquilizers are widely prescribed by physicians, and all these drugs are available through nonmedical (illegal) sources. Most of these drugs are classified as "habit forming." The minor tranquilizers are commonly associated with habituation and may induce physical dependence and severe withdrawal symptoms. The amphetamines and cocaine intoxicate at high dosages, and both are capable of inducing serious toxic and psychotic reactions under heavy use. The barbiturates are the leading cause of death by suicide. They are judged to be a danger to health by both the World Health Organization Expert Committee and the United Nations Commission on Narcotic Drugs, which have recommended strict control on their production, distribution, and use. The nonnarcotic drugs in widespread use among middle and upper class citizenry manifest considerable untoward consequences for the individual and for society when abused—thus placing their problem in a different perspective than that normally associated with the opiates, LSD, and marijuana.

BARBITURATES

Barbiturates are organic compounds used in medicine as sedatives (to produce a calming effect), as hypnotics (to produce sleep), or as an adjunct in anesthesia. Barbiturates are derivatives of barbituric acid (malonyl urea), which is formed from malonic acid and urea.

Barbital was first synthesized in 1903, and phenobarbital became available in 1912. Barbiturates act by depressing the central nervous system, particularly on certain portions of the brain, though they tend to depress the functioning of all the body's tissues. Most of them exert a sedative effect in small doses and a hypnotic effect in larger doses.

Barbiturates are classified according to their duration of action. The effects of long-acting barbiturates, such as barbital and phenobarbital, may last for as long as 24 hours. These drugs are used in conjunction with other drugs for the treatment of epilepsy, in which their prolonged depressant action helps prevent convulsions. Barbiturates of intermediate duration of action, such as amobarbital and butabarbital sodium, act for six to 12 hours and are used to relieve insomnia. Short-acting barbiturates, such as pentobarbital and secobarbital, are used to overcome difficulty in falling asleep. Ultrashort-acting barbiturates, such as thiopental sodium and thiamylal, are used intravenously to induce unconsciousness smoothly and rapidly in patients about to undergo surgery, after which gaseous anesthetics are used to maintain the unconscious state. The barbiturates have largely been replaced as sedatives by the benzodiazepines and other minor tranquilizers.

The prolonged use of barbiturates—especially secobarbital and pentobarbital—may cause the development of a tolerance to them and require amounts much larger than the original therapeutic dose. Denial of a barbiturate to the habitual user may precipitate a withdrawal syndrome that is indicative of physiological dependence on the drug. An overdose of barbiturates can result in coma and even death due to severe depression of the central nervous and respiratory systems.

The abuse of barbiturate drugs became highly prevalent in Western societies between the 1940s and '70s. In North America barbiturates were widely used by youth gangs and deviant subcultures as depressants and attracted notoriety because they were often taken in combination with other substances (e.g., stimulants such as amphetamines). Alcohol greatly intensifies the depressant effect of barbiturates, and in the 1950s and '60s, barbiturates taken with alcohol became a common agent in suicide cases. Collectively, barbiturates became known as "thrill-pills" or "goofballs," and they became a frequent target of antidrug campaigns. The use and availability of barbiturates in the United States declined steeply following the federal Comprehensive Drug Abuse Prevention and Control Act of 1970. As a street drug, barbiturates were largely replaced by other substances during the 1970s, especially by PCP.

STIMULANTS

A stimulant is any drug that excites any bodily function, but more specifically those that stimulate the brain and central nervous system. Stimulants induce alertness, elevated mood, wakefulness, increased speech and motor activity, and decreased appetite. Their therapeutic use is limited, but their mood-elevating effects make some of them potent drugs of abuse.

The major stimulant drugs are amphetamines and related compounds, methylxanthines (methylated purines), cocaine, and nicotine. Amphetamines achieve their effect by increasing the amount and activity of the neurotransmitter norepinephrine (noradrenaline) within the brain. They facilitate the release of norepinephrine by nerve cells and interfere with the cells' reuptake and breakdown of the chemical, thereby increasing its availability within the brain. Among the most commonly used amphetamines are methamphetamine (Methedrine), amphetamine sulfate (Benzedrine), and dextroamphetamine sulfate (Dexedrine).

Certain drugs related to the amphetamines have the same mode of action but are somewhat milder stimulants. Among them are phenmetrazine (Preludin) and methylphenidate (Ritalin). The latter drug is widely used to "slow down" hyperactive children and improve their ability to concentrate. The methylxanthines are even milder stimulants. Unlike the amphetamines and methylphenidate, which are synthetically manufactured, these compounds occur naturally in various plants and have been used by humans for many centuries. The most important of them are caffeine, theophylline,

and theobromine. The strongest is caffeine, which is the active ingredient of coffee, tea, cola beverages, and maté. Theobromine is the active ingredient in cocoa. It is used in the treatment of severe asthma because of its capacity for relaxing the bronchioles in the lungs.

Cocaine is one of the strongest and shortest-acting stimulants and has a high potential for abuse owing to its euphoric and habit-forming effects. Nicotine, the active ingredient in cigarettes and other tobacco products, may also be regarded as a stimulant.

CAFFEINE

Caffeine is a nitrogenous organic compound of the alkaloid group, substances that have marked physiological effects. Caffeine occurs in tea, coffee, guarana, maté, kola nuts, and cacao. Pure caffeine (trimethylxanthine) occurs as a white powder or as silky needles, which melt at 238 °C (460 °F). It sublimes at 178 °C (352 °F) at atmospheric pressure. It is very soluble in hot water, and upon cooling, the solution deposits crystals of caffeine monohydrate. Caffeine is generally less soluble in organic solvents than in hot water. It is odourless but has a bitter taste.

Caffeine is present in ground coffee in amounts ranging between 0.75 and 1.5 percent by weight. The average cup of coffee thus contains about 100 mg (0.003 ounce) of caffeine. The caffeine content of tea varies greatly depending on the strength of the tea, but it averages

Caffeine is present naturally in ground coffee beans, tea leaves, and cacao beans. Kola nuts, which also contain caffeine, are used to flavour various soft drinks. Greg Samborski/ Flickr/Getty Images

COFFEE

The coffee plant is a tropical evergreen shrub of the genus Coffea, in the madder family. The plant's seeds, called beans, are sometimes referred to as coffee. The term coffee, however, is most widely used to describe the beverage made by brewing the roasted and ground beans with water. Two of the 25 or more species, C. arabica and C. canephora, supply almost all the world's coffee. Arabica coffee is considered to brew a more flavourful and aromatic beverage than Robusta, the main variety of C. canephora. Arabicas are grown in Central and South America, the Caribbean, and Indonesia, Robustas mainly in Africa. The shrub bears bouquets of small white flowers with a jasminelike fragrance. The fruit, 0.5–0.75 inch (13–19 mm) long and red when mature, is called a cherry. Coffee contains large amounts of caffeine, the effects of which have always been an important element in the drink's popularity. Coffee drinking began in 15th-century Arabia. It reached Europe by the mid 17th century and immediately became hugely popular. Coffee is now consumed by about one-third of the world's population.

about 40 mg. There are also about 40 mg (0.0014 ounce) of caffeine in a 12-ounce glass of carbonated cola beverage.

Caffeine has a stimulating effect on the central nervous system, heart, blood vessels, and kidneys. It also acts as a mild diuretic. Caffeine's potent stimulatory action makes it a valuable antidote to respiratory depression induced by drug overdose (e.g., from morphine or barbiturates). The positive effects that have been described in people who use caffeine include improved motor performance, decreased fatigue, enhanced sensory activity, and increased alertness. These positive effects may partly explain the compulsion of many adults to consume coffee or other caffeine-containing beverages as part of the morning ritual of awakening. However, caffeine intake may also produce in people such negative effects as irritability, nervousness

or anxiety, jitteriness, headaches, and insomnia. By the mid-1980s decaffeinated coffee and soft drinks had become widely available, giving consumers the choice of regulating their caffeine intake while continuing to enjoy these beverages.

COCAINE

Cocaine is a white, crystalline alkaloid that is obtained from the leaves of the coca plant (*Erythroxylum coca*), a bush commonly found growing wild in Peru, Bolivia, and Ecuador and cultivated in many other countries. The chemical formula of cocaine is $C_{17}H_{21}NO_4$. Cocaine acts as an anesthetic because it interrupts the conduction of impulses in nerves, especially those in the mucous membranes of the eye, nose, and throat. More importantly, cocaine when ingested in small amounts produces feelings of well-being and euphoria, along with a decreased appetite, relief from fatigue, and increased mental alertness. When taken in larger amounts and upon prolonged and repeated use, cocaine can produce depression, anxiety, irritability, sleep problems, chronic fatigue, mental confusion, paranoia, and convulsions that can cause death.

For centuries the Indians of Peru and Bolivia have chewed coca leaves mixed with pellets of limestone or plant ashes for pleasure or in order to withstand strenuous working conditions, hunger, and thirst. In other cultures the active alkaloid is chemically extracted from coca leaves and is converted into the hydrochloric salt of cocaine, cocaine hydrochloride. This fine white powder is sniffed through a hollow tube and is readily absorbed into the bloodstream through the nasal mucous membranes. Cocaine is an irritant, however, and acts to constrict blood vessels, causing a chronic runny nose or, in severe cases, ulcerations in the nasal cavity. The euphoric effects

COCA

Coca (Erythroxylum coca) is a tropical shrub of the family Erythroxylaceae. Its leaves are the source of the drug cocaine.

The plant, cultivated in Africa, northern South America, Southeast Asia, and Taiwan, grows about 2.4 metres (8 feet) tall. The branches are straight, and the lively green leaves are thin, opaque, oval, and more or less tapering at the extremities. A marked characteristic of the leaf is an areolated portion bounded by two longitudinal curved lines, one on each side of the midrib, and more conspicuous on the under face of the leaf. The flowers are small and disposed in little clusters on short stalks. The corolla is composed of five yellowish white petals, the anthers are heart-shaped, and the pistil consists of three carpels united to form a three-chambered ovary. The flowers are succeeded by red berries.

The plants thrive best in hot, damp situations, such as the clearings of forests. The leaves most preferred are obtained in drier localities, on the sides of hills. The leaves are considered ready for plucking when they break on being bent. The green leaves (matu) are spread in thin layers and dried in the sun. They are then packed in sacks, which, in order to preserve the quality, must be kept from damp.

The composition of different specimens of coca leaves is very inconstant. Good samples have a strong tealike odour. When chewed they

Coca (Erythroxylum coca). W.H. Hodge

produce a sense of warmth in the mouth and have a pleasant, pungent taste. Besides the important alkaloid cocaine, there are several other alkaloids. Coca leaves and preparations of them have physiologically no external action. Internally their physiological action is similar to that of opium.

of sniffing cocaine are relatively transitory and wear off after about 30 minutes. Cocaine is habit-forming and may also be physically addicting. Cocaine is also injected in solution or smoked in a chemically treated form known as freebase. Either of these methods produces a markedly more compulsive use of the drug. In the 1980s a new preparation of cocaine appeared, called crack. The smoking of crack produces an even more intense and even more short-lived euphoria that is extremely addicting. This form of cocaine consumption is also the one most detrimental to health. Another smokable and highly addictive form is cocaine paste, which is an intermediate stage in the processing of coca leaves into cocaine.

The prolonged or compulsive use of cocaine in any of its purified forms can cause severe personality disturbances, inability to sleep, and loss of appetite. A toxic psychosis can develop involving paranoid delusions and disturbing tactile hallucinations in which the user feels insects crawling under his skin. Cocaine abuse, which had been a marginal drug problem throughout much of the 20th century, grew alarmingly in the late 20th century in several countries, and cocaine has become responsible for a markedly increased proportion of drug-induced deaths.

AMPHETAMINE AND METHAMPHETAMINE

Amphetamines were first used in the 1930s to treat narcolepsy and subsequently became prescribed for obesity and fatigue. They have been used to alleviate depression, postencephalitic Parkinsonism, enuresis, and nausea of pregnancy. These drugs also partially reverse the depressant effects of anesthetics, narcotics, hypnotics, and alcohol. All amphetamines cause profound psychic effects, including wakefulness, mental alertness, increased initiative and confidence, euphoria, lessened sense of fatigue, talkativeness, and increased ability to concentrate.

Amphetamines are used (sometimes illicitly) by pilots, truckers, and soldiers on long-term missions where prolonged wakefulness is required. The amphetamines have had a major role in the management of hyperactive children because the drugs calm such children and enable them to concentrate, usually within a day after treatment is begun.

More recently, the amphetamines have been used in combination with one of the barbiturates, such as amobarbital or phenobarbital, to produce mood elevating effects. It is the effects of the amphetamines on mood that have led to their widespread abuse. A toxic psychosis with hallucinations and paranoid delusions may be produced by a single dose as low as 50 mg if no drug tolerance is present. Although the normal lethal dose for adult humans is estimated to be around 900 mg, habitual use may increase adult tolerance up to 1,000 mg per day.

The ability of amphetamine to produce a psychosis having paranoid features was first reported in 1938, shortly after its introduction as a central stimulant. Sporadic reports of psychosis followed, and in 1958, a monograph on the subject of amphetamine psychosis included these statements:

Psychosis associated with amphetamine usage is much more frequent than would be expected from the reports in the literature. . . . The clinical picture is primarily a paranoid psychosis with ideas of reference, delusions of persecution, auditory and visual hallucinations in a setting of clear consciousness. . . . The mental picture may be indistinguishable from acute or chronic paranoid schizophrenia. . . . Patients with amphetamine psychosis recover within a week unless there is demonstrable cause for continuance of symptoms; e.g., continued excretion of the drug or hysterical prolongation of symptoms.

There have been subsequent attempts to distinguish between amphetamine psychosis and paranoid schizophrenia. Whatever the outcome, amphetamine induces a psychosis that comes closer to mimicking schizophrenia than any of the other drugs of abuse, including LSD. Some behavioral symptoms such as loss of initiative, apathy, and emotional blunting may persist long after the patient stops taking the drug. Methamphetamine was used extensively by the Japanese during World War II, and by 1953 the habitual users of the drug in Japan numbered about 500,000 persons. This large-scale usage created such a serious social problem that the amphetamines were placed under governmental control in Japan in 1954. This Japanese experience has provided the opportunity for systematic studies on chronic methamphetamine intoxication. One group of 492 addicts who had been institutionalized showed a 14 percent rate of chronic psychosis with evidence of permanent organic brain damage. In the language of the street, "Meth is death." The amphetamines produce habituation, drug dependency, physiological tolerance, and toxic effects, but no physical addiction.

Amphetamine itself is a colourless liquid with an acrid taste and a faint odour. The most widely used preparation of the drug is amphetamine sulfate, marketed under the name Benzedrine, a white powder with a slightly bitter, numbing taste. Dextroamphetamine sulfate, marketed under the name Dexedrine, is the more active of the two optically isomeric forms in which amphetamine exists. Other members of the amphetamine series include methamphetamine and benzphetamine.

Amphetamines can produce undesirable effects, the most common of which is overstimulation, with restlessness, insomnia, tremor, tenseness, and irritability. Physical tolerance to amphetamines develops rapidly, so that progressively larger doses must be consumed by the chronic user. The letdown effect that occurs in such users after the drug has worn off consists of a deep mental depression. The most severe aftereffect of large doses of amphetamines is a toxic psychosis whose symptoms resemble those of paranoid schizophrenia. Amphetamine addiction frequently is associated with similar abuse of barbiturates and alcohol.

Methamphetamine (d-desoxyephedrine) is widely known as speed. It is a potent and addictive synthetic stimulant drug. It was used widely for legal medical purposes throughout much of the 20th century. In the United States it was marketed under the brand names Methedrine and Desoxyn, and it was widely administered to industrial workers in Japan in the 1940s and '50s to increase their productivity.

Methamphetamine, which increases physical activity and suppresses the appetite, is of limited usefulness in the treatment of attention deficit disorder, narcolepsy, and obesity. However, heavy or prolonged use may produce powerful side effects, including aggression and paranoia, kidney and lung disorders, brain and liver damage, chronic depression, immune deficiency disorders, convulsions, and schizophrenia. It is normally taken in pill form or, as a crystalline powder ("crystal meth"), sniffed through a hollow tube. It may also be taken intravenously.

Methamphetamine was viewed with deep suspicion and hostility in the United States by the 1960s, not only by law-enforcement officials, politicians, the media, and medical professionals but also by large sections of the drug subculture. After the Controlled Substances Act (1970) severely restricted its availability, a large illicit manufacturing industry, relying on hundreds of clandestine "meth labs," arose in the Southwest and West and spread to parts of the Midwest in the 1990s. Despite periodic police crackdowns, large quantities of the drug continue to be produced in these labs.

Methamphetamine use has been particularly widespread in Pacific Rim nations, where it has become a serious social problem. Partly because of its association with energy and aggression, its growing use was often correlated with rapid modernization and industrialization. Although reliable figures were very hard to find, some studies suggested that a substantial increase in usage did not occur in the 1990s. Nevertheless, in the United States a survey in the mid-1990s claimed that nearly five million people had tried methamphetamine, representing an increase of approximately 240 percent from 1990.

ECSTASY

Ecstasy, or MDMA (3,4, methyl-enedioxymethamphetamine), is a euphoria-inducing stimulant and hallucinogen. The use of Ecstasy, commonly known as "E," has been widespread despite the drug's having been banned worldwide in 1985 by its addition to the international Convention on Psychotropic Substances. It is a derivative of the amphetamine family and a relative of the stimulant methamphetamine. Ecstasy, which is taken in pill form, also has a chemical relationship to the psychedelic drug mescaline.

Developed in 1913 as an appetite suppressant and patented by Merck & Co. the following year, the drug was not originally approved for release. In the 1950s and '60s, advocates of the drug, including the author and chemist Alexander T. Shulgin, claimed that it could benefit people in psychotherapy by helping to engender trust between therapist and patient, and by the late 1970s Ecstasy was being widely administered for this purpose. It was adopted enthusiastically in the 1970s and '80s by adherents of the New Age movement, who explored the similarities between the mental and emotional states induced by Ecstasy and the mystical states of awareness described by some traditional religions. Members of this group expected MDMA to be the basis of a sweeping "neuroconsciousness revolution."

Ecstasy increases the production of the neurotransmitter serotonin and blocks its reabsorption in the brain. It also increases the amount of the neurotransmitter dopamine. Stimulation of the central nervous system gives users feelings of increased energy. Other effects include heightened self-awareness, reduced social inhibitions, and feelings of happiness and well-being. Ecstasy generally does not produce severe sensory distortions such as those associated with LSD and other hallucinogens. Harmful effects can include increased blood pressure, dehydration, severe muscle tension, confusion, depression, and paranoia.

By the 1980s, parties and dances that featured Ecstasy use (known as "raves") had become popular among young people. Despite its ban in the United States and the rest of the world, the drug retained a huge following, and it came to play an important role in youth subcultures, similar to that of LSD during the 1960s. By the end of the 20th century, Ecstasy was reportedly used regularly by 500,000 people in Great Britain, and a 1998 study found that 3,400,000 Americans had tried the drug.

TRANQUILIZERS

Serendipity has played a major role in the discovery of tranquilizers (as it has in all facets of medicine). Tranquilizers were unknown to medical science until the middle of the 20th century when the therapeutic value of reserpine and chlorpromazine in psychiatry was discovered by chance. Reserpine was originally derived in the 1930s from *Rauwolfia serpentina*, a woody plant that grows in the tropical areas of the world, but it has since been synthesized. Because this drug has many undesirable side effects such as low blood pressure, ulcers, weakness, nightmares, nasal congestion, and depression, however, it has been largely replaced in psychiatric practice by chlorpromazine (Thorazine) and a number of other phenothiazine derivatives synthesized in the 1950s. These phenothiazines are inexpensive, easily available, produce little immediate pleasurable effects, can usually be taken in large amounts without harm, and are not physically addicting. They are used extensively in the treatment of various hyperactive and agitated states, and as antipsychotic agents. These drugs, however, may produce jaundice, dermatitis, or, infrequently, convulsive seizures, and they do not combine well with the drinking of alcohol. Chlorpromazine is effective in reversing "bad trips" such as an LSD-induced panic reaction, but it tends to strengthen rather than reverse the powerful hallucinogenic effects of STP (DOM). There is a second group of drugs, inappropriately called minor tranquilizers, that has achieved popularity in the management of milder psychiatric conditions, particularly anxiety and tension. The major form is meprobamate (Miltown, Equanil). Although these minor tranquilizers are considered to be entirely safe in terms of side effects, they do produce serious complications, for they are commonly associated with habituation and psychological dependence. Heavy, prolonged use may result in physical dependence and severe withdrawal symptoms including insomnia, tremors, hallucinations, and convulsions.

Cannabis

Cannabis is the general term applied internationally to the Indian hemp plant, *Cannabis sativa*, when the plant is used for its pleasure-giving effects. The plant may grow to a height of about 5 metres (16 feet), but the strains used for drug-producing effects are typically short

Valium

Valium is the trade name of a tranquilizer drug introduced by the pharmaceutical company Hoffmann-La Roche in 1963. Safer and more effective than earlier sedative-hypnotic drugs, Valium quickly became a standard drug for the treatment of anxiety and one of the most commonly prescribed drugs of all time. Its association in the popular mind with harried middle-class housewives won it the nickname "Mother's Little Helper" in a 1966 song of that name by the British rock band the Rolling Stones.

stemmed and extremely branched. The resinous exudate is the most valued part of the plant because it contains the highest concentration of tetrahydrocannabinol (THC), an active hallucinogenic principle associated with the plant's potency. The term *cannabis* also encompasses the use of the flowering tops, fruit, seeds, leaves, stems, and bark of the hemp plant even though the potency of these plant parts is considerably less than that of the pure resin itself. Hemp grows freely throughout the temperate zones of the world, but the content of the resin in the plant differs appreciably according to the geographic origin of the plant and the climate of the region in which the plant is grown. A hot, dry, upland climate is considered most favourable in terms of the potency of the plant. Careful cultivation is also considered to be an important factor in resin production. The prevention of pollination and the trimming of top leaves to produce dwarfing enhances the content of resin at plant maturity.

TYPES OF CANNABIS PREPARATIONS

Marijuana, hashish, charas, ganja, bhang, kef, and *dagga* are names that have been applied to various varieties and preparations of the hemp plant. Hashish, named after the Persian founder of the Assassins of the 11th century (Ḥasan-e Ṣabbāḥ), is the most potent of the cannabis preparations, being about eight times as strong as the marijuana used in the United States. Very few geographic areas are capable of producing a plant rich enough in resins to produce hashish. Unless sifted and powdered, hashish appears in a hardened, brownish form with the degree of darkness indicating strength. The North African either eats it in a confection or smokes it, the water pipe often being used to cool the smoke. The effects are more difficult to regulate when hashish is either ingested as a confection or drunk. In India, this resinous preparation of cannabis is called charas.

Ganja is a less active form of cannabis. Whereas hashish and charas are made from the pure resin, ganja is prepared from the flowering tops, stems,

Marijuana (Cannabis sativa). John Kohout/Root Resources

leaves, and twigs, which have less resin and thus less potency. Ganja is nevertheless one of the more potent forms of cannabis. It is prepared from specially cultivated plants in India, and the flowering tops have a relatively generous resinous exudate. Ganja is consumed much in the manner of charas.

Bhang is the least potent of the cannabis preparations used in India. It does not contain the flowering tops found in ganja. As a result, bhang contains only a small amount of resin (5 percent). It is either drunk or smoked. When drunk, the leaves are reduced to a fine powder, brewed, and then filtered for use. Bhang is also drunk in Hindu religious ceremonials.

Marijuana is the variety of cannabis grown in the Western Hemisphere. Considered mild in comparison to other forms of cannabis, it is similar in potency to the bhang used in India. The term *marijuana* is often used to describe the crude drug composed of *C. sativa* leaves and flowers. It is usually dried and crushed and put into pipes or formed into cigarettes (joints) for smoking. The drug—known by a variety of other names, including pot, tea, grass, and weed—can also be added to foods and beverages. Marijuana varies in potency, depending on where and how it is grown, prepared for use, or stored.

History of Cannabis Use

Mentioned in a Chinese herbal dating from 2700 BCE, cannabis has long been considered valuable as an analgesic, an anesthetic, an antidepressant, an antibiotic, and a sedative. Although it was usually used externally (e.g., as a balm or smoked), in the 19th century its tips were sometimes administered internally to treat gonorrhea and angina pectoris.

The worldwide use of marijuana and hashish as intoxicants has raised various medical and social questions, many of which have been under continuing scientific investigation, especially since the mid-1960s, when THC was first isolated and produced synthetically. Research was directed toward identifying the short- and long-term physical effects of marijuana. In the late 20th century, medical research revealed various therapeutic effects of marijuana and THC. They were found to be useful in lowering internal eye pressure in persons suffering from glaucoma and in alleviating nausea and vomiting caused by chemotherapeutic drugs used to treat cancer patients and those with AIDS. Marijuana also has been found to reduce the muscle pain associated with multiple sclerosis and to prevent epileptic seizures in some patients. In the late 1980s researchers discovered a receptor for THC and THC-related chemicals in the brains of certain mammals, including humans. This finding indicated that the brain naturally produces a THC-like substance that may perform some of the same functions that THC does. Such a substance subsequently was found and named anandamide, from the Sanskrit *anada* ("bliss").

International trade in marijuana and hashish was first placed under controls during the International Opium Convention of 1925. By the late 1960s most countries had enforced restrictions on trafficking and using marijuana and hashish and had imposed generally severe penalties for their illegal possession, sale, or supply. Beginning in the 1970s, some countries and jurisdictions reduced the penalty for the possession of small quantities. The Netherlands has long tolerated the sale of small amounts of marijuana, and in 1999 its legislature debated the decriminalization of the drug. In 1998 Swiss voters overwhelmingly rejected a broad referendum that would have legalized many drugs, including marijuana, heroin, and cocaine, but the government took steps to legalize marijuana two years later. Other European countries also began debating the decriminalization of so-called "soft drugs," including marijuana.

In the United States, several states passed legislation in the late 1970s and early '80s to fund research on or to legalize the medicinal use of marijuana, though some of these statutes were later repealed or lapsed. Renewed decriminalization efforts in the 1990s led to the legalization of medicinal marijuana in more than a dozen states, including Alaska, Arizona, California, Colorado, Nevada, Oregon, and Washington. In 2001, however, the U.S. Supreme Court ruled against the use of marijuana for medical purposes. Later that year Canada passed legislation easing restrictions on medicinal marijuana.

The country's new regulations included licensing marijuana growers to produce the drug for individuals with terminal illnesses or chronic diseases. In 2009 U.S. attorney general Eric Holder issued a new set of guidelines for federal prosecutors in states where the medical use of marijuana was legalized. The policy shift mandated that federal resources were to be focused primarily on prosecuting illegal use and trafficking of marijuana, thereby rendering cases of medical use, in which those individuals in possession of the drug are clearly in compliance with state laws, less prone to excessive legal investigation.

PHYSIOLOGICAL AND PSYCHOLOGICAL EFFECTS OF CANNABIS

Hashish or charas would be expected to produce a greater degree of intoxication than marijuana or bhang. Whether the drug is smoked, drunk, eaten, or received as an administration of synthetic tetrahydrocannabinol (THC) can also determine the extent of effect. In general, hashish produces effects similar to those of mescaline or, in sufficient quantity, to those of LSD—extreme intoxication being more typical when the substance is swallowed. Marijuana, on the other hand, is more apt to produce effects at the opposite or mild end of the continuum from those of LSD. When smoked, physiological manifestations are apparent within minutes. These include dizziness, lightheadedness, disturbances in coordination and movement, a heavy sensation in the arms and legs, dryness of mouth and throat, redness and irritation of the eyes, blurred vision, quickened heartbeat, tightness around the chest, and peculiarities in the sense of hearing such as ringing, buzzing, a feeling of pressure in the ears, or altered sounds. Occasionally drug use is accompanied by nausea and an urge to urinate or defecate. There is also a feeling of hunger that may be associated with a craving for sweets. Toxic manifestations are rare and include motor restlessness, tremor, ataxia, congestion of the conjunctivae of the eye, abnormal dilation of the pupil, visual hallucinations, and unpleasant delusions. Marijuana is not a drug of addiction. Use does not lead to physical dependence, and there are no withrawal symptoms when the drug is discontinued. Psychological dependence does occur among certain types of users. Infrequently, a "cannabis psychosis" may occur, but generally this type of psychiatric reaction is associated only with heavy, long-term use of hashish, such as in India and Morocco. Other effects of chronic hashish use are a debilitation of the will and mental deterioration.

Psychological manifestations are even more variable in response to cannabis. Alterations in mood may include giggling, hilarity, and euphoria. Perceptual distortions may also occur, involving space, time, sense of distance, and sense of the organization of one's own body image. Thought processes may also become disorganized, with fragmentation, disturbances of memory,

and frequent shifts of attention acting to disrupt the orderly flow of ideas. One may also experience some loss of reality contact in terms of not feeling involved in what one is doing. This may lead to considerable detachment and depersonalization. On the more positive side, there may be an enhancement in the sense of personal worth and increased sociability. Undesired subjective experiences include fear, anxiety, or panic. These effects vary considerably with practice and with the setting in which the drug is taken.

Many articles have been written on the subject of cannabis, but data that definitively outlines its benefits and harms is often conflicting or inconclusive. Some research has suggested that marijuana is a very mild substance that requires considerable practice before its full (desired) effects are achieved. Alcohol clearly appears more potent and far more deleterious.

From the point of view of those who favour the legalization of marijuana, the drug is a mild hallucinogen that bears no similarity to the narcotics. They feel that the evidence clearly indicates that marijuana is not a stepping stone to heroin and that its use is not associated with major crimes. As a means of reducing tension and achieving a sense of well-being, they believe that it is probably more beneficial and considerably safer than alcohol. The current hysteria over the use of marijuana and the harsh penalties that are imposed are perceived by users as a greater threat to society than would be a more rational and realistic approach to drug use.

PERFORMANCE-ENHANCING DRUGS AND PRACTICES

Although performance-enhancing drugs were known as early as the 19th century, when professional cyclists used strychnine as a stimulant, the widespread use of drugs began in the 1960s. It is a practice that cuts across national and ideological boundaries. Sociologists investigating the phenomenon of drug use in sports normally put aside the moral outrage that characterizes media coverage of and political commentary on this issue. Media personnel tend to focus on the actions of high-profile stars such as Canadian sprinter Ben Johnson and Irish swimmer Michelle Smith, whose Olympic gold medals were stripped away (Johnson) or tarnished by the suspicion of drug use (Smith). Whenever a prominent athlete tests positive for a banned substance, journalists, politicians, and sports administrations are likely to respond with calls for zero-tolerance policies. In contrast, sociologists ask: What is a drug? What are the social and sporting roots of drug usage? Why is the focus almost exclusively on drugs that enhance performance? What would constitute a viable policy for drug usage?

Three broad categories of drugs have been identified: recreational, restorative, and additive, or performance-enhancing, drugs. While attention is focused on recreational drugs such as marijuana and cocaine or on anabolic steroids (synthetic compounds of the male hormone testosterone) and other performance-enhancing drugs, little or no attention is given to drugs that restore athletes to fitness. This is unfortunate because the overuse of vitamins and food supplements can also be detrimental to an athlete's health. Greater consideration should be given to all categories of drug consumption, not just to the abuse of cocaine and anabolic steroids.

One hindrance to the formulation of a rational policy about drugs is the often tenuous distinction between the natural and the artificial. This is especially true for vitamins, special diets, human growth hormones, and blood doping (the extraction and later infusion of an athlete's own blood). In addition, there is no hard-and-fast distinction between different categories of drugs. Some drugs, such as beta-blockers, fall into both the restorative and performance-enhancing categories.

In examining the case for and against the implementation of bans on athletes who test positive for drug use, several key arguments can be identified. The most widely used argument for a ban is that performance-enhancing drugs confer an unfair advantage on those who use them. This argument brings the ethics of sports into play, along with the notion that athletes have a moral duty not only to adhere to the rules but also to serve as role models. Also widely used is the argument that drugs harm the athletes' health. The "harm principle" asserts or implies that athletes must be protected from themselves. Closely associated with both arguments is the notion that bans act as a deterrent, preventing athletes from cheating and from inflicting harm on themselves.

The counterargument is twofold. The argument based on fairness is said to be unpersuasive because drugs would confer no special advantage if they were legalized and made available to all athletes. Proponents of this viewpoint also note that the rules now in force allow athletes from wealthy nations to train more efficiently, with better coaching and equipment, than athletes from poorer countries, a situation that is manifestly unfair. The argument based on the "harm principle" is said to treat athletes as children. Adult athletes should be allowed to decide for themselves whether they want to harm their health by drug use.

Sociologists have contributed to the debate on drugs by pointing out that focusing on the actions of the athlete individualizes the issue of drug usage rather than examining the social roots of drug consumption. Among the causes of drug usage that have been identified are the medicalization of social life and the vastly increased importance of sports as a source of self-esteem and material benefits. Victory has always brought greater rewards than defeat, but the differences are now on an unprecedented scale. Sociologists have also

raised questions about privacy rights being violated by mandatory drug testing and about the meagre resources being provided for the rehabilitation of drug offenders.

Discussions of performance-enhancing drugs are also complicated by the fact that most spectators say they disapprove of drugs even as they turn out to support athletes who have tested positive for banned substances. After the French police uncovered massive doping during the 1998 Tour de France, roadside crowds increased.

The debate over drugs is further complicated when "unnatural" factors influencing performance are considered—for example, the use of psychological techniques and biotechnological intervention. The role of sports psychology began to increase significantly in the 1990s. Goal setting, focus, and visualization exercises were designed to ensure that athletes would concentrate on reaching their peak performance. Distractions were to be eliminated.

The growth of biotechnological intervention in human affairs, including the potential impact of genetic engineering, also raises many issues for sports. While many people uncritically accept this type of intervention in the context of restorative medicine, the boundary line between rehabilitation and enhancement, as in the case of drugs, is not clear. Reconstructive surgery, implants, and technological adjustments contribute, along with drug use and masochistically intense training regimes, to the creation of what sports scientist and historian John M. Hoberman calls "mortal engines." These interventions into the "natural" body have to be considered within the broader debate concerning sports and what it is to be human.

ANABOLIC STEROIDS

An anabolic steroid is a steroid hormone that increases tissue growth. Anabolic steroids are given to promote muscle growth and tissue regeneration in, for example, elderly or postoperative patients. A growing number of amateur and professional athletes have made use of synthetic analogs of testosterone to accelerate muscular development and to improve strength. Among anabolic steroids, the synthetic drug known as stanozolol is among the most widely abused by athletes.

Unsupervised use by athletes to build muscle and improve strength can have serious harmful effects, including

U.S. cyclist Floyd Landis was stripped of his 2006 Tour de France title after testing positive for doping. Among the drugs Landis admitted to taking is the blood-oxygenator erythropoietin. Bryn Lennon/Getty Images

coronary heart disease, immunodeficiencies, liver damage, stunted growth, aggressive behaviour, and susceptibility to connective-tissue injury. Androgens secreted or administered in abnormally large amounts can cause development of male characteristics in the female and precocious sexual development in the male. Conversely, hypogonadism of the male (inadequate testicular function) leads to retarded sexual development and retention of feminine bodily characteristics (eunuchoidism), which can sometimes be remedied by administration of androgenic steroids. Several esters of testosterone are commonly used by injection for this purpose. Many orally active analogs of testosterone are also available in which activity is greatly enhanced, and often the ratio of androgenic activity to anabolic activity is shifted markedly in favour of the latter. This ratio primarily determines the therapeutic value of these compounds as anabolic agents. They are used together with growth hormone to promote growth

ERYTHROPOIETIN

Erythropoietin is a hormone produced largely in the kidneys that influences the rate of production of red blood cells (erythrocytes). When the number of circulating red cells decreases or when the oxygen transported by the blood diminishes, an unidentified sensor detects the change, and the production of erythropoietin is increased. This substance is then transported through the plasma to the bone marrow, where it accelerates the production of red cells.

The erythropoietin mechanism operates like a thermostat, increasing or decreasing the rate of red cell production in accordance with need. When a person who has lived at high altitude moves to a sea level environment, production of erythropoietin is suppressed, the rate of red cell production declines, and the red cell count falls until the normal sea level value is achieved. With the loss of 1 pint (.5 l) of blood, the erythropoietin mechanism is activated, red cell production is enhanced, and within a few weeks the number of circulating red cells has been restored to the normal value. The precision of control is extraordinary so that the number of new red cells produced accurately compensates for the number of cells lost or destroyed.

Erythropoietin has been produced in vitro (outside the body) using recombinant DNA technology. The purified recombinant hormone has promise for persons with chronic renal failure, who develop anemia because of a lack of erythropoietin. Erythropoietin was the first hematopoietic growth factor to be developed for therapeutic purposes. In addition to treating anemia associated with chronic renal failure, it is used to treat anemia associated with zidovudine (AZT) therapy in patients infected with HIV. It may also be useful in reversing anemia in cancer patients receiving chemotherapy. Erythropoietin also has been administered after strokes in an effort to induce or enhance the growth of neurons, thereby staving off brain damage and spurring functional recovery.

in children in whom physical development is retarded. They are also used to promote physical recovery from debilitating diseases.

BLOOD-OXYGEN ENHANCERS

Blood-oxygen enhancers are substances that increase the number of red blood cells (erythrocytes) in the circulation or that increase the oxygen-carrying capacity of hemoglobin. One example is erythropoietin, a hormone that is naturally produced by the kidneys. It travels to the bone marrow to stimulate erythrocyte production, which allows more oxygen to be carried in the blood and delivered to muscles. The administration of cobalt enhances transcription of the erythropoietin gene, resulting in greater production of the hormone.

Tests to detect increased physiological production of erythropoietin are being developed. Because the hormone could not be detected, and because the margin of advantage it was believed to give athletes was narrow, the substance was long used in professional sports without consequence. In the early 21st century, however, a number of retired Tour de France riders admitted to using erythropoietin in the 1990s. Among these individuals was renowned Danish cyclist Bjarne Riis, who was taking the hormone when he won the Tour in 1996. In 2008 a new form of the hormone, known as continuous erythropoiesis receptor activator (CERA), was discovered circulating among cyclists competing in the race.

GENE DOPING

Gene doping makes use of substances and methods that are designed to manipulate cells, genes, and genetic elements. Although relatively new to the collection of performance-enhancing techniques available to athletes, the manipulation of genes to improve their function has been an intense area of scientific investigation for non-sports-related applications ranging from gene therapy for disease to the development of genetically modified organisms. One example of gene doping involves hypoxia-inducible factor (HIF) stabilizers. The HIF molecule has been studied primarily for its role in stimulating the growth of new blood vessels during tumour formation. The HIF gene is activated under hypoxic, or low-oxygen, conditions, and its activity stimulates the erythropoietin gene and therefore augments production of the hormone. HIF is turned off when tissue oxygen levels return to normal. HIF stabilizers, however, keep the gene active, regardless of oxygen levels. The stabilizers can be taken as pills.

CHAPTER 5

ALCOHOL CONSUMPTION AND HEALTH

Alcohol produces effects on the human body that parallel the quantity and rate of its consumption. Under the influence of alcohol the functions of the brain are depressed in a characteristic pattern. The most complex actions of the brain—judgment, self-criticism, the inhibitions learned from earliest childhood—are depressed first, and the loss of this control results in a feeling of excitement in the early stages. For this reason, alcohol is sometimes thought of, erroneously, as a stimulant. Under the influence of increasing amounts of alcohol, however, the drinker gradually becomes less alert, awareness of his or her environment becomes dim and hazy, muscular coordination deteriorates, and sleep is facilitated. Because of the effects that alcohol has on the body and on behaviour, governments often regulate its use.

TYPES OF ALCOHOLIC BEVERAGES

Alcoholic beverages are fermented from the sugars in fruits, berries, grains, and other ingredients, such as plant saps, tubers, honey, and milk. A ferment may be distilled to reduce the original watery liquid to a liquid of much greater alcoholic strength. Beer is the best-known member of the malt family of alcoholic beverages, which also includes ale, stout, porter, and malt liquor. Wine is made by fermenting the juices of grapes or other fruits such as apples (cider), cherries, berries, or plums. The making of distilled spirits begins with the mashes of grains, fruits, or other ingredients. The resultant fermented liquid is heated until the alcohol and flavourings vaporize and can be drawn off, cooled, and condensed back into a liquid. Water remains behind and is discarded. The concentrated liquid, called a distilled beverage, includes liquors such as whiskey, gin, vodka, rum, brandy, and liqueurs, or cordials.

WINE

Although wine was known by the ancients, it was not drunk in its matured form until the development of the bottle and cork in the late 17th century. In wine manufacture, grapes are crushed and strained, and the juice (called must) is sealed in vats along with yeast (*Saccharomyces cerevisiae*) and often sulfur dioxide, which suppresses wild yeasts and organisms. Fermentation continues for several weeks, and then the wine is drawn off

A California winery employee evenly distributes grape skins in a vat of fermenting wine. Wooden barrels, seen behind the man, hold wine as it goes through a second fermentation. Justin Sullivan/Getty Images

("racked") into wooden barrels or other containers for a second fermentation ("aging"). It is clarified and bottled before undergoing final maturation.

Wines may be classified according to colour as red, rosé (pink), or white. The colour depends on whether the skins of red grapes are allowed to ferment with the juice. Wine taste is described as sweet or dry, sweet wines being high in sugar content and dry wines containing little or no sugar. Sparkling wines, such as champagne, contain suspended carbon dioxide, the result of bottling the wine before fermentation is complete. Fortified wines, such as port and sherry, contain added brandy. The leading wine-producing countries are France, Italy,

ETHYL ALCOHOL

Ethyl alcohol (also known as ethanol, grain alcohol, or alcohol) is a member of a class of organic compounds that are given the general name alcohols. Its molecular formula is C_2H_5OH. Ethyl alcohol is an important industrial chemical. It is used as a solvent, in the synthesis of other organic chemicals, and as an additive to automotive gasoline (forming a mixture known as a gasohol). Ethyl alcohol is also the intoxicating ingredient of many alcoholic beverages such as beer, wine, and distilled spirits.

There are two main processes for the manufacture of ethyl alcohol: the fermentation of carbohydrates (the method used for alcoholic beverages) and the hydration of ethylene. Fermentation involves the transformation of carbohydrates to ethyl alcohol by growing yeast cells. The chief raw materials fermented for the production of industrial alcohol are sugar crops such as beets and sugarcane and grain crops such as corn (maize). Hydration of ethylene is achieved by passing a mixture of ethylene and a large excess of steam at high temperature and pressure over an acidic catalyst.

Ethyl alcohol produced either by fermentation or by synthesis is obtained as a dilute aqueous solution and must be concentrated by fractional distillation. Direct distillation can yield at best the constant-boiling-point mixture containing 95.6 percent by weight of ethyl alcohol. Dehydration of the constant-boiling-point mixture yields anhydrous, or absolute, alcohol. Ethyl alcohol intended for industrial use is usually denatured (rendered unfit to drink), typically with methanol, benzene, or kerosene.

Pure ethyl alcohol is a colourless, flammable liquid (boiling point 78.5 °C [173.3 °F]) with an agreeable ethereal odour and a burning taste. Ethyl alcohol is toxic, affecting the central nervous system. Moderate amounts relax the muscles and produce an apparent stimulating effect by depressing the inhibitory activities of the brain, but larger amounts impair coordination and judgment, finally producing coma and death. It is an addictive drug for some persons, leading to the disease alcoholism. Ethyl alcohol is converted in the body first to acetaldehyde and then to carbon dioxide and water, at the rate of about half a fluid ounce (15 ml) per hour. This quantity corresponds to a dietary intake of about 100 calories.

Spain, the United States, Argentina, Germany, Australia, South Africa, Portugal, and Romania.

BEER

Beer is an alcoholic beverage that is made usually from malted barley, flavoured with hops, and brewed by slow fermentation. Known from ancient times, beer was especially common in northern climates not conducive to grape cultivation for wine. It is produced by employing either a bottom-fermenting yeast, which falls to the bottom of the container when fermentation is completed, or a top-fermenting yeast, which rises to the surface. Lager beers (from *lagern*, "to store"), of German origin, are bottom-fermented and stored at a low temperature for several months. Most lagers are light in colour, with high carbonation, medium hop flavour, and

alcohol content of 3–5 percent by volume. Top-fermented beers, popular in Britain, include ale, stout, and porter. They are characterized by a prominent head of released carbon dioxide, a sharper and more strongly hopped flavour than lagers, and an alcohol content of 4–6.5 percent by volume.

DISTILLED SPIRITS

Distilled spirits (distilled liquors) are alcoholic beverages (such as brandy, whisky, rum, or arrack) that are obtained by distillation from wine or other fermented fruit or plant juice or from a starchy material (such as various grains) that has first been brewed. The alcoholic content of distilled liquor is higher than that of beer or wine.

The production of distilled spirits is based upon fermentation, the natural

PROOF

In liquor distilling, proof is a measure of the absolute alcohol content of a distilled liquor, which is a mixture of alcohol and water. The measurement is made by determining the specific gravity of the liquor (the weight per unit volume of the liquid compared to that of water). The measurement of the alcohol content is expressed in terms that vary from country to country: specific gravity, percentage by volume of alcohol, percentage by weight of alcohol, percentage by volume of proof spirit, or by gradations on an arbitrary scale. The measurement is done at an index temperature, as specific gravity varies with temperature.

In Great Britain, the Customs and Excise Act of 1952, declared proof spirits (100 proof) to be those in which the weight of the spirits is $^{12}/_{13}$ the weight of an equal volume of distilled water at 51 °F (11 °C). Thus, proof spirits are 48.24 percent alcohol by weight or 57.06 percent by volume. Other spirits are designated over or under proof, with the percentage of variance noted. In the United States, a proof spirit (100 proof) is one containing 50 percent alcohol by volume.

process of decomposition of organic materials containing carbohydrates. It occurs in nature whenever the two necessary ingredients, carbohydrate and yeast, are available. Yeast is a vegetative microorganism that lives and multiplies in media containing carbohydrates—particularly simple sugars. It has been found throughout the world, including frozen areas and deserts.

Distilled spirits are all alcoholic beverages in which the concentration of ethyl alcohol has been increased above that of the original fermented mixture by a method called distillation. The principle of alcoholic distillation is based upon the different boiling points of alcohol (78.5 °C [173.3 °F]) and water (100 °C [212 °F]). If a liquid containing ethyl alcohol is heated to a temperature above 78.5 °C but below 100 °C and the vapour coming off the liquid is condensed, the condensate will have a higher alcohol concentration, or strength.

ALCOHOL AND THE INDIVIDUAL

In the ingestion of an alcoholic beverage, the alcohol is rapidly absorbed in the gastrointestinal tract (stomach and intestines) because it does not undergo any digestive processes. Thus, alcohol rises to high levels in the blood in a relatively short time. From the blood the alcohol is distributed to all parts of the body and has an especially pronounced effect on the brain, on which it exerts a depressant action.

Although the general effects of alcohol on the body can be characterized by a basic, common sequence of events, there may occur variations in individual responses to alcohol with respect to alcohol metabolism and the behavioral symptoms produced by intoxication. Differences in alcohol metabolism are primarily the result of variations in the activity of enzymes known as alcohol dehydrogenase (ADH) and aldehyde dehydrogenase (ALDH). For example, a less-active form of ALDH found in individuals of Asian descent causes unpleasant flushing reactions in the skin within minutes of alcohol consumption. It can also lead to the buildup of toxic metabolites in the body, causing nausea and vomiting following the consumption of small amounts of alcohol.

ABSORPTION THROUGH THE STOMACH AND INTESTINES

When an alcoholic beverage is swallowed, it is diluted by gastric juices in the stomach. A small portion of the alcohol is diffused into the bloodstream directly from the stomach wall, but most passes through the pyloric junction into the small intestine, where it is very rapidly absorbed. However, up to half the alcohol is degraded in the stomach before it passes into the small intestine. In general, a lower percentage of the alcohol is degraded in a young woman's stomach than in a young man's because a young woman's gastric secretions contain lower levels of the enzyme alcohol dehydrogenase (ADH), which breaks down alcohol prior to absorption.

The rate at which alcohol is absorbed can be affected by a number of factors. For example, a strong alcoholic drink, when taken into an empty stomach, may cause a spasm of the pylorus that will impede passage into the small intestine, resulting in a slower overall rate of absorption. The presence of food in the stomach, especially some fatty foods, will also delay absorption. Naturally carbonated alcohol such as champagne or alcohol taken with a carbonated beverage such as soda water will ordinarily be absorbed more rapidly than noncarbonated alcohol. Other factors, such as the emotional state of the drinker, may also affect the rate of absorption.

Alcohol is diffused in the body in proportion to the water content of the various tissues and organs, appearing in greater concentration in the blood and brain than in fat or muscle tissue. The absorbed alcohol is greatly diluted by the body fluids. Thus, 1 ounce of whiskey at 50 percent alcohol by volume (100 U.S. proof, or 87.6 British proof) will be diluted, in a man of average build, to a concentration of about 2 parts per 10,000 in the blood (0.02 percent). The same amount of alcohol will lead to higher blood levels (up to 50 percent higher) in a woman because of differences in size, ratios of body water to body fat, and levels of gastric ADH.

The body begins to dispose of alcohol immediately after it has been absorbed. An insignificantly small proportion of alcohol is exhaled through the lungs, and a tiny amount is excreted in sweat. A small proportion is excreted by the kidneys and will be accumulated and retained in the bladder until eliminated in the urine. However, only between 2 and 10 percent of the alcohol is eliminated by these means. The remainder, 90 percent or more of the absorbed alcohol, is disposed of by metabolic processes, mainly in the liver.

PROCESSING IN THE LIVER

As absorbed alcohol is passed through the liver by the circulating blood, it is acted upon by ADH present in the liver cells. The alcohol molecule is converted by this action to acetaldehyde, itself a highly toxic substance, but the acetaldehyde is immediately acted upon by another enzyme, aldehyde dehydrogenase, and converted to acetate, most of which enters the bloodstream and is ultimately oxidized to carbon dioxide and water. Considerable utilizable energy—200 calories per ounce of alcohol (about 7.1 calories per gram)—is made available to the body during these processes, and in this sense alcohol serves as a nutrient.

The two enzymatic reactions—that of ADH and of aldehyde dehydrogenase—require a coenzyme, nicotinamide adenine dinucleotide (NAD), the acceptor of hydrogen from the alcohol molecule, for their effects. The NAD is thus changed to NADH and becomes available again for the same reaction only after its own further oxidation. While adequate ADH seems always

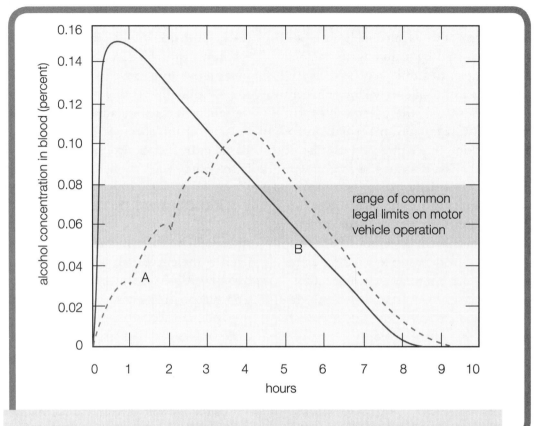

Percent of blood alcohol concentration in an average man at hourly intervals after drinking 2 ounces of spirits each hour for four hours (curve A) and eight ounces all at once (curve B). Encyclopædia Britannica, Inc.

present for the first step of alcohol metabolism, the temporary reduction of the available NAD apparently acts as a limit on the rate at which alcohol can be metabolized. That rate per hour in an average-size man is about half an ounce (15 ml) of alcohol. In other words, the body is able to process approximately one standard bar drink of spirits, beer, or wine per hour.

ACCUMULATION IN THE BODY

Whenever drinking proceeds at a faster rate than the alcohol is metabolized, alcohol accumulates in the body. If the average-size man drinks and absorbs 4 ounces (120 ml) of whiskey at 50 percent alcohol within an hour, he will have a blood alcohol concentration near 0.07 percent—above many established legal

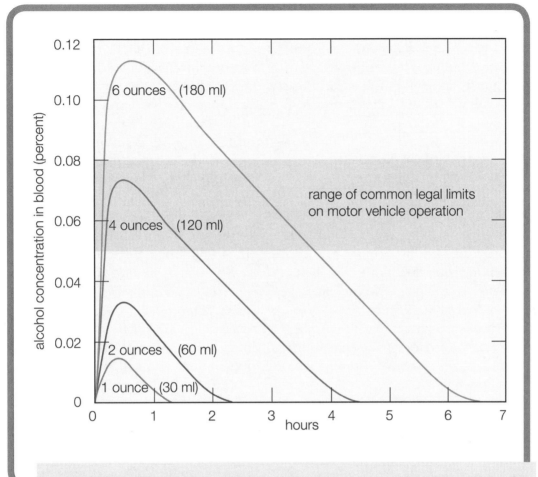

Percent of blood alcohol concentration in an average man at hourly intervals after drinking 1, 2, 4, or 6 ounces of spirits containing 50 percent alcohol. Encyclopædia Britannica, Inc.

limits to operate an automobile. Likewise, if he drinks 6 ounces (180 ml), he will have a blood alcohol concentration of about 0.11 percent—a level at which his speech will be slurred and his muscle movements clearly impaired.

Sustained drinking over time at rates greater than the body's ability to process alcohol leads to greater intoxication. This effect is illustrated by what happens if an average-size man drinks 2 ounces (60 ml) of spirits four times an hour apart. At the end of the first hour (that is, just before the second drink), the blood alcohol concentration has passed its peak and begun to decline. With the second drink, however, the concentration starts rising again, and this process is repeated after each drink. The highest blood alcohol concentration is reached at the end of four hours—an hour after the last drink. Only with the cessation of drinking does it decline steadily.

Effects of Alcohol on the Brain

Alcohol is a drug that affects the central nervous system. It belongs in a class with the barbiturates, minor tranquilizers, and general anesthetics, and it is commonly classified as a depressant. The effect of alcohol on the brain is rather paradoxical. Under some behavioral conditions alcohol can serve as an excitant, under other conditions as a sedative. At very high concentrations it acts increasingly as a depressant, leading to sedation, stupor, and coma. The excitement phase exhibits the well-known signs of exhilaration, loss of socially expected restraints, loquaciousness, unexpected changes of mood, and unmodulated anger. Excitement actually may be caused indirectly, more by the effect of alcohol in suppressing inhibitory centres of the brain than by a direct stimulation of the manifested behaviour. The physical signs of excited intoxication are slurred speech, unsteady gait, disturbed sensory perceptions, and inability to make fine motor movements. Again, these effects are produced not by the direct action of alcohol on the misbehaving muscles and senses but by its effect on the brain centres that control the muscle activity.

The most important immediate action of alcohol is on the higher functions of the brain—those of thinking, learning, remembering, and making judgments. Many of the alleged salutary effects of alcohol on performance (such as better dancing, happier moods, sounder sleeping, less sexual inhibition, and greater creativity) have been shown in controlled experiments to be a function of suggestion and subjective assessment. In reality, alcohol improves performance only through muscle relaxation and guilt reduction or loss of social inhibition. Thus, mild intoxication actually makes objectively observed depression (and dancing for that matter) worse. Experiments also indicate a dependence of learning on the mental state in which it occurs. For example, what is learned under the influence of alcohol is better recalled under the influence of alcohol, but what is learned in the sober state is better recalled when sober.

Effects on Behaviour

People ordinarily drink alcohol to obtain effects that they have been taught to expect. The state of expectation combines with the pharmacological action of the drug to produce the desired effect. Small amounts of alcohol are drunk in the expectation of reducing feelings of tension, relieving feelings of anxiety, and, conversely, experiencing

Police watch as a man takes a roadside sobriety test. Loss of balance is just one indication that high blood alcohol content may have impaired a person's ability to drive. Doug Menuez/Photodisc/Getty Images

exhilaration and a loss of inhibition. The anxiety-suppressing action of alcohol is largely a function of muscle relaxation and the removal of social inhibitions. But anxiety reduction is also a function of suggestibility and of the cultural permissiveness present in drinking settings. Shy people become outgoing or bold, well-behaved people become disorderly, the sexually repressed become amorous, the fearful become brave, and the quiescent or peaceful become verbally or physically aggressive. In people with clinically diagnosed anxieties and phobias, however, alcohol is little better than a placebo, and alcohol consumption actually worsens sleep patterns, depression, and the risk of suicide.

In folklore, whiskey is popular for treating colds and snakebites, brandy for treating faintness, spirits as a spring tonic, beer for lactation, and any alcoholic beverage for treating sleeplessness or overexcitement. Such uses depend on popular belief, not medical fact. Physicians often prescribe "a drink" for a variety of purposes: to stimulate a sluggish appetite, to help relieve premenstrual tension in women, to act as a vasodilator (an agent used to widen the lumen of the blood vessels) in arteriosclerosis, and to relieve the vague aches and pains that beset the elderly. These salutary effects, however, are psychological more than they are pharmacological. Alcohol is important pharmacologically for use with some active medicines that are poorly soluble in water but readily dissolve in alcohol and for preventing delirium tremens during alcohol withdrawal in alcoholics.

Blood Alcohol Concentration

Because brain alcohol concentrations are difficult to measure directly, the effects of alcohol on the brain are calculated indirectly by noting the physical and mental impairments that typically arise at various levels of blood alcohol concentration, or BAC. Inefficiency in performing some

BREATHALYZER

A breath analyzer, or breathalyzer, is a device used primarily by law-enforcement officials to determine the amount of alcohol in the system of persons suspected of being intoxicated. In the analyzer, a precise amount of the suspect's exhaled breath is passed through a solution of potassium dichromate and sulfuric acid. The change in the colour of the solution is proportional to the amount of alcohol in the air sample, which, in turn, is directly related to the alcohol content of the blood. Driving ability is seriously impaired when the alcohol concentration in the blood exceeds 80 mg per 100 ml.

tasks may begin at concentrations as low as 0.03 percent. The impairments at these concentrations may not be visibly manifested by all individuals, but laboratory tests show that alertness, visual acuity, and capacity to distinguish between sensory signals are all diminished. Reflex responses and the time of reaction to a signal, as well as neuromuscular functions, are slowed. Complex reactions, such as those that require the brain to process more than one type of incoming information simultaneously, are impaired at BACs too low to affect simple reflexes and reaction times.

The majority of drinkers begin to show measurable impairment at just above 0.05 percent, and in fact most jurisdictions in Western countries make it illegal to operate a motor vehicle at various levels between 0.05 to 0.08 percent. Most people exhibit some degree of functional sedation and motor incapacitation at a BAC of 0.10 percent, and most people are considered intoxicated at 0.15 percent. Habitual heavy drinking, however, does produce increased tolerance to alcohol.

As BACs rise above 0.15 percent, intoxication steadily increases. Well-adapted, very heavy drinkers may continue to function fairly well in some motor and mental tasks even up to concentrations of 0.30 percent, but, long before this level of alcohol concentration is reached, most people will appear visibly drunk, showing the common symptoms of slurred speech, unsteady gait, and confused thinking. At a 0.40-percent BAC,

most people will be anesthetized to the extent that they will be asleep, difficult to rouse, and incapable of voluntary activity—indeed, they will be in a state in which they can undergo surgery. At yet higher BACs, deep coma sets in. Between 0.40 and 1 percent, the breathing centre in the brain or the action of the heart may be anesthetized, and then death will quickly follow directly from alcohol intoxication. Ordinarily, however, it is not likely that anybody would attain a BAC above 0.40 percent by drinking. In a man of average build such a level would require the ingestion and unmetabolized absorption of between a pint and a quart (that is, almost a half-litre to a full litre) of spirits.

LONG-TERM HEALTH EFFECTS OF DRINKING

The drinking of a small amount (1 ounce [30 ml] of absolute alcohol, or two standard drinks per day), even if done regularly for years, does not have any conclusively demonstrated pathological effect except for a small increased risk for some cancers. An exception to this rule is drinking during pregnancy— even one standard drink a week may harm the fetus.

Drinking just 0.5 ounce (15 ml) of alcohol a day has been shown to be a mild anticoagulant and, like small doses of aspirin, to reduce the risk of stroke and heart attack. Mild infrequent intoxication produces a variety of temporary biochemical disturbances in the body: the adrenal glands may discharge hormones, sugar may be mobilized from stores in the liver, the electrolyte balance may be slightly altered, and the metabolism and equilibrium of the liver may be disturbed. However, these changes leave no chronic aftereffects, and the body rapidly returns to normal.

Severe or frequent intoxication, on the other hand, may produce more serious disturbances, including temporary extensive imbalances in the body chemistry, cardiac arrhythmias, acute hepatitis, and loss of memory (blackouts, passing out). Numerous hangover effects—nausea, headache, gastritis, dehydration, physical and mental incompetence, and a generalized residual malaise—may last as long as 24 hours after all the consumed alcohol has been metabolized. Some drinkers are willing to suffer the mild and even the more severe aftereffects of occasional intoxication for the sake of the temporary dissociation, euphoria, or socialization associated with it, but frequent intoxication, even of moderate degree, imposes a severe and debilitating burden on the drinker. Four or more standard drinks a day, consumed regularly, can produce liver damage and atrophy of the cerebral cortex (the "gray matter" of the brain) in vulnerable people.

The irritating effects of alcohol, especially in undiluted strong beverages, can result in damage to the tissues of the mouth, pharynx, esophagus, and stomach and an increased susceptibility to cancer in these organs. Laryngeal and stomach cancers are often associated with chronic alcohol consumption. Laryngeal cancer is

a malignant tumour of the larynx (voice box). A type of laryngeal cancer known as carcinoma occurs more often in males and frequently arises from chronic irritation, overuse of the voice, or alcohol and tobacco abuse. It begins as a small hard patch or papillary tumour. There may be extensive destruction, ulcers, and abscesses. Laryngeal cancer is a relatively common disease that can be treated in the early stages. Unfortunately, 8 to 10 months may elapse before the first symptoms of hoarseness appear and a diagnosis is made. Similar to laryngeal cancer, tobacco and alcohol use are among the main risk factors for stomach cancer. Males develop stomach cancer at approximately twice the rate of females. Symptoms may be abdominal pain or swelling, unexplained weight loss, vomiting, and poor digestion. Surgery is the only method for treating stomach cancer, although radiation therapy or chemotherapy may be used in conjunction with surgery or to relieve symptoms.

The liver is likely to suffer serious damage if it must cope for extended periods with the detoxication of large amounts of alcohol. There can also be damage to the heart muscle and the pancreas. Frequent heavy drinking that leads to severe intoxication or the prolonged steady maintenance of a high alcohol concentration in the body has been shown to be linked to many impairments or injuries. Disorders commonly linked to alcoholism are diseases caused by nutritional deficiencies, cardiomyopathy, accidents, suicide, cirrhosis, and impaired resistance to infection. Worldwide, such chronic alcohol abuse causes as much death and disability as measles and malaria and results in more years lost to death and disability than are caused by tobacco or illegal drugs.

FETAL ALCOHOL SYNDROME

There is evidence that even occasional drinking by an expectant mother can endanger the development of the fetus and result in a variety of birth defects. These defects are referred to together as fetal alcohol syndrome (FAS). The principal symptoms of a child born with FAS are retarded growth both before and after birth, various abnormalities of the central nervous system, and certain characteristic abnormalities of the face and head. The latter include microcephaly (small head); short palpebral fissures (small eye openings); ptosis (eyelid droop); epicanthic folds (skin folds over the inside eye corner); short, upturned nose; long, smooth philtrum (area between nose and mouth); thin upper lip; and a small jaw. The central nervous system abnormalities result in delayed intellectual development and intellectual disability and various behavioral problems such as poor concentration, impulsiveness, and an inability to consider the consequences of one's actions. Behavioral problems may be the principal symptoms in persons who show little sign of facial abnormalities or intellectual disability. Those born with FAS also may have abnormalities of the upper respiratory passageways, heart, joints, and limbs.

FAS is apparently caused by the effects of ethyl alcohol or its breakdown product acetaldehyde on the developing human embryo or fetus. FAS occurs with a frequency of anywhere from 0.2 to 1.5 live births per thousand in the United States. The syndrome commonly appears in the newborns of mothers who are chronic alcoholics. The more heavily a mother drinks during pregnancy, the greater the risk to the developing fetus. It is estimated that between 30 and 40 percent of all women who drink heavily during pregnancy will have a child afflicted with FAS. Although not strictly defined, the phrase "heavy drinking" can be quantified as a daily intake of eight or more drinks, amounting to 4 ounces or more of absolute alcohol.

Even moderate consumption of alcohol during pregnancy, however, may be associated with milder symptoms of FAS, and women are often counseled to abstain from imbibing any amount of alcohol shortly before and during pregnancy. In 2005 the U.S. Surgeon General issued an advisory that "no amount of alcohol consumption can be considered safe during pregnancy." It is also often advised to prolong this period of abstinence throughout breast-feeding, or at least to avoid drinking alcohol during specified hours before nursing, because various other disorders of the newborn have been linked to alcohol in breast milk.

CHAPTER 6

ALCOHOL AND SOCIETY

Alcoholic beverages are consumed largely for their physiological and psychological effects, but they are often consumed within specific social contexts and may even be a part of religious practices. The different social contexts of alcohol use often influence how and the extent to which alcohol is consumed. For example, coworkers gathered at a formal dinner are more likely to limit their consumption than are young drinkers at a college party. The latter situation predisposes individuals to the unhealthy and dangerous practice of binge drinking—the consumption of large amounts of alcohol in a short span of time.

Such instances of alcohol consumption, often considered a form of irresponsible drinking, have long been a source of concern for societies, particularly because of the dangerous and risky behaviours that they seem to encourage. The negative reputation that alcohol has gained from its abuse overshadows the fact that many people worldwide engage in moderate alcohol consumption. Distinguishing between the two practices, however, is difficult, and many young drinkers unfortunately learn moderation only through intoxication. Those who learn to temper their alcohol consumption often perceive drinking as a relaxing activity, something to be enjoyed responsibly throughout life.

ALCOHOL CONSUMPTION IN SOCIETY

Alcohol has been consumed by humans for thousands of years. In early societies, it was often an important component of rituals and a valuable source of nutrients. In ancient Greece, alcohol was believed to be consumed by the Greek gods, and in many other ancient societies, it fulfilled a vital role in religious ceremonies. Later, in Europe and the United Kingdom, alcohol was popularized as a social lubricant in public houses (pubs) and taverns.

Throughout history and across all societies, there has always existed a tendency toward alcohol abuse. Even in the early eras, there were conflicted perceptions of alcohol. In some instances, religious doctrines were invoked to control alcohol consumption. In other cases, governments implemented measures for prohibition. Regardless of the diversity of approaches taken, it was clear to citizens in very early societies that regulations providing some semblance of alcohol control were needed to discourage drunkenness. These early systems of alcohol control provided the framework needed for the development of modern alcohol regulation.

HISTORY OF ALCOHOL USE: EARLY SOCIETIES

The origin of alcoholic beverages is lost in the mists of prehistory. Fermentation can occur in any mashed sugar-containing food—such as grapes, grains, berries, or honey—left exposed in warm air. Yeasts from the air act on the sugar, converting it to alcohol and carbon dioxide. Alcoholic beverages were thus probably discovered accidentally by preagricultural cultures. Early peoples presumably liked the effects, if not the taste, and proceeded to purposeful production. From merely gathering the wild-growing raw materials, they went on to regular cultivation of the vine and other suitable crops. Few preliterate groups did not learn to convert some of the fruit of the earth into alcohol. In the case of starchy vegetation, quite primitive agriculturists learned how to convert the starch to fermentable sugar through preliminary chewing. (Saliva contains an enzyme that carries out this conversion.)

Alcohol is the oldest and still one of the most widely used drugs. The making of wines and beers has been reported from several hundred preliterate societies. The importance of these alcoholic beverages is evident in the multiplicity of customs and regulations that developed around their production and uses. They often became central in the most valued personal and social ceremonies, especially rites of passage, and were ubiquitous in activities such as births, initiations, marriages, compacts, feasts, conclaves, crownings, magic rites, medicine, worship, hospitality, war making, peace making, and funerals.

The manufacture and sale of alcoholic beverages was already common in the earliest civilizations, and it was commercialized and regulated by government. The oldest known code of laws, the Code of Hammurabi of Babylonia (c. 1770 BCE), regulated drinking houses. Sumerian physician-pharmacists prescribed beer (c. 2100 BCE) in relatively sophisticated pharmacopoeias found on clay tablets. Later Egyptian doctors, in their medical papyri (c. 1500 BCE), included beer or wine in many of their prescriptions. Semitic cuneiform literature of the northern Canaanites, in prebiblical Ugarit, contains abundant references to the ubiquitous religious and household uses of alcohol.

Water, a precious commodity in the earliest agriculturally dependent civilizations, was probably the original fluid used as offering in worship rites. In time, other fluids—milk, honey, and later wine (in some religions, beer)—were substituted. That alcoholic beverages should have displaced other fluids in early religions, both as offering and drink, is not surprising. The capacity of alcohol to help the shaman or priest and other participants reach a desired state of ecstasy or frenzy could not long have escaped observation, and its powers were naturally attributed to supernatural spirits and gods. The red wine in religious uses was eventually perceived as symbolizing the blood of life and, in this spiritual sense, ultimately passed into the Christian Eucharist. The records of the ancient Egyptian as well as of the Mesopotamian civilizations attest that drinking and drunkenness had passed from the state of religious rite to common practice, often troublesome to government and accompanied by acute and chronic illnesses. There are ample indications that some people so loved drink and were so abandoned to drunkenness that they must be presumed to have been alcoholics.

HISTORY OF ALCOHOL USE: CLASSICAL PEOPLES

The significance of the Classical history of drinking arises from the fact that after about 300 BCE the Greek, Hebrew, and Roman cultures became mingled in a manner that was to influence powerfully the development of European culture. The surviving records of ancient Greek and Roman culture, in Classical pictorial and plastic art as well as in the literature transmitting prehistoric memories enshrined in myths, reveal the common and copious use of wine by the gods, as well as by people of all classes. The worship of Dionysus, or Bacchus, the wine god, was the most popular. His festival, the Bacchanalia, has given English one of its literary names for a drunken orgy. His female devotees, the Maenads, worshipped him in drunken frenzies. The Greco-Roman classics abound with descriptions of drinking and often of drunkenness. The wine of the ancient Greeks, like that of the Hebrews of the same time, was usually drunk diluted with an equal part or two parts of water, and so the alcohol strength of the beverage was presumably between 4 and 7 percent. But diluted wine, as a standard

Caravaggio portrait of Bacchus, the Roman name for Dionysus, the god of wine. Superstock/
Getty Images

drink, was apparently more common than plain water, and there were topers who preferred their wine straight.

The literature of the Greeks does not lack warnings against the evil effects of excessive drinking, but in this it is surpassed by the classics of the Hebrews. The earliest references in the Bible show that abundant wine was regarded not only as a blessing, on a par with ample milk and honey, grain, and fruit, but also as a curse to alcohol abusers such as Noah.

In the national religious culture that developed into the Judaism of today, drinking was an important aspect of all important ceremonial occasions—from the celebration of the eight-day-old boy's circumcision to the toasting of the soul of the departed and, in between, the wedding, the arrival and departure of every Sabbath and festival, and, indeed, any sort of celebration. Drinking thus became integrated with a strict attitude of reverence for the sanctity or importance of the occasion, to the extent that overdrinking and becoming tipsy would manifestly be inappropriate and disapproved. Drunkenness then became a culturally negative, rejected behaviour, and it generally vanished from Jewish communities. In contemporary terms, drinking was under effective social control, and the result has been the seeming paradox, fascinating to modern students of sociocultural phenomena, that some peoples with a very high proportion of drinkers will exhibit relatively low rates of alcoholism and other alcohol-related problems.

A different kind of religious control was adopted later (in the 7th century) in Islam: the Qur'ān (Koran) simply condemned wine, and the result was an effective prohibition wherever the devout followers of Muhammad in Arabia and other lands prevailed. A similar process occurred some 1,000 years later in Europe after the Reformation and later still in the United States, when a number of ascetic Christian sects, resting their ideology on the Bible, made abstinence a fundamental tenet.

Like the early agriculturists of the Middle East, the people of East Asia discovered the technology of manufacturing alcoholic beverages in prehistoric times. Barley and rice were the chief crops and the raw materials for producing the beverages that, as in the Middle East, were incorporated into religious ceremonies, both as drink and libation, with festivals featuring divine states of drunkenness. Here too, in time, sacred drink became secularized, even while its religious uses survived, and evoked public as well as private disorders. The history of China includes several abortive efforts at control or prohibition, but prohibition was effective only when religiously motivated. The Hindu Ayurvedic texts skillfully describe both the beneficent uses of alcoholic beverages and the consequences of intoxication and alcoholic diseases. Most of the peoples in India and China, as well as in Sri Lanka, the Philippines, and Japan, have continued, throughout, to ferment a portion of their crops and nourish as well as please themselves with the alcoholic product. However, devout adherents of Buddhism, which arose in India in the 5th and 6th centuries BCE and spread over southern and eastern Asia, abstain to this day, as do the members of the Hindu Brahman caste.

In Africa, corn (maize), millet, sorghum, bananas, honey, the saps of the palm and bamboo, and many fruits have been used to ferment nutrient beers and wines, the best-known being sorghum beer and palm wines. Most of the peoples of Oceania, on the other hand, seem to have missed the discovery of fermentation. Many of the pre-Columbian Indians of North America were also exceptional in lacking alcoholic beverages until they were introduced by Europeans, with explosive and disastrous consequences. But the Papago Indians of the southwestern United States made a cactus wine, and the Tarahumara of northern Mexico made beers from corn and species of agave, while throughout Central and South America the indigenous peoples made chicha and other alcoholic beverages from corn, tubers, fruits, flowers, and saps. For the most part, their drinking appears to have been regulated so as to inhibit individual alcoholism and limit drunkenness to communal fiestas.

TAVERN

A tavern is an establishment where alcoholic beverages are sold for consumption on the premises. Tavern keeping has paralleled the growth of trade, travel, and industry throughout history and virtually worldwide. The Code of Hammurabi of ancient Babylonia (c. 1750 BCE) provided that the death penalty could be imposed upon a proprietor for diluting beer. In ancient Greece the lesche, *which was primarily a local club, served meals to strangers as well as to its local members. By the 5th century BCE there were sumptuous Greek establishments called* phatnai *that served a local and transient clientele of traders, envoys, and government officials.*

In ancient Rome no man of any social standing could be seen in a tavern, although one type of establishment, the lupanar, *flourished behind locked doors on the quietest of side streets, and men with veiled heads entered in the dark of night to dine, drink, or gamble. Nor was the reputation undeserved, for the* deversoria, tabernae, cauponae, *and* bibulae *of republican and imperial Rome were haunts of the jaded and degraded at best, and of criminal types at worst. Yet cooked delicacies and full meals were traditionally served in the* caupona *(low-class inn) and* taberna meritoria *(better-class tavern). These were long chambers having vaulted ceilings, with serving boys standing at semiattention and the proprietor sitting at a raised platform at one end.*

The hostelries of Roman England were derived from the cauponae *and the* tabernae *of Rome itself. These were followed by alehouses, which were run by women (alewives) and marked by a broom stuck out above the door. The English inns of the Middle Ages were sanctuaries of wayfaring strangers, cutthroats, thieves, and political malcontents. The tavern, the predecessor of the modern restaurant, originated the custom of providing a daily meal at a fixed time.*

By the middle of the 16th century the dining-out habit was well established among townsmen of all classes. Most taverns offered a good dinner for one shilling or less, with wine and ales as extras. Tobacco was also sold after its introduction into England in 1565. Taverns offered companionship as well as refreshment, and some of the better houses became regular meeting places and unofficial clubhouses. Among the more famous London taverns of Tudor times were the Mermaid, frequented by Ben Jonson and his friends; the Boar's Head, associated with Shakespeare's Sir John Falstaff; and the Falcon, where actors and theatre managers of the day gathered.

The identity of the first public drinking and dining establishment in the United States is obscure. It is certain, however, that it was known as an inn, tavern, or ordinary, names not always interchangeable. It is probable that taverns appeared in the United States almost as soon as the first Dutch settlers arrived. Boston's first tavern, Cole's, opened its doors in 1634. New York's first tavern was opened in Dutch Colonial days by Governor Kieft, who stated that he was tired of entertaining strangers and travelers in his own home and thus opened a tavern to lodge and feed them. The building became New Amsterdam's (and later New York's) city hall and was used for that purpose until about 1700, when a new city hall (now Federal Hall) was built. Colonial courts generally required that some kind of public house be established in each community. These early American taverns were under the strict guardianship of the government, which regulated prices. During the American Revolution, the tavern was the customary locus of political planning sessions. In the 19th, 20th, and 21st centuries, the tavern remained a centre of social activity primarily as the neighborhood bar of towns and cities and the roadhouse of more rural areas.

ALCOHOL IN MODERN SOCIETIES

In early societies, alcoholic beverages had multiple uses. First, they had important nutritional value. Second, they were the best medicine available for some illnesses and especially for relieving pain. (In any case, a patient given a prescription to be taken in beer or wine, with the instruction to drink it liberally, was likely to feel better regardless of whether the various ingredients affected his disease.) Also, they facilitated religious ecstasy and communion with the mystical supernatural powers thought to control tribal and individual fate. They enabled periodic social festivity and the personal jollification of the participants, thus also serving as the mediator of popular recreation.

By helping to reduce tension and fears and preoccupation with safety, alcohol can reduce as well as stimulate the impulse to engage in aggressive or dangerous activities. Just as drinking facilitates dangerous and uninhibited sex and driving by reducing stranger anxiety and fear of punishment, it also facilitates peaceful associations and commercial or ceremonial relations. In individuals with extraordinary responsibilities, such as chiefs, shamans, and medicine men, alcohol helped to assuage the personal anxieties and tensions connected with those exceptional roles. In some cases a formalized public binge could serve to loosen interpersonal aggressions and allow an interlude of verbal or even physical hostility within the family or clan group that otherwise would be forbidden by the mores of the cohesive small society. Any insults and wounds suffered during the discordant interlude could easily be forgiven by blaming them on alcohol-induced irresponsibility. Under these circumstances drunkenness could be approved or even be mandatory and still serve an integrative social function. In short, the most general effect of alcohol, suggested by its very equivocal uses, appears to be as a facilitator of mood change in any desired direction.

The conditions of early societies foreshadow the conditions of modern societies, including the contemporary highly industrialized ones. As food, alcohol retains little value beyond its caloric content. As a medicine, it has survived only as a solvent for water-insoluble compounds and as a "tonic." In religion, where not completely eliminated, wine has been relegated to a highly specific, essentially symbolic role. Indeed, the most distinctive features of alcohol in complex technological societies are social, from Andean fiestas to Irish pub life to Greek weddings.

Not that the ancient uses of alcohol have been forgotten: a drink is still the symbolic announcer of friendship, peace, and agreement, in personal as well as in business or political relations. In modern society, however, many people discover that drinking can often help them to suppress the overwhelming inhibitions, shyness, anxieties, and tensions that frustrate and interfere with urgent needs to function effectively, either socially or economically. In cultures characterized by various inhibitions against gratifying interpersonal relationships, the capacity of alcohol to serve as a social lubricant is highly valued.

CONFLICTS OVER DRINKING

Modern societies are troubled by a lack of consensus around many issues of right and wrong or proper and improper behaviour. Since the latter part of the 18th century, drinking alcohol has been a focus of disagreement, sometimes amounting to political warfare among subgroups making up larger national societies. In the United States, the late 19th-century temperance movement became, by the early 20th century, an antialcohol movement that culminated in national Prohibition, enacted by constitutional amendment in 1919 (and repealed in 1933). Similar movements in other countries had somewhat similar histories.

The lack of consensus regarding who may drink, how much of what may be drunk, and where and when and with whom one may drink is illustrated by the crazy quilt of local regulations extant in the United States. In some localities there is total prohibition or prohibition only of distilled spirits and strong wines. In other localities, only those over 18 or over 21

TEMPERANCE MOVEMENT

The temperance movement was dedicated to promoting moderation and, more often, complete abstinence in the use of intoxicating liquor. Although an abstinence pledge had been introduced by churches as early as 1800, the earliest temperance organizations seem to have been those founded at Saratoga, New York, in 1808 and in Massachusetts in 1813. The movement spread rapidly under the influence of the churches. By 1833 there were 6,000 local societies in several U.S. states.

Some temperance advocates, notably Carry Nation, worked to great effect outside the organized movement. The earliest European organizations were formed in Ireland. The movement began to make effective progress in 1829 with the formation of the Ulster Temperance Society. Thereafter, the movement spread throughout Ireland, to Scotland, and to Britain. The Church of England Temperance Society, the largest such organization at mid-20th century, was founded in 1862 and reconstituted in 1873. In 1969 it was united with the National Police Court Mission to form the Church of England Council for Social Aid. On the continent, the earliest temperance organizations seem to have been in existence in Norway and Sweden in 1836 and 1837.

Temperance and abstinence became the objects of education and legislation in many regions. Besides combining moral and political action, the modern temperance movements were

A poster for the Prohibition Party, 1888. Library of Congress, Washington, D.C.

characterized by international scope and the organized cooperation of women. The first international temperance organization appears to have been the Order of Good Templars (formed in 1851 at Utica, New York), which gradually spread over the United States, Canada, Great Britain, Scandinavia, several other European countries, Australasia, India, parts of Africa, and South America. In 1909 a world prohibition conference in London resulted in the foundation of an International Prohibition Confederation.

As the extreme wing of the temperance movement, prohibition was one of the hallowed reforms from the 1840s. As the wave of U.S. state prohibition laws passed in the 1850s began to be repealed, prohibition agitators began to organize formally. The strictly political Prohibition Party, founded in 1869, and the Woman's Christian Temperance Union (WCTU) of 1874, which employed educational and social as well as political means in promoting legislation, represented the two strategic approaches. When a second wave of state prohibition in the 1880s receded, both were superseded by the Anti-Saloon League, founded in 1893.

Founded in Cleveland, Ohio, the national WCTU later became an international association. During the 1880s the organization spread to other lands, and in 1883 the World's Woman's Christian Temperance Union was formed.

years of age may buy drinks or married underage women may buy alcohol but married underage men may not. At one time, some localities did not allow Native Americans to buy alcohol. Certain places only allow liquor to be sold by the bottle, not by the drink. In some places, drinks may be served only with food, whereas in others only without food. Sometimes drinking in public places is permitted only if the drinkers are curtained or only if they are uncurtained or only when they are seated. In other instances, men may stand to drink, but women must be seated. Dissonant attitudes toward a custom as common as drinking are believed by many sociologists to account for the inability of a society to establish firm rules inhibiting immoderate behaviour, with a resulting high incidence of damaging use, drunkenness, and many other problems related to alcohol. The Chinese and Italians, as well as the Jews, are cited as examples of groups having a well-developed cultural consensus against drinking to drunkenness, with resulting low rates of alcohol problems. In parallel, France and Great Britain are cited as countries with a consensus favouring steady copious drinking, with a resulting high rate of alcoholism.

The modern conflict over drinking reflects the complex interactions of the individual with small groups and larger society. Small groups, formed by common interests in business, occupation, recreation, neighbourhood, politics, ethnicity, or religion, use communal drinking to facilitate mixing, engender solidarity, reduce normal inhibitions against trust and promote collaboration with "strangers," symbolize and ratify accord, and

PROHIBITION

Prohibition is the legal prevention of the manufacture, sale, or transportation of alcoholic beverages with the aim of obtaining partial or total abstinence through legal means. Some attempts at prohibition were made in Aztec society, ancient China, feudal Japan, the Polynesian islands, Iceland, Finland, Norway, Sweden, Russia, Canada, and India, but only a few countries—most notably, certain Muslim countries—have maintained national prohibition. Most countries that have experimented with the ban have soon lifted it. Finland, for instance, adopted prohibition in 1919 and repealed it in 1931, and the United States adopted it in 1919 and repealed it in 1933.

In northern European countries liquor control has reflected concern for the prevention of alcoholism. The Finnish prohibition outlawed the sale of spirits in an attempt to redirect the population toward greater consumption of beer (with lower alcoholic content). Sweden experimented with a system of liquor-ration books with the aim of limiting the individual's use of liquor.

Various cultures differ considerably in their attitudes toward drinking as well as their systems of control. Among the Japanese, for example, drunkenness is not strongly condemned, and

Two men pour alcohol into a sewer during Prohibition in the United States. Library of Congress, Washington, D.C.

the drunkard is simply prevented from harming himself or others. Other cultures may show high acceptance of drinking as a social custom with a norm directing moderate use. With regard to control, efforts have been directed toward the drinker, as in Sweden, or toward the seller, as in the United States.

In the United States an early wave of movements for state and local prohibition arose out of the intensive religious revivalism of the 1820s and '30s, which stimulated movements toward perfectionism in humans, including temperance and the abolition of slavery. The precedent for seeking temperance through law was set by a Massachusetts law, passed in 1838 and repealed two years later, which prohibited sales of spirits in less than 15-gallon quantities. The first state prohibition law was passed in Maine in 1846 and ushered in a wave of such state legislation before the Civil War.

New York City Deputy Police Commissioner John A. Leach (right) *watching agents pour liquor into the sewer following a raid, c. 1920.* New York World-Telegram and the Sun Newspaper Photograph Collection/Library of Congress, Washington, D.C. (neg. no. LC-USZ62-123257)

The drive for national prohibition emerged out of a renewed attack on the sale of liquor in many states after 1906. The underlying forces at work to support national prohibition included antipathy to the growth of cities (the presumed scene of most drinking), evangelical Protestant middle-class anti-alien and anti-Roman Catholic sentiment, and rural domination of the state legislatures, without which ratification of the Eighteenth Amendment would have been impossible. Other forces included the corruption existing in the saloons and the industrial employers' increased concern for preventing accidents and increasing the efficiency of workers.

The Anti-Saloon League, founded in 1893, led the state prohibition drives of 1906–13. During World War I a temporary Wartime Prohibition Act was passed to save grain for use as food. By January 1920 prohibition was already in effect in 33 states covering 63 percent of the total population. In 1917 the resolution for submission of the Prohibition Amendment to the states received the necessary two-thirds vote in Congress. The amendment was ratified on Jan. 29, 1919, and went into effect on Jan. 29, 1920. On Oct. 28, 1919, the National Prohibition Act, popularly known as the Volstead Act (after its promoter, Congressman Andrew J. Volstead), was enacted, providing enforcement guidelines.

Federal government support of enforcement of Prohibition varied considerably during the 1920s. Illegal manufacture and sales of liquor went on in the United States on a large scale. In general, Prohibition was enforced wherever the population was sympathetic to it. In the large cities, where sentiment was strongly opposed to Prohibition, enforcement was much weaker than in rural areas and small towns. Increased price of liquor and beer, however, meant that the working classes probably bore the restrictions of urban Prohibition to a far greater degree than the middle-class or upper class segments of the population.

Prohibition brought into being a new kind of criminal—the bootlegger. The career of Al Capone was a dramatic instance of the development of bootlegging on a large scale. His annual earnings were estimated at $60,000,000. The rise of the bootlegging gangs led to a succession of gang wars and murders. A notorious incident was the St. Valentine's Day Massacre in Chicago in 1929, when the Capone gang shot to death seven members of the rival "Bugs" Moran gang. Historians of the underworld, however, suggest that by the late 1920s bootlegging was on the verge of semimonopoly control and that the end of gang wars was approaching.

The temperance movement itself changed during the 1920s. The fundamentalist and nativist groups assumed greater leadership, tending to drive away less hostile and urban forces. Major supporters of Prohibition gradually became disenchanted with it, citing the increase in criminal liquor production and sale, the development of the speakeasy, and increased restriction on individual freedom as its results. In 1932 the Democratic Party adopted a platform calling for repeal, and the Democratic victory in the presidential election of 1932 sounded the death knell of the Eighteenth Amendment.

In February 1933 Congress adopted a resolution proposing the Twenty-first Amendment to the Constitution to repeal the Eighteenth. On Dec. 5, 1933, Utah became the 36th state to ratify the amendment, and repeal was achieved. After repeal a few states continued statewide prohibition, but by 1966 all had abandoned it. In general, liquor control in the United States came to be determined more and more at local levels.

ensure that gatherings for celebration will succeed as festive occasions. Individuals use alcoholic beverages as an agreeable effector of desired mood alteration, such as altering dysphoric mood or masking unease and pain, and to enable participation in the various small groups with which they are required to associate.

Given favourable contexts and consensual practices, moderate amounts of drink have an integrative function within families and in common-interest groups. This is thought to account for the survival of drinking customs from early times in spite of the problems drinking has engendered and the opposition it has provoked. Nevertheless, individuals and sometimes groups, whether formally or informally organized, also indulge in immoderate, self-injurious, and socially damaging drinking. These dysfunctional behaviours account, in part, for the organized societal opposition to any drinking. Alcohol has been, from olden times, a facilitator of risk-taking and morally lax, hedonistic behaviour. As such, it has evoked the displeasure and condemnation of those favouring moral strictness and an ascetic way of life.

DRINKING PATTERNS

Patterns of drinking are displayed in a great variety of ways and customs in different parts of the world and among various subgroups and subcultures within larger societies. Based on the presence or absence of subsequent regret and negative consequences, celebratory drunkenness should be distinguished from alcoholism. The places of drinking vary greatly: even the home may be the only place where one can drink or the one place where drinking is forbidden. Drinking may be a ceremonial or informal family affair, with or before meals. It may be a solitary practice at home, in commercial drinking places, or in private hideaways, or it may be a group practice in membership clubs, neighbourhood taverns, beer gardens, sidewalk cafés, or skid-row alleys. The purposes and occasions are infinitely disparate. It may be the benign drunkenness of men in a quasi-religious fiesta in Central or South America, the festal abandonment in song and dance—after relatively little drinking—of members of a Hasidic sect, the drunken celebrations of collegiate fraternity brothers, or the exhibitionistic libationism of business meetings and professional conventions. It may be the repeated "killing" of bottles by men or women fixed mindlessly before the television set, the quick "high" at cocktail parties, or the "chugging" of forbidden liquors by defiant, rebellious youths seeking to assert their independence.

Not only one's taste, predilection, or psychological need but also one's sex, age, residential neighbourhood, education, associations, church and other memberships, and socioeconomic status may determine whether, when, what, how much, or with whom one shall drink. In the United States, where nearly one-third of adults are abstainers, the better educated and the economically advantaged are more likely to be drinkers than the poor—though, among the poor who do drink, the proportions of heavy drinkers are higher. By contrast, in France, where abstainers are in a very small minority, they are more likely to be found among the better educated and upwardly mobile. The attitudes toward drinking and abstaining, among or within different countries, are as varied as the practices.

ALCOHOL CONSUMPTION WORLDWIDE

The worldwide per capita consumption of distilled spirits, beer, and wine has generally increased since 1950, with beer consumption increasing more than the consumption of either spirits or wine. Although the consumption of all alcoholic beverages generally rose during the second half of the 20th century and into the 21st century, deviations from these general tendencies were evident in many countries. Countries with traditionally high levels of total alcohol consumption (e.g., France, Italy, Portugal, Spain, and Switzerland) exhibited stable or only slightly increased per capita consumption. Beer consumption in traditionally heavy beer-drinking countries (e.g., Germany, Belgium, Australia, New Zealand, Ireland, the United Kingdom, and Denmark) did not increase as much as did the world-wide pattern. Wine consumption on a per capita basis actually declined in some countries with traditionally high levels of consumption (e.g., France and Italy), while it rose in some countries with relatively low wine consumption, especially the United States and Australia. In the 1990s alcohol consumption declined in most of the developed countries but increased in many developing countries.

Many factors are believed to have affected these patterns in total alcohol consumption. One factor is the increased use of alcohol—primarily beer and wine—with meals, in part a result of long-term increases in per capita income in many countries and in part a result of fermentation technology that has kept the price of some alcoholic beverages relatively low, facilitating the purchase of beer and wine. Another factor is improved marketing and advertising. For example, in North America, particularly in the United States, the introduction of low-calorie beer and wine in the early 1970s was instrumental in the increased per capita consumption of alcohol in the late 20th and early 21st centuries.

The countries leading in total alcohol consumption per drinking-age person in the early 21st century were Luxembourg, Hungary, the Czech Republic, Ireland, and Germany. There were significant disparities in the level of consumption across countries among different types of alcoholic beverages. For example, although most of the leading consumers of alcoholic beverages drank significant quantities of wine, many drank relatively low quantities of distilled spirits. The leading beer-drinking countries were the Czech Republic, Ireland, Germany, Austria, and Luxembourg. Russia, Latvia, Cyprus, the Czech Republic, and Japan were among the leading consumers of distilled spirits. Ireland and Russia had the highest rates of heavy alcohol consumption among women, while Russia, Hungary, and Austria had very high rates among men. Portugal and Spain had high rates of per capita consumption, but, since they also had high rates of abstinence, the per capita number of very heavy drinkers was higher than it was for countries such as France with few abstainers.

EUROPE

In both France and Italy, wine consumption is high, but attitudes as well as patterns and amounts differ in the two countries in many ways. French parents tend to exhibit strong attitudes, either favourable or negative, toward their children's drinking. Italian parents typically introduce their children to wine drinking without any emotional overtones. Italian standards of respectable limits for drinking are lower than those of the French, and the Italians typically regard getting drunk with disdain, while the French look on it with good humour or even, in men, as a mark of virility. Although these generalized patterns are not always consistent among the various regional populations

PUBLIC HOUSE

A public house (or pub) is an establishment providing alcoholic liquors to be consumed on the premises. The traditional pub is an establishment found primarily in Britain and regions of British influence. English common law early imposed social responsibilities for the well-being of travelers upon the inns and taverns, declaring them to be public houses that must receive all travelers in reasonable condition who were willing to pay the price for food, drink, and lodging.

In Tudor England (1485–1603), selected innkeepers were required by a royal act to maintain stables. In addition, some innkeepers acted as unofficial postmasters and kept stables for the royal post. In the mid-1600s, some public houses even issued unofficial coins which the innkeepers guaranteed to redeem in the realm's currency. By the 1800s, many of these establishments were divided internally to segregate the various classes of customers. Public houses—inns or taverns—were considered socially superior to alehouses, beerhouses, and ginshops.

The early inns or taverns were identified by simple signs, such as lions, dolphins, or black swans. Many colourful pub names (e.g., Bag o'Nails, Goat and Compass, and Elephant and Castle) are actually corrupted forms of historical, ecclesiastical, or other proper phrases and titles (e.g., "Bacchanals," "Great God Encompassing," and "Infanta de Castile," respectively). In the 18th century, the word Arms was appended to many pub names, indicating that the establishment was under the protection of a particular noble family, although some heraldic signs were references to the original ownership of the land on which the inn or tavern stood. Although public houses were traditionally owned and operated by licensed victuallers or publicans, by the early part of the 20th century many of them were owned or otherwise connected to a comparatively small number of brewery companies.

and socioeconomic groupings of either country, they are thought to be significant in accounting for the much higher mortality and morbidity from alcoholism in France.

Among the Scandinavian countries, the alcohol consumption pattern typically is one not of drinking daily or with meals but rather of very heavy drinking on weekends or special occasions. This is believed to account for the relatively high rate of alcohol-connected problems, such as intoxication, even though the total alcohol consumption there is relatively low. The Scandinavian countries also have strong temperance (antialcohol) movements, often supported by government funds, and have large populations that abstain from alcohol consumption. It is probable, therefore, that alcohol is consumed by a smaller number of drinkers than is represented by the drinking-age population.

In England and Ireland, the pub maintains its popularity as a main locus of drinking. In both countries, beer is the most popular alcoholic beverage. The marked preference for beer is seen in other countries that are overwhelmingly settled and influenced by British populations—Australia, New Zealand, and much of Canada. In these countries, too, the pub tends to dominate the drinking style. Drinking to a moderate grade of intoxication is generally acceptable, a permissive societal attitude that facilitates the development of alcoholism.

The drinking patterns of few European countries have been subject to formal examination by social scientists. Studies have focused primarily on segments of the population regarded as problematic, such as alcoholics, traffic offenders, criminals, patients of mental hospitals, or youths, especially students. Research has suggested that in eastern Europe alcohol consumption dropped by approximately 7 percent in the first decade after the fall of communism in that region. However, there are indications that in Poland the shift of a young population from rural areas to new urban-industrial centres increased the rate of alcoholism. In Russia there was a concerted effort to establish sobering-up stations and treatment clinics in many cities, often with research-oriented staffs. This action indicated recognition of the serious problem that alcoholism presented there. Vodka is the national drink. The situation is quite varied in different parts of eastern Europe. In the Transcaucasian country of Georgia, a viticultural region, wine is the favoured drink, and the drinking patterns are much more like those of Italy than those of western Russia or the rest of eastern and central Europe.

LATIN AMERICA

There has been even less systematic research on drinking patterns in Latin America, Africa, or Oceania. The limited evidence suggests that people in Latin America drink significantly less than do people in Europe, North America, or Oceania. For example, one study found that the total per capita alcohol consumption in Latin America in 1998 was 40 percent lower than in eastern Europe and North America and 50 percent lower than in Europe overall. However, most research has consisted of occasional reports on special populations, either local or problematic. One study in Chile found a middle-class population that exhibited patterns characteristic of some European populations, including typically consuming a moderate amount, drinking at home with meals, and frowning on drunkenness. The much larger working class customarily drank outside the home, in male company, on weekends or paydays, and sought intoxication that was valued as signaling both friendship and virility. A third population, identified as indigenous, displayed a pattern similar to that of the working class. The favoured drinks were generally pisco, which is a strong native brandy, and wine. Drinking accompanied secular and religious holidays, as well as the celebrations of births, baptisms, marriages, and funerals. Women, however, were expected to drink very moderately. Similar drinking patterns were reported from various areas in Bolivia and Peru.

JAPAN

In Japan, heavy drinking and drunkenness are traditionally permitted in well-delimited social situations and are socially integrative. The traditional beverage is sake, often called rice wine but more properly referred to as a beer, brewed to a strength of at least 14 percent alcohol up to 17 percent. A great many drinking customs and rituals involving sake have been connected with religious and social occasions. Next to sake the common beverage is shochu, a sake mash distillate that contains about 25 percent alcohol. There is historical evidence of heavy drinking and alcoholism, as well as various attempts to impose prohibition. Abstinence was practiced by some followers of Buddhism and of some revered Japanese philosophers. In the last quarter of the 19th century, modernization was accompanied by a temperance movement stimulated, in part, by the Woman's Christian Temperance Union and the Salvation Army. After World War II the influence of American culture on Japan resulted in a growing popularity of beer and an increased use of imported beverages, especially whiskey.

UNITED STATES

Drinking patterns and attitudes in the United States have been studied more systematically and completely than those of any other country. The results indicate there is no pattern or set of attitudes typical of the nation as a whole. Instead, there is a variety of patterns, customs, and attitudes reflective of many immigrant and indigenous populations and modified somewhat by changing historical and economic circumstances and political developments. Nevertheless, certain generalizations are possible. In the post-Prohibition and post–World War II era, several changes in American drinking practices and attitudes were observed and confirmed by formal studies. The proportion of abstainers declined after World War II, especially among women. By the early 1970s, approximately 77 percent of adult men and 60 percent of adult women were drinkers. The figures stabilized thereafter. There was evidence that underage drinking decreased, though heavy drinking on college campuses—especially so-called binge drinking—remained a considerable problem. As people aged, abstention generally increased. In part, this may have been an artifact of birth cohort and of a wish of former alcoholics to recover from their disorder.

Throughout the 20th century there were significant disparities in alcohol consumption across groups. Whereas 30 percent of whites were abstainers, nearly 50 percent of African Americans and Hispanics and 65 percent of Asians and Pacific Islanders abstained from alcohol consumption. As compared with urban populations, people in rural areas—who generally had fewer years of education, lower incomes, attended religious services more frequently, and belonged in larger proportions to fundamentalist Protestant denominations—also contained larger proportions of abstainers. In much of the United States, per capita consumption decreased in the latter part of the 20th century, especially in California and New York, though consumption increased from relatively low levels in most southern states.

In general, styles and customs of drinking are influenced by ethnic and geographic backgrounds, but Americans tend to be members of multiple small societies, and, to some extent, they drink differently within each of these societies. People from diverse origins may drink alike when joined in some special association—as fellow collegians, members of a business convention, comrades in one of the armed services, or guests at a special kind of social function. Even then, the expected manner and amount of drinking is likely to be at least modified by an individual's background.

The fact that most Americans drink—that drinking rather than abstinence is the norm—does not prevent a paradoxical existence of ambiguous attitudes about the behaviour among drinkers themselves, many of whom believe that alcohol consumption is harmful. These ambivalences account for the massive array of regulations on the sale and distribution of alcohol, most of them intended to interfere with the availability of beverages at certain times, in certain places, or to certain classes of persons. An example is the tolerance sometimes found for driving under the influence of alcohol. In response to the large percentage of automobile fatalities involving alcohol consumption—according to some studies alcohol use was present in more than 40 percent of fatal crashes in the United States in the 1980s—and pressure from interest groups (e.g., Mothers Against Drunk Driving), many states in the 1990s lowered the legal limit of blood alcohol content (BAC) for drivers from 0.10 mg of alcohol per 100 ml of blood to 0.08 and increased the penalties for driving under the influence.

ALCOHOL PROBLEMS AND CONTROLS

Alcohol is so commonly discussed in terms of its negative effects that it is often seen as being wholly detrimental. As a result, the personally functional and socially integrative uses of alcohol tend to be overlooked. The vast majority of drinkers in most of the world are occasional and moderate drinkers—normal drinkers who experience no harm from their own use of alcoholic beverages. Thus, relatively small minorities fall into the class of heavy, excessive, or problem drinkers, including alcoholics. Nevertheless, problem drinkers invoke so many troubles for themselves, their families, their employers, their occupational or social associates, and their communities and society that "alcohol problems" are major and costly causes of disorder and suffering.

INDIVIDUAL AND SOCIAL EFFECTS

In the realm of health, the most serious and detrimental effect of alcohol is alcoholism. Although drinking itself is hardly ever regarded as sufficient to cause alcoholism, this disease could not arise without the use of alcohol. Next in seriousness come the alcoholic diseases—physical and mental disorders that are caused directly or indirectly by alcoholism or heavy drinking. As indicated previously, these include acute hepatitis, cancer of the esophagus, larynx, stomach, and other organs, and cirrhosis of the liver. Alcoholics and heavy drinkers are also especially susceptible to the development of some other diseases, not specifically alcoholic, and are then less able to withstand the vicissitudes of ill health. For example, although worldwide far more people die from the complications of smoking and high blood pressure than from alcoholism, the disability-adjusted life years (a technical measure for computing the loss of healthy life as the result of disability) resulting from alcohol abuse nearly equals that from high blood pressure and smoking combined. Alcoholics and problem drinkers also undoubtedly contribute to the deterioration of the mental health of other members of their families through verbal, physical, and sexual abuse. Indeed, alcoholism may be the greatest single cause of the breakdown of family life. Finally, a great portion of the work of police departments and the costs of local courts and jails is attributable to arrests, prosecutions, and brief incarcerations for public intoxication and other incidents in which alcohol is involved.

The social and economic costs of alcoholism and heavy drinking are essentially incalculable. The annual costs of health and welfare services provided to alcoholics and their families in the United States alone is in the billions of dollars and suggests the measure of effects worldwide. Furthermore, the millions of problem drinkers who have jobs and businesses are more frequently absent and often less efficient than their occupational associates. Almost a quarter of all patients in general hospitals are estimated to be alcoholic, and their per capita cost is more than twice that of other patients.

ALCOHOL CONTROL

Governmental efforts to control alcoholic beverages go back as far as recorded history. That the laws have often failed to produce the desired effects—temperance and good public order and perhaps revenue exceeding the social costs of excess—is inferred from the frequent legislative attempts at total prohibition in numerous lands throughout history, all apparently without lasting success. The most resounding failure was Prohibition in the United States from 1919 to 1933. Current prohibitions of alcohol consumption in parts of India appear to be equally ineffective.

Less-totalitarian efforts include licensing systems that limit the number and locations of places of sale, restriction of days and hours of sale, and prohibitions of sale to the young, with ages varying in different localities. Other secular efforts at control include regulation of the alcohol content of beverages, the size of containers, advertising, prices, or profits. Some governments—for instance, those of Finland and several U.S. states—have sought to eliminate the private-profit motive from the sale of alcoholic beverages by reserving a monopoly in the trade

to themselves. There are few indications, however, that this has made any marked difference in the kinds, degree, or severity of alcohol-related problems. In contrast, faith-based efforts to promote abstinence have been astonishingly effective.

Since reducing per capita alcohol consumption reduces future rates of alcoholism, some governments—for instance, those of Sweden, Finland, and the U.S. state of Ohio—have attempted to control individual drinking by a system of personal ration books for purchases. In Sweden this system was abandoned after 38 years of trial. Evidently, those who needed to drink a lot could find supplies—even when their ration books were withdrawn. The most universal regulation of alcoholic beverages takes the form of taxation (or, in government monopolies, an added profit), and, within limits, price in relation to discretionary income is the most effective single way that society has to affect per capita consumption of alcohol. However, none of the common forms of governmental or religious control has proved itself able to promote temperance in those already alcoholic.

A special offense related to drinking is alcohol-impaired driving of motor vehicles and the resulting high rate of accidents, with fatalities, personal injuries, and property damage. For example, in 2002 alcohol was involved in about one-third of the more than 40,000 annual road traffic fatalities in the United States, in possibly 500,000 injuries to persons, and in more than $1 billion worth of property damage. Although people with extremely low alcohol concentrations in their blood do not figure in accidents more often than those with no alcohol, the chances of being involved in a traffic accident rise precipitously with increasing blood alcohol concentrations beyond minimal levels. Therefore, laws making specified blood alcohol concentrations prima facie evidence of being drunk, impaired, under the influence of alcohol, or unfit to drive have been passed in most jurisdictions. In most countries the limit falls between 0.05 and 0.08 percent, though in some countries the limit is even lower. Attempts to curb alcohol-influenced driving have included the imposition of severe punishments—heavy fines, mandatory jail sentences, and the loss of a driving license for a specified period.

The rate and severity of alcohol problems have been more consistently influenced by nongovernmental movements and agencies. The most obvious example is the success of religious movements, such as Buddhism, Islam, and numerous Christian denominations and sects, in confirming their followers as total abstainers. Mormons, Christian Scientists, Seventh-day Adventists, Jehovah's Witnesses, and Baptists are examples of Christians whose churches have made abstinence a condition of loyal membership. In several European countries the abstinence movement also drew some support from the socialist-influenced labour movement and found some organizational expression in the form of fraternal orders, particularly the Order of Good Templars. The importance of religious orientation is indicated by the larger proportion of abstainers in the United States than in countries where the ideal of abstinence has been more politically motivated. The decline in the numbers of American abstainers in recent times may reflect the changing character of religious adherence in the United States.

MODERN TRENDS IN UNDERSTANDING ALCOHOL CONSUMPTION

In the past generation the character and influence of citizen movements have changed markedly. Whereas in former times the personnel, teaching aids, and ideologies of the temperance movement generally dominated research and education regarding alcohol, the tendency now is toward deriving objective information from academic and scientific sources. Among major efforts in the United States to bring a scientific orientation to bear on the consideration of alcohol problems has been the founding of the National Institute on Alcohol Abuse and Alcoholism in 1970. The trend has had repercussions on international cooperation as well. The International Bureau Against Alcoholism, founded in 1907, became, in 1964, the International Council on Alcohol and Alcoholism. In 1968 it was renamed the International Council on Alcohol and Addictions. The change of name represented a change in aims and policies, from total opposition to any drinking to advocacy of an objective consideration of alcohol problems. This change was manifested also in the character of the international congresses convened by antialcohol organizations once devoted essentially to descriptions of the horrible effects and denunciations of the evils of alcohol.

Beginning in the 1960s, these organizations were infiltrated by presentations from the scientific-academic world. By the 1970s the remnants of the old temperance movement had vanished. The papers and lectures offered by representatives of religious organizations and societies were now on an equal level of scholarship and objectivity with those from the scientific and academic community. This was in contrast to labeling alcoholism as "drunkenness," describing it as a vice and not a disease, and asserting that the only treatment was prolonged involuntary institutionalization.

Other governments have shown recognition of the potential of science-oriented approaches and have supported research and education as well as therapeutic activities, sometimes through special institutions such as Canada's Centre for Addiction and Mental Health; the Finnish Foundation for Alcohol Studies; the Norwegian National Institute for Alcohol and Drug Research; and the Nordic Council for Alcohol and Drug Research, with membership from the Scandinavian countries. The new excitement discernible in the late 20th and early 21st centuries concerning the study of problems related to alcohol consumption was stimulated mainly by consciousness of the human and economic costs of existing problems. At present the most effective methods of reducing per capita alcohol consumption and alcohol abuse are increased taxation, limits on availability and advertising, and random highway breath-analyzer tests with quick and certain sanctions. Among other methods, preventive educational efforts in schools have not lived up to expectations.

CHAPTER 7

ALCOHOLISM

Alcoholism is the excessive and repetitive drinking of alcoholic beverages to the extent that the drinker repeatedly is harmed or harms others. The harm may be physical or mental, and it may also be social, legal, or economic. Because such use is usually considered to be compulsive and under markedly diminished voluntary control, alcoholism is considered by a majority of, but not all, clinicians as an addiction and a disease.

The concept of inveterate drunkenness as a disease appears to be rooted in antiquity. The Roman philosopher Seneca classified it as a form of insanity. The term *alcoholism*, however, appeared first in the classical essay "Alcoholismus Chronicus" (1849) by the Swedish physician Magnus Huss. The phrase *chronic alcoholism* rapidly became a medical term for the condition of habitual inebriety, and the bearer of the "disease" was called an *alcoholic* or *alcoholist* (e.g., Italian *alcoolisto*, French *alcoolique*, German *Alkoholiker*, Spanish *alcohólico*, Swedish *alkoholist*).

DEFINING ALCOHOLISM

Alcoholism is a complex, many-sided phenomenon, and its many formal definitions vary according to the point of view of the definer. A simplistic definition calls alcoholism a disease caused by chronic, compulsive drinking. A purely pharmacological-physiological   definition   of   alcoholism classifies it as a drug addiction that requires imbibing increasing doses to produce desired effects and that causes a withdrawal syndrome when drinking is stopped. This definition is inadequate, however, because alcoholics, unlike other drug addicts, do not always need ever-increasing doses of alcohol. Opium addicts, on the other hand, become so adapted to the drug that they can survive more than a hundred times the normal lethal dose, but the increased amounts to which alcoholics become adapted are rarely above the normal single lethal dose. Moreover, the withdrawal syndromes in alcoholism occur inconsistently, sometimes failing to appear in a person who has experienced them before and never occurring in some drinkers whose destructive behaviour is otherwise not distinguishable from that of someone who is pharmacologically dependent on alcohol.

A third definition, behavioral in nature, defines alcoholism as a disorder in which alcohol assumes marked salience in the individual's life and in which the individual experiences a loss of control over its desired use. In this definition, alcoholism may or may not involve physiological dependence, but invariably it is characterized by alcohol consumption that is sufficiently great to cause regret and repeated physical, mental, social, economic, or legal difficulties. Clinicians call such a behavioral disorder a disease because it persists for years, is strongly hereditary, and is a major cause of death and disability. In addition,

alcohol permanently alters the brain's plasticity with regard to free choice over beginning or stopping drinking episodes. As with other medical diseases but unlike most bad habits, prospective studies demonstrate that willpower per se is of little predictive significance.

An informed minority opinion, especially among sociologists, believes that the medicalization of alcoholism is an error. Unlike most disease symptoms, the loss of control over drinking does not hold true at all times or in all situations. The alcoholic is not always under internal pressure to drink and can sometimes resist the impulse to drink or can drink in a controlled way. The early symptoms of alcoholism vary from culture to culture, and recreational public drunkenness may sometimes be mislabeled alcoholism by the prejudiced observer. In the general population, variation in daily alcohol consumption is distributed along a smooth continuum. This characteristic is inconsistent with the medical model, which implies that alcoholism is either present or absent—as is the case, for example, with pregnancy or a brain tumour.

For such reasons, the sociological definition regards alcoholism as merely one symptom of social deviance and believes its diagnosis often lies in the eyes and value system of the beholder. For example, periodic intoxication can cause sickness necessitating days of absence from work. In a modern industrial community, this makes alcoholism similar to a disease. In a rural Andean society, however, the periodic drunkenness that occurs at appointed communal fiestas and results in sickness and suspension of work for several days is normal behaviour. It should be noted that this drunkenness at fiestas is a choice and does not produce regret. If the sociological model were entirely correct, alcoholism should often be expected to disappear with maturation as is the case with many other symptoms of social deviance. This does not occur, however.

Finally, epidemiologists need a definition of alcoholism that enables them to identify alcoholics within a population that may not be available for individual examination. To define alcoholism they may rely on quantity and frequency measurements of reported community drinking and alcohol-related hospitalizations, on a formula based on the frequency of deaths from cirrhosis within the population, or on arrests for alcohol-related misbehaviour.

CAUSES OF ALCOHOLISM

Many theories of the causes of alcoholism rest on the limited perspectives of specialists in particular disciplines or professions. These theories range from heredity, environmental contagion, bad character, and economic misery (or affluence) to bleak childhoods, preexisting depressive disorder, ready and inexpensive availability of alcoholic beverages, or sociopathy. More discerning theories take into account the complexity of the disorder and acknowledge that

ELVIN M. JELLINEK

(b. Aug. 15, 1890, New York, N.Y., U.S.—d. Oct. 22, 1963, Palo Alto, Calif.)

American physiologist Elvin M. Jellinek was a pioneer in the scientific study of alcoholism.

Jellinek studied at several European universities and received a master's degree in 1914 from the University of Leipzig. He became a biometrician (i.e., one concerned with the statistics of biological studies) and worked for various institutions and organizations in Budapest (1914–20), Sierra Leone (1920–25), Honduras (1925–30), and at the Worcester State Hospital, Mass. (1931–39). In 1939 he began directing that hospital's studies on the effects of alcohol, and in 1941 he became an associate professor of applied physiology at Yale University, where he directed the Yale University School of Alcohol Studies from 1941 to 1950. From 1962 until his death he taught and conducted research at the Institute for the Study of Human Problems at Stanford University.

Jellinek was a pioneer in research having to do with the nature and causes of alcoholism and in descriptions of its symptomatology. He was an early proponent of the disease theory of alcoholism, arguing with great persuasiveness that alcoholics should be treated as sick people. Jellinek gathered and summarized his own research and that of others in the important and authoritative works Alcohol Explored *(1942) and* The Disease Concept of Alcoholism *(1960).*

alcoholism is usually caused by a combination of factors.

Prospective studies of lifetimes have often shown that some theories of alcoholism were incorrect because they confused cause with association. For example, on the basis of current evidence, alcoholism is seen to be associated with but not caused by growing up in a household with alcoholic parents. Likewise, alcoholism is associated with but not usually caused (in men, at least) by depression, and alcoholism is associated with but not caused by self-indulgence, poverty, or neglect in childhood. Rather, alcoholism in individuals often leads to depression and anxiety. Indeed, self-medication with alcohol makes depression worse, not better. Again, alcoholism in parents often leads to childhood poverty and childhood unhappiness. The same parental alcoholism also increases the risk of later alcoholism in such children, but for genetic, not environmental, reasons.

Studies of twins and adoptees have confirmed the common belief that alcoholism can be inherited. This genetic component is not inexorable, but reflects a predisposition that renders some people significantly more vulnerable to alcoholism than others. At present there is no evidence that this predisposition depends upon a single gene. Rather, there are probably a large number of genes, each with rather small individual effects, that affect the risk of developing alcoholism. Recent evidence indeed suggests that much of the genetic risk is not

due to neurological vulnerability but to a heightened resistance to the unpleasant side effects of heavy alcohol consumption. As a corollary to this evidence, a genetic defect has been identified that interferes with the degradation of acetaldehyde (a metabolic product of alcohol). Many people of Asian descent who are homozygous (carry two identical copies of the gene) for this defect have a marked and often uncomfortable flushing response to even small quantities of alcohol, which makes it unlikely that they will develop alcoholism. Another hereditary factor causes young women (but not young men) to break down less alcohol in the stomach prior to absorption through the digestive system. Young women therefore experience higher blood-alcohol levels from a given dose of alcohol.

Besides heredity, there are at least five other major contributing causes to alcoholism: peer influence, cultural influence, certain coexisting psychiatric conditions, availability, and occupation. Peer social networks (friends, clubs, or spouses) that include heavy drinkers and alcohol abusers increase the individual's risk of alcoholism. Cultural attitudes and informal rules for drinking are also important. Cultures that permit the use of low-proof alcoholic beverages with food or religious ritual, but have well-established taboos against drunkenness (as in Israel and Italy), enjoy low alcoholism rates. Cultures that do not have traditions of consuming alcohol with food or ritual, yet are tolerant of heavy drinking (as in the United States and Ireland), experience high alcoholism rates. Cultures that have no well-established rules at all for alcohol use (as among indigenous rural immigrants to large cities in Australia and Africa) and cultures in which high-proof alcohol is drunk in the absence of food or ritual (as among Native Americans and Russians) are at increased risk for alcoholism. Certain psychiatric conditions also increase the risk of alcoholism, including attention deficit disorder, panic disorder, schizophrenia, and, especially, antisocial personality disorder. Easy availability also increases risk. Communities or countries that have low alcohol taxes, cheap alcohol with extensive advertising, and limited societal control over sales suffer high rates of alcoholism. Finally, persons who are unemployed or who have occupations with irregular working hours (e.g., writers) or close sustained contact with alcohol (e.g., diplomats and bartenders) may be prone to the development of alcoholism.

A return to normal drinking is often possible for individuals who have abused alcohol for less than a year, but, if alcohol dependence has persisted for more than five years, efforts to return to social drinking usually lead to relapse. Thus, although the frequency of alcohol-related problems is highest among men aged 18–30, the development of chronic alcohol dependence for both men and women is most common from ages 25 to 50. Put differently, the process of becoming a chronic alcoholic with loss of control over initiation and cessation of drinking often takes several years. There are several million young persons whose heavy drinking has the potential to lead to alcoholism, but in many cases the process is not carried to completion, and by age 30 many such drinkers will have returned to a pattern of social (volitional) drinking.

PREVALENCE OF ALCOHOLISM

Estimates of the prevalence of alcoholism vary depending on the definition used and upon the methods of estimation. In the United States 10 to 20 percent of men and 5 to 10 percent of women at some point in their lives will meet criteria for alcoholism, depending on the stringency of the criteria employed. These rates are similar to the rates for many countries in western Europe, and the rates are a little higher in eastern European countries. Rates in countries around the eastern Mediterranean and in Southeast Asia are much lower. Overall, rates in Africa are low, but they are very high in the new urban slums.

Variations in the definition of alcoholism, however, make it difficult to compare rates in different countries. In England and Wales, estimates of the prevalence of alcoholism have suggested rates that range from 1.1 to 11 percent, and in Switzerland the suggested rates range from 2.2 to 13 percent. The prevalence of alcoholism in France has been estimated at as high as 15 percent of the adult population, but more conservative estimates suggest 9 percent.

National per capita consumption of alcohol is an important factor in the prevalence of alcoholism, yet Portugal, with one of the highest per capita alcohol-consumption rates in the world, did not even recognize alcoholism as a problem until the late 20th century. In the mid-20th century, the death of Soviet dictator Joseph Stalin resulted in a shift from official denial that any significant alcohol problem existed in the Soviet Union to an outcry that alcoholism involved 40 percent of adult males. In both circumstances, however, statistics were inadequate. In short, there is a strong subjective element in statistics of alcoholism. In addition, comparative data invariably fail to take account of changes in diagnostic policies and whether illicit, untaxed alcoholic beverages are included in estimates of national consumption.

DISEASES ASSOCIATED WITH ALCOHOLISM

Excessive users of alcohol have been shown to suffer in varying degrees from both acute and chronic diseases. Worldwide, morbidity due to alcohol abuse is on a par with malaria and unsafe sex, greater than that from smoking, and far greater than morbidity from illegal drug use. These numbers place alcoholism in the front rank of public-health problems. Among alcoholics, mortality is 2.5 times the expected. Heavy

JACQUES BERTILLON

(b. Nov. 11, 1851, Paris, France—d. July 7, 1922, Valmondois)

French statistician and demographer Jacques Bertillon was known for his application of quantitative methods to the analysis of a variety of social questions. His work gave impetus to the increased use of statistics in the social sciences.

Educated as a physician, Bertillon in the 1870s turned to the analysis of statistics, publishing articles on comparative divorce and suicide rates among nations. In 1883 he succeeded his father, Louis-Adolphe Bertillon, as head of the Paris bureau of vital statistics. Over the next 30 years the bureau, under his direction, increased the kinds of data gathered and developed more elaborate kinds of analysis.

Bertillon worked to establish uniform international statistical standards and saw his "Bertillon classification" of causes of deaths come into use in many nations. To facilitate the collection of data in French government offices, he wrote an elementary course in administrative statistics (1895). Increased alcoholism in France and a decline in French population growth relative to the rates in other countries were problems that particularly interested Bertillon. These questions gave rise to several works, including L'Alcoolisme et les moyens de le combattre jugés par l'expérience (1904; "Alcoholism and Ways of Combating It Judged from Experience") and La Dépopulation de la France (1911; "The Depopulation of France").

smoking shortens life by roughly 8 years—alcoholism shortens it by 15 years. In the United States, active alcoholics account for as many as 25 percent of the patients in general hospitals.

Although the magnitude of social and psychological pathology associated with alcoholism is more difficult to calculate—in part because of public denial—it is enormous. The number of patients hospitalized for depression and personality disorder resulting from alcoholism, often undiagnosed, is large if uncalculated. Alcoholism in parents vastly increases the chances that their children will fail in school, become delinquent, or misuse drugs.

ACUTE DISEASES

Alcohol intoxication produces a wide variety of disturbances of neuromuscular and mental functions and of body chemistry. In addition, the intoxicated person is more liable to accidents and injuries. Alcoholics—who chronically experience severe intoxication—are said to be 30 times more liable to fatal poisoning, 16 times more liable to death from a fall, and 4.5 times more liable to death in a motor-vehicle accident. Risk of death by suicide, homicide, fire, and drowning are roughly doubled. These liabilities reflect not only the effects of immediate intoxication but also poor self-care by alcoholics. For example, in Hungary 52 percent of suicide victims have been found to have a fatty liver (a symptom of chronic alcohol intoxication). In contrast, fatty liver is present in only 3 percent of the general population.

Other acute conditions associated with alcoholism are those that occur in the postintoxication state—the alcohol-withdrawal syndromes. The most common and least debilitating of these syndromes is the hangover—a general malaise typically accompanied by headache and nausea. After a prolonged bout of drunkenness, however, severe withdrawal phenomena often supervene. These phenomena include tremulousness, loss of appetite, inability to retain food, sweating, restlessness, sleep disturbances, seizures, and abnormal changes in body chemistry (especially electrolyte balance).

In cases of severe alcohol withdrawal, it is common for seizures, mental clouding, disorientation, and hallucinations (both visual and auditory) to occur during the first 48 hours. Depending on the amount and quality of care and treatment as well as on the possible occurrence of additional disease, delirium tremens can develop, usually after 36 hours. Prolonged drinking that interferes with an adequate diet may lead to Wernicke disease, which results from an acute complete deficiency of thiamin (vitamin B1) and is marked by a clouding of consciousness and abnormal eye movements. It also can lead to Korsakoff syndrome, marked by irreversible loss of recent memory. Vitamin deficiency associated with alcoholism can also lead to polyneuropathy, a degenerative disease of the peripheral nerves with symptoms that include tenderness of calf muscles, diminished tendon reflexes, and loss of vibratory sensation. Inflammation and fatty infiltration of the liver are common, as are disorders of the gastrointestinal tract (gastritis, duodenal ulcer, and, less often, severe pancreatitis).

Delirium Tremens

Delirium is a mental disturbance marked by disorientation and confused thinking in which the patient incorrectly comprehends his or her surroundings. The delirious person is drowsy, restless, and fearful of imaginary disasters, often suffering from hallucinations, such as seeing terrifying imaginary animals or thinking the building is on fire. Maniacal excitement may follow.

Delirium usually results from some intoxication or other physical disorder that affects the brain, such as fever, heart failure, or a blow on the head. It often results from an overdose of sedatives, especially bromide, and can be provoked by the too-abrupt discontinuance of barbiturates in addicts. Alcoholic delirium—known specifically as delirium tremens—is a result not merely of excessive consumption of alcohol but of a complicating exhaustion, lack of food, and dehydration. Delirium tremens involves a gross trembling of the whole body, fever, and frank delirium. Prior to an outbreak of delirium tremens, the patient has usually been deteriorating physically because of vomiting and restlessness. The condition can last from 3 to 10 days, with a reported fatality rate, if untreated, ranging from 5 to 20 percent. Rarely, chronic alcoholic hallucinosis develops, with or without preceding delirium tremens, and can persist for weeks to years.

Korsakoff Syndrome

Korsakoff syndrome, also known as Korsakoff psychosis (or Korsakoff disease), is a neurological disorder characterized by severe amnesia (memory loss). Many cases result from severe chronic alcoholism. Patients with Korsakoff syndrome typically are unable to remember events in the recent or even the immediate past, and some can store information for only a few seconds before they forget it. The patient may also have forgotten a much longer time period, extending back for as many as 20 years. Another feature that is sometimes present is confabulation—the patient recounts detailed and convincing memories of events that never happened. Korsakoff syndrome is often a transient manifestation of some other brain disorder, but some cases are chronic. In chronic alcoholism, Korsakoff syndrome may occur in combination with Wernicke disease.

Chronic Diseases

The chronic disorders associated with alcoholism are psychological, social, and medical. Among the psychological disorders are depression, emotional instability, anxiety, impaired cognitive function, and, of course, compulsive self-deleterious use of alcohol. After some six months of abstinence, the mild cortical atrophy and impaired cognition often associated with alcoholism disappear. After an extremely variable period of abstinence, ranging from weeks to years, there is usually marked improvement on tests assessing chronic depression and anxiety. Among the social disorders associated with alcoholism are 2- to 10-fold increases in driving and sexual offenses, petty crime, child and spousal abuse, and divorce. Homicide, homelessness, and chronic unemployment are several times more common among alcoholics than nonalcoholics.

Many of the chronic medical consequences of alcoholism are caused by dietary deficiencies. Alcohol provides large numbers of calories, but, like those from refined sugar, they are empty calories—that is, devoid of vitamins and other essential nutrients, including minerals and amino acids. The small amounts of vitamins and minerals present in beers and wines are insufficient for dietary needs. During bouts of heavy drinking, alcoholics neglect normal eating or, because of digestive difficulties, cannot absorb enough of the essential food elements. These nutritional defects are the cause of many of the chronic diseases associated with alcoholism.

In long-lasting alcoholism, one or more of the chronic nutritional-deficiency diseases may develop. Probably most common are the more severe effects of long-term thiamin deficiency—degeneration of the peripheral nerves (with permanent damage in extreme cases) and beriberi heart disease. Another nutritional disease in alcoholism is pellagra, caused by deficiency of niacin. Other diseases include scurvy, resulting from vitamin C deficiency; hypochromic macrocytic anemia, caused by iron deficiency; and pernicious anemia, resulting from vitamin B12 deficiency. Severe open sores on the skin of alcoholic derelicts whose usual drink is the cheapest form of alcohol—low-quality fortified wines—are sometimes miscalled "wine sores," but they result from a combination of multiple nutritional deficiencies and poor hygiene.

Chronic hepatitis is characterized by liver cell death and inflammation over a period greater than six months. Although most cases of chronic hepatitis are caused by the hepatitis viruses B, C, and D, other factors, including alcoholism, lead to development of the disease. Alcoholic hepatitis results from sustained consumption of excessive amounts of alcohol. The condition can be reversed if it is caught in its early stages and if the individual either significantly reduces or entirely curtails intake of alcohol. If untreated, it can result in alcoholic cirrhosis.

The classic disease associated with alcoholism is cirrhosis of the liver (specifically, Laënnec cirrhosis), which is commonly preceded by a fatty enlargement of the organ. The relationship between alcohol and cirrhosis is unquestioned, but the mechanism of injury remains unknown. Besides cirrhosis, the affected person may show jaundice,

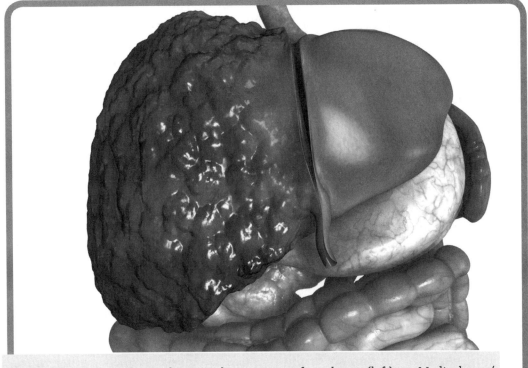

Model of a human liver, showing the ravages of cirrhosis (left). 34Medical.com/ Getty Images

gastrointestinal bleeding, and kidney failure.

In the early stage of cirrhosis, the disease can be stabilized by abstention from alcohol and by an adequate diet. In this stage, the liver first enlarges. Its outer capsule becomes smooth and stretched, and its colour turns yellow because of an increase in fat. Fibrous tissue and extra bile ducts may develop. In the next stage, the quantity of fibrous tissue increases so that the liver is granular. The blood vessels thicken, and their channels may become obstructed, which reduces blood flow in the organ. Complications at this stage include coma, kidney failure, jaundice, infection, and hemorrhages. In the advanced stage of the disease, the liver shrinks and the surface usually has a roughened appearance. The normal lobular structure of the liver is lost; there is no longer fat but only poorly functioning residual liver tissue.

The final complications of cirrhosis include high blood pressure in the portal vein, which can lead to hemorrhages in the esophagus and stomach. The imbalance in blood chemicals from malfunctioning of the liver can affect the brain and cause hepatic coma. Hepatic coma usually starts with drowsiness and confusion and culminates in loss of consciousness. Jaundice may complicate any stage of cirrhosis. Edema—fluid retention in the tissues—and ascites, an accumulation of fluid in the peritoneal cavity that results in abdominal swelling, also are commonly seen. Liver damage caused by portal cirrhosis can be halted by abstention from alcohol.

In addition to the mental symptoms that may accompany pellagra, other mental disorders more specifically related to the consumption of alcohol include mild dementia, which may persist for up to six months after cessation of alcohol ingestion, and a relatively uncommon chronic brain disorder called Marchiafava-Bignami disease, which involves the degeneration of the corpus callosum, the tissue that connects the two hemispheres of the brain. Other brain damage occasionally reported in alcoholics includes cortical laminar sclerosis, cerebellar degeneration, and central pontine myelinolysis. Alcoholics, especially older ones, frequently experience enlargement of the ventricles as a result of atrophy of brain substance caused in part by the direct effects of alcohol on the central nervous system. In some cases, however, brain atrophy is the result of damage caused by accidents and blows. Many of those who survive long years of alcoholism show a generalized deterioration of the brain, muscles, endocrine system,

and vital organs, giving an impression of premature old age.

Finally, chronic alcohol abuse heightens the risk of stroke and heart disease through cardiomyopathy, high blood pressure, and failed smoking cessation. It also greatly increases the risk of diabetes (by placing stress on the pancreas), of unwanted pregnancy and sexually transmitted diseases (through unsafe sex practices), and of infection (by alcohol-induced suppression of the immune system).

TREATMENT OF ALCOHOLISM

The various treatments of alcoholism can be classified as physiological, psychological, and social. Many physiological treatments are given as adjuncts to psychological methods, but sometimes they are applied in "pure" form, without conscious psychotherapeutic intent.

PHYSIOLOGICAL THERAPIES

The most important physiological medical treatment is detoxification—the safe withdrawal of the patient from alcohol, usually in a hospital setting. This process prevents life-threatening delirium tremens and also provides attention to neglected medical conditions. In addition, sophisticated hospital detoxification programs also provide patients and their families hope for recovery and begin the alcoholic's education in relapse prevention. As is the case with smoking cessation, relapse prevention is critical.

One of the popular modern drug treatments of alcoholism, initiated in 1948 by Erik Jacobsen of Denmark, uses disulfiram (tetraethylthiuram disulfide, known by the trade name Antabuse). Normally, as alcohol is converted to acetaldehyde, the latter is rapidly converted, in turn, to harmless metabolites. However, in the presence of disulfiram—itself harmless—the metabolism of acetaldehyde is blocked. The resulting accumulation of the highly toxic acetaldehyde results in unpleasant symptoms such as flushing, nausea, vomiting, a sudden sharp drop of blood pressure, pounding of the heart, and even a feeling of impending death. The usual technique is to administer one-half gram of disulfiram in tablet form daily for a few days. Then, under carefully controlled conditions and with medical supervision, the patient is given a small test drink of an alcoholic beverage. The patient then experiences symptoms that dramatically show the danger of attempting to drink while under disulfiram medication. A smaller daily dose of disulfiram is prescribed, and the dread of the consequences of drinking acts as a "chemical fence" to prevent the patient from drinking as long as he or she continues taking the drug.

Other, less scientific physical and drug therapies that have been tried in the treatment of alcoholics include apomorphine, niacin, LSD (lysergic acid diethylamide), antihistaminic agents, and many tranquilizing and energizing drugs. More recently, antidepressants and mood stabilizers (e.g., lithium) have been tried. In controlled studies of more than a year, however, none of these treatments, including disulfiram, has been shown more effective than a placebo in preventing relapse to alcohol abuse. Naltrexone (an opiate antagonist) and acamprosate, or calcium acetylhomotaurinate (a modulator of gamma-aminobutyric acid [GABA] and N-methyl-D-aspartate [NMDA] receptors), have, like disulfiram, been effective in reducing relapse over periods up to a year. But there is no evidence that either of these agents reduces the risk of relapse over the long-term.

Another form of aversion therapy that is designed to cause a patient to reduce or avoid an undesirable behaviour pattern by conditioning the person to associate the behaviour with an undesirable stimulus is electrical therapy. In this form of therapy, the patient is given a lightly painful shock whenever the undesirable behaviour is displayed. In covert conditioning, developed by American psychologist Joseph Cautela, images of undesirable behaviour (e.g., smoking) are paired with images of aversive stimuli (e.g., nausea and vomiting) in a systematic sequence designed to reduce the positive cues that had been associated with the behaviour.

PSYCHOLOGICAL THERAPIES

Psychotherapy employs an entire range of strategies, including individual and group techniques, to treat the psychoneuroses and character disorders associated with alcoholism. The aim varies from eliminating underlying putative psychological causes to effecting just enough shift in the patient's emotional and volitional state so that he or she can abstain from drink entirely or only drink in moderation. Psychoanalysis is rarely tried, having shown little success in treating alcoholism. Analytically oriented and cognitive-behavioral therapies are more common, often in conjunction with supportive aims. Unfortunately, as with pharmacotherapy, the effects of most psychotherapies upon alcoholism are impressive mainly over the short term.

In the 1990s a promising psychological technique sometimes called "motivational interviewing" was developed specifically for alcoholism and consists of identifying a patient's motivation for change. The patient first learns to recognize his or her loss of control over alcohol and the deleteriousness of the situation in order to develop a wish and a hope for change. Only then is the patient likely to become actively engaged in the process of change.

With alcoholics, group therapies are often regarded as more effective than individual treatment. Such group therapies range from instructional lectures and superficial discussions to deep analytic explorations, psychodrama, hypnosis, psychodynamic confrontation, and marathon sessions. Mechanical aids include didactic motion pictures, movies of the patients while intoxicated, and recordings of previous sessions. Many institutional programs rely on a "total-push approach," in which the patient is bombarded with multiple methods of treatment with the hope that one or more methods will affect the patient favourably. Other institutional programs rely on merely removing the patient from a stressful outside environment, with a period of enforced abstinence. The therapists may be psychoanalysts, psychiatrists, clinical psychologists, pastoral counselors, social workers, nurses, police or parole officers, or lay counselors—the latter often being former alcoholics with special training. Careful, controlled, long-term studies of institutional programs have not shown intensive inpatient therapies to be superior to much briefer outpatient interventions. However, brief outpatient interventions are most successful when the process of addiction is still in very early stages. Treatments have been developed for spouses and occasionally for whole families, either separately or jointly, in recognition of the fact that in alcoholism the "patient" is not just the alcoholic but also the family.

Over the past few decades, psychologists have repeatedly tried to develop cognitive-behavioral techniques for teaching a problem drinker how to return to controlled drinking. In early stages of problem drinking, before plasticity regarding choice has been lost and physiological dependence initiated, brief interventions that help pre-alcoholics to become conscious of how much they drink, of the risks involved, and of the regret they experience after heavy drinking have been helpful in reducing consumption to safe amounts. These techniques have been repeatedly proved effective and inexpensive. However, once sustained loss of control is established and once plasticity of choice has been lost—a characteristic of most individuals who receive a diagnosis of alcoholism—efforts to teach ways to return to moderate drinking have proved difficult. Long-term studies have consistently demonstrated that once the patient's own voluntary efforts to cut down on drinking have repeatedly failed, sustained abstinence is the practical answer.

The treatment of diabetes provides a helpful analogy to why most professional treatment of alcoholism has enjoyed only limited success. In diabetes, as in alcoholism, medical intervention is often life-saving, but successful long-term treatment of diabetes depends not upon elaborate medical intervention but upon strict self-care (diet and self-administration of insulin) to prevent relapse. The same principles apply to alcoholism.

SOCIAL TREATMENT

Long-term naturalistic studies of addicts have revealed four types of nonmedical community interventions that facilitate self-care and relapse prevention. The first is external unavoidable community supervision, such as an employee-assistance program that is connected with the alcoholic's place of work and requires the alcoholic to participate in order to stay employed. The second consists of substitutes for the addiction that behaviorally compete with it, such as compulsive hobbies, weight gain, or increased smoking. The third is what Swiss psychologist Carl Jung called the "protective wall of human community," which is found, for example, in therapeutic and religious communities or in new love relationships. Obviously, such interactions can also create substitute dependences. Unfortunately, because of the alcoholic's past behaviour toward his or her family, old relationships often are less valuable for relapse prevention than new ones. The fourth community intervention is a deepening spiritual commitment that often facilitates successful abstinence. In this vein it is useful to reflect that faith communities (e.g., Islam and Mormonism) have been successful in promoting lifelong abstinence, in contrast to governmental interventions such as the American experiment with prohibition.

A notable example that combines these last two types of community intervention is Alcoholics Anonymous (AA). A voluntary fellowship of men and women, AA enables its members to share their common experiences in a spiritual setting and to help each other become and stay sober. AA was founded in the United States in 1935 by two alcoholics, Robert Holbrook Smith and William Griffith Wilson, both of whom had been strongly influenced by a spiritual revival movement called the Oxford Group. The members of AA strive to follow the 12 Steps, a nonsectarian spiritual program that includes reliance on God—or any "higher power" as understood by each individual—to help prevent a relapse into drinking. It also includes self-examination; personal acknowledgment of, confession of, and taking responsibility for the harm caused by the member's alcohol-related behaviour; and assistance to other alcoholics in trying to abstain. At meetings members narrate the stories of their alcoholic experiences and their recovery in AA. Today AA is a worldwide community of more than two million. The fellowship is organized in local groups of indeterminate size, has no dues, and accepts contributions for its expenses only from those who attend meetings. Affiliation of the fellowship or of its groups with churches, politics, fundraising, or powerful leaders is strongly discouraged by AA's 12 Traditions. Existing research suggests that finding a sponsor, joining a home group, asking others for help when fearing relapse, providing service to others, and striving for a more spiritual life all appear to help sustain abstinence.

Paradoxically, severity of alcoholism often facilitates both abstinence and AA involvement. Just as many individuals do not adopt an effective program of weight reduction and exercise until after their first heart attack or accept a hip replacement until severely disabled, so the more symptomatic alcoholics are more prone than other alcoholics to join AA.

AA apparently meets deep-seated needs among its members. It enables them to associate with kindred sufferers who understand them, and it helps them to accept the disease concept of alcoholism, to admit their powerlessness over alcohol and their need for help, and to depend—without shame or stigma—on others. The 12 Steps provide a regimented, concrete training program that supports responsibility for self-care and relapse prevention. The fellowship of AA also provides community supervision and substitute gratifying behaviours (e.g., around-the-clock meetings on holidays) that compete with relapse to alcohol dependence.

Professionals in the field of alcoholism now regard AA as, at worst, an inexpensive addition to any therapeutic regimen and, at best, the relapse-prevention technique of choice. AA has spawned allied but independent organizations, including Al-Anon, for spouses and other close relatives and friends of alcoholics, and Alateen, for their adolescent children. The aim of such related groups is to help the members learn how to be helpful and to forgive alcoholic relatives.

AA groups, found in more than 150 countries, resemble each other and generally use the same "approved" literature (including translations) published by its central office in New York City. AA members include felons and physicians, young and old, minorities and atheists, and Catholics, Buddhists, and Hindus as well as Protestants. There are always some variations in style and conduct among AA groups, each of which is autonomous. In some countries, AA groups are sponsored by or affiliated with national

Alcoholics Anonymous (AA)

The voluntary fellowship of alcoholic persons who seek to get sober and remain sober through self-help and the help of other recovered alcoholics is among the most effective interventions for alcoholism. Although general conventions meet periodically and Alcoholics Anonymous World Services, Inc., is headquartered in New York City, all AA groups are essentially local and autonomous. To counteract self-indulgence and promote the group's welfare, members identify themselves only by first name and surname initial. Much of the program has a social and spiritual, but nonsectarian, basis.

AA began in May 1935 in the meeting of two alcoholics attempting to overcome their drinking problems: a New York stockbroker, "Bill W." (William Griffith Wilson [1895–1971]), and a surgeon from Akron, Ohio, "Dr. Bob S." (Robert Holbrook Smith [1879–1950]). Drawing upon their own experiences, they set out to help fellow alcoholics and first recorded their program in Alcoholics Anonymous (1939; 3rd ed., 1976). By the early 21st century, AA had some 2,000,000 members forming more than 110,000 groups in about 180 countries and territories (most of them, however, in the United States and Canada).

temperance societies or accept financial support from government health agencies, but this is not encouraged by AA's central office.

Results of Treatment

The success of treatment in any behavioral or personality disorder is always difficult to appraise, and this also is true of alcoholism. Some clinicians believe that one or another of the therapies discussed in this section works better for certain patients, but such beliefs have not been demonstrated by experiment. It is possible that the most effective therapy is the one in which the therapist or the patient most believes. This factor of subjectivity may account for the inferior results achieved in controlled experiments contrasting different treatments compared with uncontrolled reports of alcohol treatment. The effects of new treatments tend to be reported enthusiastically. Later, critical examination of the results and controlled studies usually diminish the claims. Follow-up studies of treated alcoholics have often been too brief to determine whether or not lasting results have been achieved, or the investigators have failed to locate a substantial portion of the former patients. Moreover, the measures of "success" are inconsistent. Some investigators regard only total abstinence as a successful outcome, whereas others are satisfied if the frequency of drinking bouts is lessened or if the patient's self-destructive behaviour or harm to others is reduced.

CHAPTER 8

SMOKING: TOBACCO AND HEALTH

Smoking is defined as the act of inhaling and exhaling the fumes of burning plant material. A variety of plant materials are smoked, including marijuana and hashish, but the act is most commonly associated with tobacco as smoked in a cigarette, cigar, or pipe. Tobacco contains nicotine, an alkaloid that is addictive and can have both stimulating and tranquilizing psychoactive effects. The smoking of tobacco, long practiced by American Indians, was introduced to Europe by Christopher Columbus and other explorers. Smoking soon spread to other areas and today is widely practiced around the world despite medical, social, and religious arguments against it.

METHODS OF TOBACCO CONSUMPTION

There are two major types of tobacco products available: those that can be smoked and those that are smokeless. Smoked products include cigarettes or cigars, as well as plant materials that are burned in tobacco pipes. Smokeless forms include chewing tobacco and snuff. The method by which tobacco is consumed is often influenced by cultural practices. For example, the use of chewing tobacco in the United States was a reflection of the lifestyle of the country's pioneers. By far, the most widespread method of tobacco consumption worldwide is smoking, primarily in the form of cigarettes.

A field of tobacco plants. © Photos.com/Jupiterimages

CHEWING TOBACCO

Tobacco used for chewing comes in a variety of forms. Among the most notable of these are: (1) "flat plug," a compressed rectangular cake of bright tobacco, sweetened lightly or not at all; (2) "navy," a flat rectangular cake of burley tobacco, highly flavoured with either licorice, rum, cinnamon, nutmeg, sugar, honey, or some other spice or sweetener; (3) "twist," tough, dark tobacco rolled and braided into ropes; (4) "fine-cut," shredded, stripped leaf, not compressed, of expensive blend; and (5) "scrap," cigar by-products consisting of loose leaf ends and clippings.

Tobacco chewing was common among certain American Indian groups.

After 1815 it became almost a distinctive mode of tobacco usage in the United States, replacing pipe smoking. Partly the switch was a chauvinistic reaction against European snuff-taking and pipe-smoking. However, it was also a matter of convenience for pioneering Americans on the move, since chewing was easier than lighting up a cumbersome pipe. The symbol of the change was the spittoon or cuspidor, which became a necessity of 19th-century America. Manufacturing statistics are revealing: of 348 tobacco factories listed by the 1860 census for Virginia and North Carolina, 335 concentrated wholly on chewing tobacco, and only 6 others even bothered with smoking tobacco as a sideline, using scraps from plug production.

The rising popularity of manufactured cigarettes by the beginning of the 20th century spelled the decline of chewing tobacco. After World War I, plug-taking fell off abruptly, though its usage increased in the 1980s and early '90s as it was believed to be a safe alternative to cigarette smoking. Studies, however, revealed that chewing tobacco was associated with numerous health problems, including cancer and heart disease.

CIGARS

A cigar is a cylindrical roll of tobacco for smoking, consisting of cut tobacco filler formed in a binder leaf and with a wrapper leaf rolled spirally around the bunch. Wrapper leaf, the most expensive leaf used in cigars, must be strong, elastic, silky in texture, and even in colour. It must have a pleasant flavour and good burning properties.

Columbus and the explorers who followed him in Cuba, Mexico, Central America, and Brazil found that the Indians of those regions smoked a long, thick bundle of twisted tobacco leaves wrapped in a dried palm leaf or corn (maize) husk. A pottery vessel discovered at Uaxactún, Guatemala, dating from the 10th century CE or earlier, shows the figure of a Maya smoking a string-tied roll of tobacco leaves. The Spanish word *cigarro*, from which "cigar" is derived, probably was an adaptation of *sik'ar*, the Mayan term for smoking. By 1600 the cigar had been introduced into Spain, where it was a symbol of conspicuous wealth for two centuries before it was widely used in other European countries. The use of cigars in New England probably followed closely the settlement of Connecticut in 1633.

Modern cigars are described by their size and shape as follows: corona is a straight-shaped cigar with rounded top (the end placed in the mouth), about 5 ½ inches (14 cm) long; petit corona, or corona chica, is about 5 inches (13 cm)long; tres petit corona is about 4 ½ inches (11 cm) long; half a corona is about 3 ¾ inches (9.5 cm) long; Lonsdale is the same shape as a corona, about 6 ½ inches (16.5 cm) long; ideales is a slender, torpedo-shaped cigar, tapered at the lighting end, about 6 ½ inches (16.5 cm) long; bouquet is a smaller, torpedo-shaped cigar; Londres is a straight cigar about 4 ¾ inches (12 cm) long. These descriptive terms appear after the brand name. A panatela is a thin cigar open at both ends, usually about 5 inches (13 cm) long with a straight shape but sometimes having a shoulder, or drawn-in portion, at the mouth end. Originally it had a finished top that had to be cut off before smoking. A cheroot is a thin cigar, open at both ends, usually thicker and stubbier than a panatela, and sometimes slightly tapered. The name whiff, used in Britain, refers to a small cigar open at both ends, about 3 ½ inches (9 cm) long.

The main colour classifications of cigars are claro (CCC), light; colorado-claro (CC), medium; colorado (C), dark; colorado-maduro (CM), very dark; and maduro (M), exceptionally dark. The last two are seldom seen in the United Kingdom or the United States. The colour of the wrapper is no indication of the strength of a cigar, but considerable care is given to the matching of colours. Good-quality cigars may be sorted into as many as 20 different shades to ensure that all cigars in a box have a uniform appearance. In modern packaging, selectors and packers, working under suitable lighting, arrange the cigars according to colour and perfection of wrapper and place them in boxes made of wood, metal, paper, or glass.

Snuff

Snuff is a powdered preparation of tobacco used by inhalation or by dipping—that is, rubbing on the teeth and gums. Manufacture involves grinding the tobacco and subjecting it to repeated fermentations. Snuffs may be scented with attar of roses, lavender, cloves, jasmine, etc.

Some of the first peoples known to use snuff were the natives of Brazil. In the late 15th century, members of Christopher Columbus's crew observed indigenous Caribbean peoples inhaling a snufflike preparation of tobacco. The following century, the practice of inhaling tobacco powder was popularized in France, following the introduction of the tobacco plant from Portugal by French diplomat and scholar Jean Nicot. Nicot, who had been to Lisbon, where he learned of the plant's medicinal properties, reportedly gave the queen of France, Catherine de

Médicis, tobacco leaves and showed her how to prepare a medicinal powder from them. Inhaling the powder as a preventive became popular among the French court. Also in the 16th century, the inhaling of powdered tobacco was practiced by the Dutch, who referred to it as *snuf*, short for *snuftabak* (from the words meaning "sniff" and "tobacco"). Tobacco and the practice of snuffing spread rapidly throughout Europe, taking hold in England around the 17th century. During the 18th century, snuff taking became widespread throughout the world.

At first, each quantity was freshly grated. Rappee (French *râpé*, "grated") is the name later given to a coarse, pungent snuff made from dark tobacco. Snuff takers carried graters with them. Early 18th-century graters made of ivory and other materials still exist, as do elaborate snuffboxes.

Snuffbox, gold and enamel, French, c. 1770; in the Victoria and Albert Museum, London. Courtesy of the Victoria and Albert Museum, London

The adverse health effects of snuffing relative to other forms of tobacco consumption such as smoking were once considered insignificant. Similar to all other tobacco products, however, snuff contains nicotine and numerous carcinogens (cancer-causing substances). Hence, snuffing is not only addictive but also associated with an increased risk for certain cancers, particularly those of the oral cavity in persons who place moist snuff between the cheek and gums.

TOBACCO PIPE

A tobacco pipe is a hollow bowl used for smoking tobacco. It is equipped with a hollow stem through which smoke is drawn into the mouth. The bowl can be made of such materials as clay, corncob, meerschaum (a mineral composed of magnesia, silica, and water), and most importantly, briar-wood, the root of a species of heather.

The smoking of tobacco through a pipe is indigenous to the Americas and derives from the religious ceremonies of ancient priests in Mexico. Farther north, American Indians developed ceremonial pipes, the chief of these being the calumet, or pipe of peace. Such pipes had marble or red steatite (or pipestone) bowls and ash stems about 30–40 inches (75–100 cm) long and were decorated with hair and feathers. The practice of pipe smoking reached Europe through sailors who had encountered it in the New World.

CIGARETTES

A cigarette is a paper-wrapped roll of finely cut tobacco for smoking. Modern cigarette tobacco is usually of a milder type than cigar tobacco. The Aztecs smoked a hollow reed or cane tube stuffed with tobacco. Other natives of Mexico, Central America, and parts of South America crushed tobacco leaves and rolled the shreds in corn (maize) husk or other vegetable wrappers. But it was the cigar rather than this prototype of the cigarette that the conquistadors brought back to Spain as a luxury for the wealthy.

Early in the 16th century beggars in Sevilla Seville began to pick up discarded cigar butts, shred them, and roll them in scraps of paper (Spanish *papeletes*) for smoking, thus improvising the first cigarettes. These poor man's smokes were known as *cigarrillos* (Spanish: "little cigars"). Late in the 18th century they acquired respectability and their use spread to Italy and Portugal. They were carried by Portuguese traders to the Levant and Russia. French and British troops in the Napoleonic Wars became familiar with them, and the French named them cigarettes. Forty years later another generation of French and British troops, fighting in the Crimean War, made the acquaintance of Turkish cigarettes. At the same time, cigarettes were becoming popular in the United States. British taste later switched to cigarettes filled with unmixed Virginia tobacco, but the U.S. market developed a preference for a blend including some Turkish tobacco.

At first, all cigarettes were made by hand either by the smoker or in factories. The factory process consisted of hand rolling on a table, pasting, and hand packaging. In 1880 James A. Bonsack was granted a U.S. patent for a cigarette machine in which tobacco was fed onto a continuous strip of paper and was automatically formed, pasted, closed, and cut to lengths by a rotary cutting knife. The Bonsack machine was imported to England in 1883. In the next few years the cigarette industry developed in several European countries.

Improvements in cultivation and processing that lowered the acid content of cigarette tobacco and made it easier to inhale contributed to a major expansion in cigarette smoking during the first half of the 20th century. During World War I the prejudice against smoking by women was broken, and the practice became widespread among women in Europe and the United States in the 1920s.

In the 1950s and '60s research produced medical evidence that linked cigarette smoking with health hazards, especially with lung cancer, emphysema, and heart disease. In some countries, notably the United Kingdom and the United States, measures were taken to

The mounting total of deaths due to smoking flashes across a billboard in Los Angeles, CA. The billboard was designed to deter people from using tobacco products. Gilles Mingasson/Getty Images

discourage the use of cigarettes. In the 1980s and '90s, despite growing awareness of the health risks involved, smoking continued to increase, with greater consumption in Third World countries offsetting the effects of antismoking sentiment elsewhere.

SMOKING AND HEALTH

At the dawn of the 20th century, the most common tobacco products were cigars, pipe tobacco, and chewing tobacco. The mass production of cigarettes was in its infancy, although cigarette smoking was beginning to increase dramatically. According to the ninth edition of *Encyclopædia Britannica* (1888), tobacco products were suspected of producing some adverse health effects, yet tobacco was also considered to have medicinal properties. Many scholars and health professionals of the day advocated tobacco's use for such effects as improved concentration and performance, relief of boredom, and enhanced mood.

By the dawn of the 21st century, in stark contrast, tobacco had become recognized as being highly addictive and one of the world's most devastating causes of death and disease. Moreover, because of the rapid increase in smoking in developing nations in the late 20th century, the number of smoking-related deaths per year is projected to rise rapidly in the 21st century. For example, the World Health Organization (WHO) estimated that in the late 1990s there were approximately 4 million tobacco-caused

deaths per year worldwide. This estimate was increased to approximately 5 million in 2003 and could reach 10 million per year by the 2020s. By the mid-21st century, a staggering 500 million of today's cigarette smokers will have died prematurely because of their smoking. Although tobacco use is declining in many countries of western Europe and North America and in Australia, it continues to increase rapidly in many countries in Asia, Africa, and South America.

The primary cause of the escalation in the number of deaths and incidents of disease from tobacco is the large increase in cigarette smoking during the 20th century. During that time cigarette smoking grew to account for approximately 80 percent of the world's tobacco market. Nonetheless, all tobacco products are toxic and addictive. In some regions of the world, the use of smokeless tobacco products is a major health concern.

Tobacco products are manufactured with various additives to preserve the tobacco's shelf life, alter its burning characteristics, control its moisture content, inhibit the hatching of insect eggs that may be present in the plant material, mask the irritative effects of nicotine, and provide any of a wide array of flavours and aromas. The smoke produced when tobacco and these additives are burned consists of more than 4,000 chemical compounds. Many of these compounds are highly toxic, and they have diverse effects on health.

The primary constituents of tobacco smoke are nicotine, tar (the particulate residue from combustion), and gases such as carbon dioxide and carbon monoxide. Although nicotine can be poisonous at very high dosages, its toxic effect as a component of tobacco smoke is generally considered modest compared with that of many other toxins in the smoke. The main health effect of nicotine is its addictiveness. Carbon monoxide has profound, immediate health effects. It passes easily from the lungs into the bloodstream, where it binds to hemoglobin, the molecule in red blood cells that is responsible for the transfer of oxygen in the body. Carbon monoxide displaces oxygen on the hemoglobin molecule and is removed only slowly. Therefore, smokers frequently accumulate high levels of carbon monoxide, which starves the body of oxygen and puts an enormous strain on the entire cardiovascular system.

The harmful effects of smoking are not limited to the smoker. The toxic components of tobacco smoke are found not only in the smoke that the smoker inhales but also in environmental tobacco smoke, or secondhand smoke—that is, the smoke exhaled by the smoker (mainstream smoke) and the smoke that rises directly from the smoldering tobacco (sidestream smoke). Nonsmokers who are routinely exposed to environmental tobacco smoke are at increased risk for some of the same diseases that afflict smokers, including lung cancer and cardiovascular disease.

Consequently, clean-air laws that prohibit cigarette smoking are becoming widespread. In the 1980s and 1990s, such laws typically required that nonsmoking areas be established in restaurants and workplaces. However, the finding that toxins in environmental smoke could easily diffuse across large spaces led to much stronger bans. Since 2000 many cities, states, and regions worldwide, including New York City in 2003, Scotland in 2006, Nairobi in 2007, and Chicago in 2008, have implemented complete smoking bans in restaurants, taverns, and enclosed workplaces. In addition, entire countries have implemented smoking bans in workplaces or restaurants or, in some cases, in all public areas, including Ireland, Norway, and New Zealand in 2004 and France and India in 2008. In 2005 Bhutan became the first country to ban both smoking in public places and the sale of tobacco products.

HEALTH CONSEQUENCES OF SMOKING

Smoking can have severe consequences on human health, including nicotine addiction, cancer, lung disease, and heart disease. Perhaps the most devastating of these conditions is lung cancer, which claims the lives of thousands of smokers worldwide each year. Smoking-related diseases, however, are not isolated to smokers. Indeed, secondhand smoke can cause serious disease in nonsmokers as well. Likewise, women who smoke while pregnant jeopardize the health of the developing fetus.

ADDICTION

A major health effect common to all forms of tobacco use is addiction, or, more technically, dependence. Addiction is not lethal in its own right, but it contributes to tobacco-caused death and disease, since it spurs smokers to continue their habit, which repeatedly exposes them to the toxins in tobacco smoke. Although there are many historical accounts of the apparent ability of tobacco use to escalate into an addiction for some smokers, it was not until the 1980s that leading health organizations such as the Office of the Surgeon General in the United States, the Royal Society of Canada, and WHO formally concluded that cigarettes are highly addictive on the basis of their ability to deliver large doses of nicotine into the lungs, from which blood quickly carries it to the brain.

Nicotine produces the entire range of physical and behavioral effects characteristic of addiction. These effects include activation of brain reward systems that create behavioral effects and physiological cravings that lead to chronic use, tolerance and physical dependence, and withdrawal upon discontinuation. Addiction to tobacco also involves a variety of constituents in tobacco smoke that, for many people, have pleasurable sensory characteristics and enhance nicotine's effects. Such constituents as ammonia, menthol, levulinic acid, and even chocolate improve a cigarette's flavour and aroma. Cigarettes are addicting,

more so than nicotine medications, such as nicotine patches and gum, whose sensory and other effects are weaker and less desirable.

Deep inhalation of nicotine-laden smoke results in rapid absorption of nicotine in the lungs—the nicotine diffuses into the bloodstream as rapidly as the inhaled oxygen. From the lungs the nicotine reaches the brain in less than 10 seconds. Nerve cells, or neurons, in the brain and peripheral nervous system have receptor proteins on their surfaces to which nicotine binds, much in the way that a key fits into a lock. When a molecule of nicotine binds to a nicotine receptor, it causes the neuron to transmit a nerve impulse to various target organs and tissues. This process stimulates the release of neurotransmitters, or chemical messengers, which produce the physiological and psychological effects of nicotine. For example, nicotine stimulates the adrenal glands and prompts the release of epinephrine and norepinephrine, which are responsible for raising heart rate and blood pressure and heightening alertness and concentration. Nicotine also stimulates the release of the neurotransmitter dopamine in the brain. Dopamine is thought to be critical to nicotine's reinforcing and pleasurable mood-altering effects.

Most smokers report that their initial experiences with smoking were far from pleasurable. The nicotine in tobacco can have toxic effects in first-time users, who commonly experience dizziness, nausea, and even vomiting.

With experience, smokers become adept at limiting their dose of nicotine to one that provides its desired effects. With continued use of tobacco, however, the body creates more and more nicotine receptors. As a result, the smoker experiences a phenomenon called tolerance—greater amounts of nicotine are needed in order to experience the same effect. Typically, when tolerance has developed and nicotine intake has increased, the body becomes physiologically dependent on nicotine, and any abrupt abstinence from smoking will trigger withdrawal symptoms. These symptoms include impaired ability to concentrate, irritability, weight gain, depressed mood, anxiety, difficulty sleeping, and persistent cravings. The symptoms typically peak within a few days and subside within a month. However, the experience varies from person to person, and, for some, powerful cravings can persist for years.

Nicotine's ability to help tobacco users control their mood and appetite and sustain their attention when working undoubtedly contributes to the persistence of tobacco use. Some of these effects interact with physical dependence. For example, increased exposure to nicotine can increase physical dependence and thereby make the effects of withdrawal stronger. During withdrawal, resumption of smoking provides rapid relief of withdrawal effects. This reaction may lead the smoker to believe that smoking in itself enhances mood and performance, when in reality the effect is mainly that of reversing the withdrawal symptoms, which occur only because of the physical dependence on nicotine. This effect can be profound, at least from the smoker's perspective. For example, cigarette smokers generally weigh some 2 to 4 kg (4.4 to 8.8 pounds) less than nonsmokers, and weight gain frequently accompanies cessation of smoking. Resumption of smoking can help people lose the gained weight. Similarly, even a few hours of tobacco abstinence can leave some people unable to get their work done, study for an exam, or perform adequately in other ways. Over time the smoker may learn that even a single cigarette can provide an immediate restoration of performance.

All widely used tobacco products deliver addicting levels of nicotine. However, the patterns of use that can lead to addiction vary with different tobacco products and are affected by many factors. For example, simply raising the cost of and limiting access to tobacco products tend to reduce tobacco use (thereby reducing the risk of addiction) and can even prompt some addicted persons to quit smoking. Cigar smoking and pipe smoking tend to be taken up later in life than cigarette smoking, and cigar smokers and pipe smokers are less likely to inhale the smoke. As a consequence, the overall rate of addiction to cigars or pipes appears to be less than the addiction rate for cigarettes, although many cigar or pipe smokers undoubtedly become highly addicted. The highest risk of addiction to nicotine occurs when the drug is absorbed very rapidly, producing its noted pleasant psychoactive effects. Oral smokeless products, such as snuff and chewing tobacco, do not produce as rapid an effect on the brain as cigarette-smoke inhalation, but the convenience and ease of use of these products are appealing to many and contribute to their addicting effects.

CANCER

It is estimated that approximately one-third of all cancer deaths worldwide are attributable to tobacco. Cigarette smoke contains more than 60 known carcinogens, including tobacco-specific nitrosamines and polycyclic aromatic hydrocarbons. Although certain of the body's enzymes metabolize carcinogens and cause them to be excreted, these enzymes sometimes function inadequately, allowing carcinogens to bind to cellular DNA and damage it. When cells with damaged DNA survive, replicate, and accumulate, cancers occur. Cancerous cells can metastasize—that is, travel to other sites in the body—causing

NICOTINE

Nicotine is an organic compound that is the principal alkaloid of tobacco. (An alkaloid is one of a group of nitrogenous organic compounds that have marked physiological effects on humans.) Nicotine occurs throughout the tobacco plant and especially in the leaves. The compound constitutes about 5 percent of the plant by weight. Both the tobacco plant (Nicotiana tabacum) and the compound are named for Jean Nicot, a French ambassador to Portugal, who sent tobacco seeds to Paris in 1560.

Crude nicotine was known by 1571, and the compound was obtained in purified form in 1828. The correct molecular formula was established in 1843, and the first laboratory synthesis was reported in 1904. Nicotine is one of the few liquid alkaloids. In its pure state it is a colourless, odourless liquid with an oily consistency, but when exposed to light or air, it acquires a brown colour and gives off a strong odour of tobacco. Nicotine's chemical formula is $C_{10}H_{14}N_2$.

Nicotine is the chief addictive ingredient in the tobacco used in cigarettes, cigars, and snuff. In its psychoactive effects, nicotine is a unique substance with a biphasic effect. When inhaled in short puffs it has a stimulant effect, but when smoked in deep drags it can have a tranquilizing effect. This is why smoking can feel invigorating at some times and can seem to block stressful stimuli at others. Nicotine is also an addictive drug, though, and smokers characteristically display a strong tendency to relapse after having successfully stopped smoking for a time. When ingested in larger doses, nicotine is a highly toxic poison that causes vomiting and nausea, headaches, stomach pains, and, in severe cases, convulsions, paralysis, and death.

Nicotine is commercially obtained from tobacco scraps and is used as an insecticide and as a veterinary vermifuge. Nitric acid or other oxidizing agents convert it to nicotinic acid, or niacin, which is used as a food supplement.

the cancer to spread. Cancer risk is partly determined by the toxicity of tobacco products. However, the risk of disease is also strongly related to the amount and duration of toxin exposure. The longer and more frequently a person smokes, the more likely a tobacco-related cancer will develop. For this reason, addiction is a strong indirect contributor to other diseases in that it promotes high-level and persistent exposure to cancer-causing agents.

Since the majority of tobacco users are cigarette smokers who inhale smoke into the lungs, it is not surprising that active smoking and exposure to environmental tobacco smoke are believed to account for 90 percent of all cases of lung cancer. A marked increase in lung cancer has occurred in all countries of the world where smoking has increased. In the United States lung cancer is responsible for more cancer deaths than any other kind of cancer and kills more women each year than breast cancer. It is estimated that 85 percent of all cases of lung cancer could be prevented if all smoking of cigarettes stopped. However, exposure to carcinogens is not limited to the respiratory system. Smoking is a major cause of bladder cancer, pancreatic cancer, laryngeal cancer, oral cancer, and esophageal cancer. When a regular tobacco user successfully quits, the risk of cancer decreases, though not to the level of someone who has never smoked.

Smokeless tobacco users, meanwhile, repeatedly expose the oral mucosa to toxins and have a substantially increased risk

of getting head and neck cancers, though the risk depends in part on the period of consumption and the nature of the product. For example, Swedish smokeless tobacco ("snus") is made to contain substantially lower levels of carcinogens than American smokeless tobacco, and the risk of tobacco-caused cancer in its users appears to be correspondingly lower. There are large geographic differences in the prevalence of oral tobacco use, with higher consumption in Sweden, India, Southeast Asia, and parts of the United States.

Lung Disease

It is not surprising that smokers suffer from many respiratory diseases other than lung cancer. One such disease is chronic obstructive pulmonary disease, or COPD, which is one of the major causes of debilitation and eventual death in cigarette smokers. More than 80 percent of those diagnosed with COPD are smokers, and most of these people die prematurely, with a greater number of women dying from COPD than men.

COPD is a general term that refers to respiratory diseases in which airflow is obstructed. Women's airways appear to be more sensitive to the effect of cigarette smoke. Women with COPD often experience greater breathlessness and a disproportionately greater thickening of airway walls relative to men with COPD. Most commonly, COPD refers to chronic bronchitis (chronic cough and phlegm production) and emphysema (permanent enlargement of air spaces accompanied

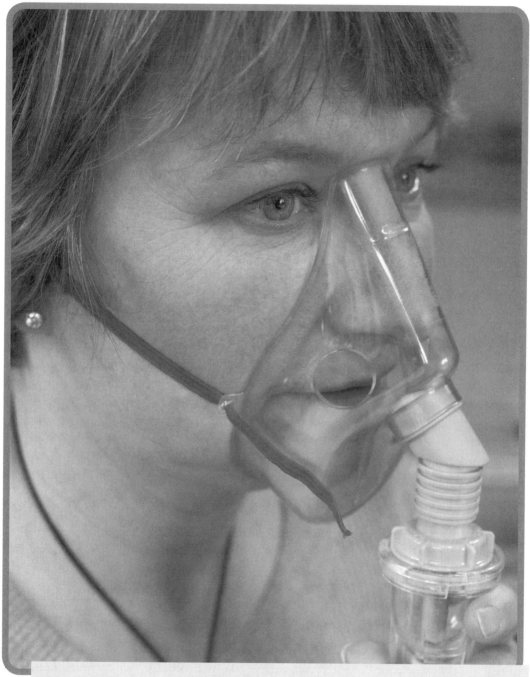

Woman using a nebulizer, which delivers medicine that eases breathing problems caused by chronic obstructive pulmonary disease (COPD). COPD is just one of the lung diseases linked to smoking. Brian Lawrence/Photographer's Choice/Getty Images

by deterioration of lung walls), although specific diagnostic criteria sometimes differ. Active smoking and exposure to environmental tobacco smoke are also responsible for increases in other respiratory ailments, such as pneumonia, the common cold, and influenza. Smokers who contract these ailments take longer than nonsmokers to recover from them.

Children are especially susceptible to the effects of environmental tobacco smoke. When raised in a household in which they are regularly exposed to environmental tobacco smoke, children are more likely to suffer from asthma and chronic cough, and they may suffer from reduced lung growth and function.

Heart Disease

Smoking has long been recognized as a major risk factor in cardiovascular disease, the risk being greater the more one smokes. As previously discussed, the carbon monoxide present in cigarette smoke binds to hemoglobin in the blood, making fewer molecules available for oxygen transport. In addition, coronary blood flow is reduced, forcing the heart to work harder to deliver oxygen to the body. Such strain places smokers at significantly greater risk for myocardial infarction, or heart attack, and stroke. There are, however, regional differences in the incidence of smoking-related cardiovascular disease. In China, for example, where smoking rates have increased steadily since the 1970s and about 63 percent of adult males smoke (as opposed to 4 percent of adult females), cardiovascular disease makes up a much smaller percentage of smoking-related deaths than in the United States and Europe, where it accounts for approximately 30 to 40 percent of all tobacco-caused deaths. After quitting, a smoker's risk for cardiovascular

Sir Richard Shaboe Doll

(b. Oct. 28, 1912, Hampton, Middlesex, Eng.—d. July 24, 2005, Oxford)

British epidemiologist Sir Richard Shaboe Doll, with his colleague Austin (later Sir Austin) Bradford Hill, definitively established the link between cigarette smoking and lung cancer. In 1947 Doll, who was already known for a study on the causes of peptic ulcers, was asked to look into the alarming increase in lung cancer in Great Britain. Environmental causes related to the rapid increase in car ownership were suspected, but Doll, a smoker, found to his surprise that smoking was by far the dominant factor. The results were so clear that he gave up smoking himself during the study. The report, co-written with Bradford Hill, was published in 1950.

Doll framed additional studies that clarified the relationship between smoking and disease. Some of his research proved that there was no link between peptic ulcers and diet and that even low-level radiation could cause cancer. Doll, the Regius Professor of Medicine at the University of Oxford from 1969, won many awards, notably the UN Award for Cancer Research in 1962. He was knighted in 1971 and made a Companion of Honour in 1996.

disease falls faster than the risk for lung cancer, with reductions in risk evident within one year of cessation.

EFFECTS ON PREGNANCY

Women who smoke are more likely to experience infertility and miscarriage (spontaneous abortion). When a pregnant woman smokes, some toxins from the smoke can be passed to the fetus. These toxins can later affect an infant's lung development and lung function. Babies of women who smoke are more likely to be born prematurely, to have a low birth weight, and to have slower initial growth. Smoking cessation within the first trimester lowers these health risks to a level comparable to those of people who have never smoked. Infants in households where there is a smoker are more likely to die from sudden infant death syndrome (SIDS).

SMOKING CESSATION

The starting point for "kicking the habit" is awareness of the harm smoking can cause. For example, after the U.S. surgeon general's report in 1964 brought to public awareness a link between smoking and cancer, smoking rates in the United States dropped precipitously. By 2000 the smoking rate was about one-half that of 1960. Furthermore, strong antismoking warnings and health-related messages generally increase smokers' motivation to quit, as was shown in Canada when it adopted strong graphic warnings on cigarette packaging. Such warnings are now promoted by WHO as an important educational tool to motivate smoking cessation and to help prevent persons from starting to smoke.

Unfortunately, the vast majority of people who try to stop smoking resume within a few weeks of quitting because of the addictive grip of nicotine. Persons who smoke any cigarettes at all usually smoke enough to develop an addiction to nicotine. In general, the more cigarettes a person smokes per day, the greater is the addiction and the more difficult it is to quit. In addition to nicotine dependency, other factors that impede quitting are easy access to cigarettes and the withdrawal symptoms that accompany any discontinuance of nicotine intake. These symptoms include cravings, depression, anxiety, irritability, difficulty concentrating, and insomnia.

Dependence and withdrawal can be managed better by some people than others, and people often learn how to deal with these problems after repeated attempts. Medical intervention, including behavioral guidance, can be critical for recovery from tobacco addiction. Scientifically based treatment strategies can have more than double the success rate of quitting "cold turkey" without assistance. Because the health benefits of quitting are so profound, leading health authorities consider treatment for tobacco dependence to be among the most important and cost-effective types of medical intervention. WHO and the governments of many countries are working aggressively to make scientifically proven treatments available to all tobacco users so that they may find a path to better long-term health. Other organizations such as the World Bank are working to support the availability of treatment in developing countries so that their struggling economies are not crippled by tobacco-caused disease and its burdens on health care systems and worker productivity.

BEHAVIORAL INTERVENTION

Quitting successfully must generally start with a plan for managing behaviour associated with tobacco addiction. Common to virtually all therapeutic approaches is the selection of and planning for a quitting date and adherence to the plan. The plan should include strategies for avoiding or managing situations that might stimulate a craving for a cigarette and therefore trigger a relapse to smoking. For example, for a few weeks or months, some people will need to avoid certain places and activities that they associate with smoking. Others will find it useful to learn methods by which to cope with stress or occasional cravings, such as breathing deeply, chewing gum, or taking a brief walk. Major health organizations provide information on a variety of successful strategies that can be tailored to an individual's situation.

Social and emotional support is often critical in sustaining an individual's efforts to quit. Support can come from a structured smoking-cessation program with group, one-on-one, or telephone counseling. Counseling need not be time-consuming or expensive. Studies have shown that even very brief counseling—as little as three minutes total—can make a difference, although more extensive treatment is generally more effective. Support from family members, friends, and health professionals can also play an integral part in the process of quitting. For many persons a nicotine medication that helps address the physical aspects of nicotine dependence and withdrawal can be as important and beneficial as medications used for the management of other disorders, such as high blood pressure, in which behavioral strategies are also important.

NICOTINE REPLACEMENT THERAPY

Nicotine replacement therapy delivers nicotine to the body in controlled, relatively small doses, typically by means of a transdermal patch, chewing gum, a nasal spray, an inhaler, or tablets. These products do not contain the tar, carbon monoxide, or other toxic ingredients that are largely responsible for the health hazards of smoking, and, because they deliver controlled doses of nicotine, they are much less addictive than cigarettes. All these products are comparably effective, and advice on making a selection can be obtained from health organizations, health professionals, and the providers of the therapy. In particular, pregnant women, adolescents, and people with heart disease should consult a health professional for advice on product selection and dosing.

In contrast to tobacco products, nicotine replacement medicines are safe when used as directed. They deliver lower doses of nicotine into the bloodstream and do so more slowly than tobacco products do. Nicotine is not a carcinogen or lung toxin, and the nicotine doses delivered by the medicines do not produce cardiovascular disease. Nicotine at higher doses than are typically prescribed can contribute to low fetal birth weight and other adverse effects during pregnancy. However, the benefit of increased success in smoking cessation for women of childbearing age who have already tried and failed to quit without medication is generally considered to outweigh this comparatively small risk.

Nicotine medications carry a very low potential for establishing addiction, and there is little evidence of their abuse. Some people may find the use of medications vital for many months to preventing a relapse to tobacco use. Such individuals are generally encouraged to take the medications as long as required in order to be confident to avoid a relapse. In fact, the most common dosing error is taking too little or not using the medicine long enough. Taking too much can produce the same short-lived symptoms of dizziness, nausea, and headache that are associated with smoking too many cigarettes, but this generally is not a serious health concern.

Nicotine Patch

Nicotine patches are available without a prescription in many countries. A new patch is applied to the skin every day and is left in place for a recommended amount of time (usually 16 to 24 hours) while it delivers a controlled amount of nicotine to the body through the skin. The patches are used over a period of six to eight weeks or longer. Patches with the highest dosage of nicotine (15 or 21 mg) are generally used for the first few weeks. Patches with lower doses are used thereafter. The most common side effect of the nicotine patch is a mild itching, burning, or tingling at the site on which it is applied. The nicotine patch can produce sleep disturbances. If they persist, they can often be remedied by removing the patch at bedtime.

Transdermal patches deliver a controlled, diminishing dose of nicotine through the skin, which then gets absorbed into the bloodstream. This and other nicotine replacement methods are designed to wean people off tobacco. Ian Hooton/Science Photo Library/ Getty Images

Nicotine Gum and Lozenges

Nicotine gum, usually available in 2- and 4-mg formulations, is available in many countries without a physician's prescription. The gum is chewed a few times and then placed between the cheek and gums to allow the nicotine to be absorbed through the mouth's mucous membrane. These actions are repeated for up to about 30 minutes. Achieving success with gum as a cessation aid depends largely on using it consistently. At least one piece of nicotine gum should be used every one to two hours over a period of one to three months. Additional pieces may be used in the event of a strong craving. Possible side effects include mouth soreness, headache, and jaw ache. Nicotine lozenges in 2- and 4-mg dosages are also available in many countries. The lozenges are similar to nicotine gum in use except that they are not chewed.

Nicotine Nasal Spray

Nicotine nasal spray was designed to deliver nicotine more rapidly than is possible with a patch or gum. It is available by prescription only because it appears to carry a somewhat higher cardiovascular risk and a potentially higher risk for abuse than other nicotine medications do. The 1 mg of nicotine commonly prescribed (a 0.5-mg dose squirted into each nostril) is rapidly absorbed by the nasal mucosa. Patients are encouraged to use at least 8 doses (16 sprays) per day for optimal efficacy but can use up to 40 doses per day, depending on their level of nicotine dependence. The most common side effects include nasal and throat irritation, watery eyes, and runny nose. The nicotine nasal spray is not recommended for persons with nasal or sinus conditions, certain allergies, or asthma.

Nicotine Inhaler

The nicotine inhaler, which consists of a nicotine-filled cartridge and a mouthpiece, was developed in order to imitate the behavioral and sensory characteristics of smoking without mimicking the actual delivery of nicotine to the lungs. The user inhales nicotine vapour into the mouth. Most of the nicotine is absorbed through the oral mucosa. The amount of nicotine delivered depends on the number of inhalations and their intensity. Depending on their needs, patients are advised to use from 6 to 16 cartridges per day. Each cartridge contains 10 mg of nicotine, of which 4 mg is delivered and up to 2 mg absorbed by the user. Side effects usually involve local irritation of the throat, together with coughing or sneezing. In most countries the nicotine inhaler is available only by prescription.

Sublingual Nicotine Tablets

The sublingual nicotine tablet is approved for use in several European countries. Each tablet commonly contains 2 mg of nicotine and is placed under the tongue until it dissolves. The nicotine is absorbed through the oral mucosa. Common side effects include irritation in the throat or under the tongue. As with nicotine gum, patients are instructed to move the tablet around within the mouth in order to alleviate these symptoms. The tablet form of nicotine is available without a prescription in many countries, but it is not available in the United States.

Bupropion

The first nonnicotine medication to gain approval for smoking cessation was the prescription drug bupropion, which was placed on the market in the United States in 1997 under the name Zyban. (The drug is also marketed as an antidepressant under the name Wellbutrin.) Bupropion seems to reduce both withdrawal symptoms and the urge to smoke by affecting the neurotransmitters dopamine and norepinephrine. Bupropion is available in the form of a 150-mg pill taken once a day for three days, then twice a day for 7 to 12 weeks, often concurrently with a nicotine replacement medication. Bupropion is not recommended for anyone who has a seizure disorder, has ever been diagnosed with an eating disorder, or takes certain kinds of antidepressants. Of the few major side effects that have been reported, insomnia and dry mouth are the most common.

OTHER APPROACHES TO SMOKING CESSATION

The most common approach to smoking cessation is that of quitting "cold turkey," which is the sudden discontinuation of smoking. This approach is rarely effective the first time it is tried, but through repeated efforts some people eventually succeed by this approach. Yet many people might have been able to quit years earlier by using a proven form of treatment. Hypnosis, acupuncture, herbal remedies, and other approaches are often advertised as ways to help quit smoking. These methods have not been proved to be any more effective than simply deciding to quit, although some individuals undoubtedly have been able to quit smoking by using them. For people with physical withdrawal symptoms, such as an impaired ability to function in the workplace (many people have difficulty concentrating on tasks), strong proven methods may be the best road to success. Nonetheless, new techniques and medicines are constantly being evaluated, so people interested in quitting should consider checking with WHO or the various national cancer organizations for information. Treatments that are under development or consideration include a vaccine to help people refrain from smoking once they have quit smoking, a medication to help prevent weight gain associated with nicotine withdrawal, and a medication to help persons reduce tobacco use when they find that they cannot abstain from it.

CHAPTER 9

SMOKING: PUBLIC POLICY AND SOCIAL AND CULTURAL HISTORY

For centuries, a major factor in setting public policy regarding tobacco products was the economic importance of the tobacco industry. Therefore, despite occasional efforts to prohibit the production of tobacco products, the main impetus of tobacco regulation throughout the world was to ensure the continued viability of the tobacco trade and to collect taxes on its products. The specific regulatory framework varied from country to country, but the result was essentially the same everywhere; tobacco was exempt from the ordinary controls to which other products were subject. In the United States, for example, tobacco products, which traditionally fell under the jurisdiction of the Bureau of Alcohol, Tobacco and Firearms, were exempt from the most basic safety and health standards required of other consumer products. However, in June 2009 the U.S. Senate voted overwhelmingly to shift the power of tobacco products regulation to the Food and Drug Administration (FDA), thereby subjecting tobacco to the same health standards as all other federally regulated food, drug, and chemical products. The anti-smoking bill, known as the Family Smoking Prevention and Tobacco Control Act, was signed into law by U.S. Pres. Barack Obama on June 22, 2009.

SMOKING AND PUBLIC POLICY

The state of affairs for tobacco regulation had begun to change in the early 1960s, when the United Kingdom's Royal College of Physicians (in 1962) and the U.S. surgeon general (in 1964) concluded that cigarette smoking caused lung cancer and other diseases. These reports were based largely on the rapidly mounting evidence from laboratory studies of smoke toxins and from population studies of disease risk in cigarette smokers in the 1950s. The reports paved the way for scientifically based health considerations to emerge as significant factors in the creation of tobacco public policy. Initial efforts were often aimed at specific issues, such as how tar and nicotine in cigarettes should be measured and advertised, health warnings on cigarette packaging, and smoking-prevention programs for young people. These limited efforts were generally thwarted or weakened by tobacco interests.

Nonetheless, smoking by adults began to subside in the 1970s and 1980s in many developed countries, particularly in the United States, Canada, Sweden, and Australia. At the same time, the prevalence of smoking was rapidly increasing in many less-developed countries, particularly in Asia and Africa. By the 1990s the toll in death and disease in these countries was mounting rapidly, and youth smoking began to shoot upward in some of the countries, including the United States and Canada, that had shown great strides in the reduction of smoking in the 1970s and 1980s.

In the 1990s several currents converged to foster major smoking-control policy initiatives around the world. The leading current was an extensive body of scientific research that proved the deadly and addictive effects of tobacco beyond the ability of even the tobacco industry to deny. This included evidence that environmental smoke was more than an annoyance—it was lethal for thousands of nonsmokers and a cause of respiratory disease in children. A second current was the sheer magnitude of the economic losses projected to be caused by tobacco use, as measured by the diversion of health care funds for the treatment of tobacco-related illnesses and by the loss of worker productivity. A third current was litigation brought against the tobacco industry by governments and individuals. These lawsuits brought to light millions of secret documents showing that the tobacco industry had long known its products were highly addictive and deadly. Finally, the growing recognition that environmental tobacco smoke was deadly even for nonsmokers led to efforts to restrain and contain smoking. These efforts further decreased smoking rates, making it possible for even stronger regulatory actions to be taken.

By the end of the 20th century, therefore, organized campaigns had led to the implementation of a wide spectrum of tobacco-related measures, including increases in the price of cigarettes and restrictions on their availability, restrictions in advertising, disclosure of information on the health consequences of tobacco use, protection of nonsmokers from environmental tobacco smoke, and regulation of manufacturing standards for tobacco companies. In the many countries that implemented such measures, per capita cigarette consumption was much reduced from earlier decades.

However, in many developing countries and in the world as a whole, cigarette consumption continued to increase. In response to this increase, the World Health Organization (WHO) and other health organizations sought to step up coordinated international efforts to regulate tobacco products in the late 1990s. In 2003 WHO adopted a tobacco-control treaty designed to serve as an international framework for tobacco regulation. It imposed controls over tobacco-industry marketing, required health-warning labels on tobacco products, and sought to reduce the exposure of users and nonusers alike to tobacco toxins. The treaty was ratified at a rapid pace by many countries, and it entered into force in early 2005. Although some major countries, including the United States and China, had not ratified it by that time, more than one-third of the signatory countries had done so, including Canada, Japan, the United Kingdom, and many developing countries.

The Goals and Strategies of Public Policy on Smoking

The goal of policy interventions on smoking is to reduce as rapidly as possible the incidence of death and disease related to smoking. Toward that end, policy measures employ a four-part strategy: (1) discourage individuals from starting to use tobacco, (2) encourage users to quit and provide support for their efforts, (3) reduce the adverse health consequences of tobacco by substantially reducing the toxins to which users are exposed through their use of tobacco products, and (4) expand clean-air nonsmoking policies to protect nonsmokers and to support prevention and cessation efforts.

No single action can accomplish these goals, but the coordination of a number of actions has proved effective in reducing tobacco use in a number of countries. These actions, encouraged by WHO, include:

- Reducing access to tobacco products by prohibiting sales to minors, raising prices, and making them more difficult to purchase.
- Promoting educational campaigns that provide detailed health information and ensuring that tobacco products include appropriate health warnings and information on how to get help in quitting.

- Restricting smoking in public areas and the workplace in order to protect nonsmokers. This action also has the effect of making it difficult to smoke and increases the pressure on smokers to quit.
- Regulating product manufacture to minimize the health risks to which tobacco users are exposed.

These goals and strategies may seem simple, but they are complex in practice because of opposition by the tobacco industry, merchants, and benefactors of tobacco sales. Furthermore, users of tobacco tend to find many reasons to keep using it and to oppose efforts to restrict it. Controlling access to tobacco products involves balancing efforts to prevent young people and nonusers from becoming tobacco users while continuing to make the products available to users. Efforts to inform consumers more thoroughly about the risks of use and the benefits of nonuse raise practical questions of how this information can be communicated most effectively to the consumer and what role, if any, the manufacturers should have in communicating such information.

REGULATION

Regulation of the design and ingredients of tobacco products is perhaps the greatest challenge for tobacco-control advocates. In the United States the FDA

A No Smoking sign greets visitors to Solana Beach in California. Some U.S. states have placed smoking bans on outdoor as well as indoor public spaces. David McNew/Getty Images

in 1996 attempted to regulate tobacco and its marketing—without banning it—in such a way that would reduce smokers' risks of developing a nicotine addiction and increase their likelihood of quitting. Key elements of the regulation were increased restrictions on appeal-enhancing marketing and reduced access by young people to tobacco products. Although this regulatory effort was overturned by the U.S. Supreme Court in 2000, the court recognized that some form of substantial regulation was not prohibited by the Constitution.

The need to protect nonsmokers from the health risks of environmental tobacco smoke has led to stricter regulation of smoking in public places, such as airports and hotels, and even to city-wide and countrywide bans on smoking in enclosed workplaces, including offices, restaurants, and taverns. Although the primary purpose of smoking restrictions is to prevent nonsmokers from being exposed to environmental tobacco smoke, a major public health benefit is that such restrictions put pressure on smokers to quit and, in general, act as a deterrent to smoking.

TAXATION

Price has likely been the single most effective policy intervention by those seeking to reduce tobacco-caused death and disease. Detailed studies have shown that in many countries price increases cause many smokers to quit

and others to reduce their smoking. The smoking practices of young people have been shown to be particularly sensitive to price. For example, between 1982 and 1992 Canada raised the real price of tobacco products by 150 percent. This price increase coincided with a reduction in total cigarette consumption of roughly 40 percent and a reduction in teenage smoking of 60 percent. In some countries, including Australia and France, increases in cigarette prices have been found to be a potent force for preventing young people from taking up tobacco and for supporting smoking-cessation efforts among adults.

LITIGATION AGAINST THE TOBACCO INDUSTRY

Litigation and the threat of litigation played a major role in shaping the environment for tobacco products at the end of the 20th century. While litigation

FAMILY SMOKING PREVENTION AND TOBACCO CONTROL ACT

In June 2009 U.S. Pres. Barack Obama signed the Family Smoking Prevention and Tobacco Control Act, legislation that gave the Food and Drug Administration (FDA) regulatory authority over the manufacturing and marketing of cigarettes and other tobacco products, including final approval of new tobacco products, cigarette ingredients, and tobacco industry advertising. The FDA's first major action in September 2009 was to ban flavoured cigarettes, including candy and clove varieties. Tobacco companies, including R. J. Reynolds Tobacco Co. and Lorillard Inc., had filed a federal lawsuit in August to protest the FDA's new power to impose marketing restrictions, claiming that it violated the companies' First Amendment rights, but in early November 2009 a U.S. District Court judge in Richmond, Va., denied a motion for a preliminary injunction sought by the tobacco companies.

seeks to accomplish the same ends as legislation, it is often a more viable strategy in regions where legislators are reluctant to act against the interests of the tobacco industry and its frequent allies, such as convenience stores and the alcohol-selling portions of the hospitality industry, which rely heavily on tobacco sales for their total revenue.

Litigation covers a wide range of issues, including product liability, consumer protection, antitrust activity, racketeering, health care reimbursement, and tax evasion. These lawsuits have been brought forward by individuals, classes of individuals (class actions), governments, and others. The ability of plaintiffs to sue tobacco companies for health care reimbursement is based on various legal theories of recovery, including negligence, gross negligence, strict liability, fraud, misrepresentation, design defect, failure to adequately warn, and conspiracy. In a landmark 1998 case, the major cigarette companies in the United States entered into an agreement with the attorneys general of a number of states as a result of lawsuits aimed at recouping health care expenditures for treating sick smokers. This agreement required the disclosure of millions of corporate documents, the discontinuation of various forms of youth-focused advertising, and the annual payment in perpetuity of roughly $10 billion per year. Although the actual payment may vary and even decrease as cigarette consumption decreases, such a substantial amount

has put pressure on tobacco companies to support legislative efforts they formerly opposed, since further litigation could bankrupt them.

A SOCIAL AND CULTURAL HISTORY OF SMOKING

In order to explain why enormous sections of the world's population continue to smoke, given the overwhelming medical evidence of its dangerous effects, one must understand the social history of the practice, the role of smoking in everyday cultural practices, and the meaning that people attach to it. Historian Jordan Goodman has argued that societies in which tobacco has been introduced have demonstrated a "culture of dependence," be it in the ceremonial rituals of Native American culture, the fiscal policies of early modern states, the coffeehouses of 18th-century Europe, or the physical and psychological addictions associated with the cigarette. This dependence is one of the reasons individuals—and societies as a whole—are aware that smoking is harmful yet continue to smoke because of the individual and communal pleasures it brings. Smoking might represent folly and foolhardiness, but its intangible qualities still encourage millions to smoke. As the dramatist Oscar Wilde wrote,

A cigarette is the perfect type of a perfect pleasure. It is exquisite and it leaves one unsatisfied. What more can one want?

Tobacco in New World Culture

Although the origin of tobacco use in Native American culture is uncertain, tobacco clearly played a far more ceremonial and structured role than it would come to play in Europe and the modern world. Along with several other hallucinogens and narcotics, a strong, dark, high-nicotine and, consequently, mind-altering tobacco was crucial to the performance of shamanistic rituals and social ceremonies. Usually smoked but also chewed, drunk, taken as snuff, and even given as an enema, tobacco was seen by Native Americans as a means for providing communication with the supernatural world through the medium of the shaman, for either medicinal or spiritual purposes. Among medical applications, tobacco was used as a cure for toothache by the Iroquois, as a cure for earache by the Indians of central Mexico, as a painkiller by the Cherokee, and as an antiseptic in Guatemala.

Beyond such practical functions, tobacco was also often exchanged as a gift, helping to forge social connections and establish community hierarchies. In many groups tobacco was given as an offering to the gods, and in some groups, in particular among the Maya, tobacco was itself deified as a divine plant. Tobacco was also linked to the fertility both of the land and of women, and it was used in initiation ceremonies for boys entering manhood. Most famously, tobacco was used in the calumet ritual, when agreements and obligations would be made binding with the passing of the ritual pipe (the calumet, or sacred pipe).

Tobacco was thus central to Native American culture, be it with the cigar in

Sacred Pipe

The sacred pipe (also called peace pipe, or calumet) is one of the central ceremonial objects of the Northeast Indians and Plains Indians of North America, it was an object of profound veneration that was smoked on ceremonial occasions. Many Native Americans continued to venerate the Sacred Pipe in the early 21st century.

The sacred pipe was revered as a holy object, and the sacrament of smoking was employed as a major means of communication between humans and sacred beings. The narcotic effect of tobacco and the symbolism of the indrawn and ascending smoke affirmed that such communication took place. The pipe itself was a symbolic microcosm. Its parts, its colours, and the motifs used in its decoration each corresponded to essential parts of the indigenous universe. The pipe was smoked in personal prayer and during collective rituals, and both of these uses commonly began with invocations to the six directions: east, south, west, north, skyward, and earthward. Among some tribes such as the Pawnee, Omaha, and Crow, complex pipe dances were developed that presented smoke offerings to the Almighty on behalf of the entire community.

the South or the pipe in the North, and its properties were known from Canada to Argentina and from the Atlantic to the Pacific. So important was it that some native groups, such as the Blackfoot and the Crow, cultivated no other crop.

TOBACCO IN OLD WORLD CULTURE

It is likely that sailors returning from the Americas to various ports in Europe in the late 15th and early 16th centuries took with them the practice of smoking. Northern Europeans adopted the practice of pipe smoking, which was prevalent along the north Atlantic seaboard, and Spaniards brought the practice of cigar smoking, which was prevalent in the regions around the Caribbean. Many Europeans believed tobacco was a panacea, a new herb that could be incorporated into Western medical traditions and celebrated as an almost universal

Depiction of a hill chief smoking, Pahari style, Basohli, late 17th century; in the National Museum of India, New Delhi. P. Chandra

curative. In the late 16th century, the Spanish doctor Nicolas Monardes claimed that tobacco alleviated hunger, acted as a relaxant and a painkiller, and was even a cure for cancer.

However, this view was opposed by others, including King James I of England. James's *Counterblaste to Tobacco*, published in 1604, described smoking as "a custom loathsome to the eye, hateful to the nose, harmful to the brain, dangerous to the lungs, and in the black, stinking fume thereof, nearest resembling the horrible Stygian smoke of the pit that is bottomless." Elsewhere, Popes Urban VIII and Innocent IX issued papal bulls excommunicating those who snuffed in church, the Ottoman sultan Murad IV made smoking a capital offense, and Russians were subject to having their noses cut off if caught smoking. Nevertheless, the acceptance of tobacco into Old World culture was assisted by the patronage it received from various aristocrats and rulers. For example, tobacco was introduced into the court of Catherine de Médicis in 1560 by Jean Nicot (from whom nicotine and tobacco's botanical name, *Nicotiana tabacum*, get their name) and into the court of Elizabeth I by Sir Walter Raleigh, who himself had been introduced to smoking by Sir Francis Drake.

After tobacco's introduction into Europe, the smoking and cultivation of it rapidly spread to other parts of the world. By the beginning of the 17th century, tobacco was being grown in India, China, Japan, Southeast Asia, the Middle East, and West Africa. With the availability of inexpensive clay pipes, tobacco became an item of mass consumption in England as early as 1670. Pipe manufacture spread throughout Europe. By the end of the 18th century, Dutch towns such as Gouda could support 350 pipe manufacturers, thanks to the smoking culture of coffeehouses and alehouses. Snuff also proliferated, often rivaling smoking as the dominant form of tobacco consumption and producing such fascinating novelties as the perhaps apocryphal but frequently cited special pockets in the clothes of Frederick the Great of Prussia, which were enlarged to cope with his considerable consumption. In southern Europe the great state-owned tobacco factories of Cádiz and Seville ensured the continued popularity of the cigar, though it was not until the Peninsular War (1808–14) that military officers began to popularize it in Britain.

When pipes were introduced into Asia, they were quickly adapted and made from materials as diverse as wood, bamboo, jade, ivory, metal, and porcelain. Arab communities took up the hookah, or water pipe, and smoking became a shared activity typically enjoyed with conversation and coffee. The hookah spread throughout Persia (present-day Iran) and into India, eventually reaching China, Southeast Asia, and many parts of Africa by the end of the 17th century. By the mid-19th century, smoking had become an established ritual throughout the world. It was celebrated in prose, in verse, in art, and on the stage, and its use

JEAN NICOT

(b. 1530, Nîmes, France—d. 1600/1604, Paris)

French diplomat and scholar Jean Nicot de Villemain introduced tobacco to the French court in the 16th century, which gave rise to the culture of snuffing and to the plant's eventual dissemination and popularization throughout Europe.

Nicot was raised in the quiet town of Nîmes in southern France, where his father worked as a notary. Nicot studied in Toulouse and Paris before entering into service of the French court in 1553. In 1559, having fallen into favour with King Henry II, Nicot became the French ambassador to Portugal. He was sent to Lisbon to oversee French trade concerns and to arrange a marriage between Margaret of Valois and Sebastian, who had become king of Portugal in 1557, at age three. The marriage arrangement fell through, but while in Lisbon, Nicot was introduced to tobacco, the plant that would ultimately make him famous. He learned of the plant and its medicinal properties from Portuguese humanist Damião de Góis. Intrigued by the details related by de Góis, Nicot decided to test a tobacco ointment on a Lisbon man with a tumour. The man was cured, and further investigation of the plant's medicinal applications convinced Nicot that it was a medical nostrum, effecting cures for conditions from cancer to gout to headache.

In 1560 Nicot sent tobacco seeds—as well as figs, oranges, and lemons—to the queen of France, Catherine de Médicis, at Paris. Along with the specimens, Nicot included a letter expounding the medicinal properties of tobacco. In 1561 Nicot returned to the court in Paris, where he presented the queen with leaves from a tobacco plant. It is believed that the queen received instructions from Nicot for preparing a simple headache remedy by crushing the leaves into a powder that could be inhaled through the nose. The remedy, which proved satisfactory, soon became popular with members of the French court, who used tobacco powder to stave off various illnesses. In this preventative role, tobacco became identified with the pleasures of nobility, and it is likely that many users developed addictions to it. Eventually the

Jean Nicot de Villemain. Archive Photos/Getty Images

plant was cultivated in France and other parts of northern Europe to fulfill demand. In the 17th century in England the crushed preparation became widely known as snuff.

Following Nicot's return to Paris, he was granted the title Villemain and given land near the village of Brie-Comte-Robert, located in the north-central region of Île-de-France. Nicot subsequently retired to his new home, where he composed the French dictionary Thresor de la langue françoyse, tant ancienne que moderne *(1606; "Treasure of the French Language"). The work was an extension of French humanist Robert Estienne's* Dictionaire françois-latin *(1531; "French-Latin Dictionary").*

In 1753 Swedish naturalist Carolus Linnaeus named the genus of tobacco cultivars Nicotiana *in recognition of Nicot's role in popularizing the plant. (The plant Nicot knew was probably* N. rustica.*) Nicot's name was also immortalized by the term* nicotine, *the name given to the active ingredient in tobacco, first isolated from the plant's leaves in 1828.*

came to be seen as a central component of manhood. Literary sources captured the paraphernalia of the smoking ritual—pipes, cleaners, holders, spills, spittoons, ashtrays, pouches, storage jars, and lighters, as well as smoking jackets, armchairs, hats, and slippers—all of which, ideally, had to be collected in "that chamber of liberty, that sanctuary of the persecuted, that temple of refuge . . . the smoking room" (Ouida, *Under Two Flags*, 1867).

The Age of the Cigarette

Tobacco use was forever changed by the introduction of the mass-produced cigarette in the late 19th century. Inexpensive manufactured cigarettes made tobacco smoking widely accessible, and mass marketing campaigns glorified and popularized an addictive habit. It was not until the late 20th century, when the detrimental health effects of cigarette smoking were firmly established, that the

disease burden left in the wake of the age of the cigarette was realized.

Mass Production and Mass Appeal

Cigarettes were originally sold as an expensive handmade luxury item for the urban elites of Europe. However, cigarette manufacture was revolutionized by the introduction of a rolling machine called the Bonsack machine, which was patented by American James Bonsack in the United States in 1880. The machine was soon put into use by the American industrialist James Buchanan Duke, who founded the American Tobacco Company (ATC) in 1890. Inexpensive mass-produced cigarettes, promoted by Duke's aggressive marketing methods and advertising, gradually led to a decline in pipe-smoking and tobacco-chewing habits in the United States.

In Britain the manufacturer Henry Wills began using the machine in Bristol in 1883, and this enabled him to dominate the cigarette trade within just a few years. Then, in 1901, Duke attempted to enter the British market. The subsequent "tobacco war" resulted in a standoff as the British manufacturers united within the Imperial Tobacco Company. An agreement in 1902 allowed both sides to claim a victory. Duke retreated to the United States, and the British market was left to Imperial, but together they formed the British-American Tobacco Company (BAT) to market and sell their products to the rest of the world, especially India, China, and the British dominions. Although other American companies entered the global market following the breakup of the ATC—the result of a 1911 Supreme Court ruling under the Sherman Antitrust Act (1890)—BAT continued to meet much success. In 1999 the company produced more than 800 billion cigarettes per year, which made it the world's third-largest tobacco company (just behind the Philip Morris USA and Philip Morris International companies, together ranking second, and the China National Tobacco Corporation, ranking first).

The success of the cigarette was due not only to the business strategies of the large firms but also to the rapid adoption by urban male youths of the relatively inexpensive and easy-to-smoke lighter flue-cured Virginia tobacco. In particular, this product became a favourite of teenage boys—a situation that led to public outcries, to the revival of antitobacco movements in France, Australia,

Cigarettes were a convenient nicotine delivery method for soldiers in the trenches. Civilians soon followed the trend. Cigarette smoking spiked in the United States following World War II. Keystone/Hulton Archive/Getty Images

Britain, Canada, and the United States (spearheaded there by the seasoned antidrink campaigners of the Woman's Christian Temperance Union), and to the eventual passing, in the 1890s and 1900s, of legislation across most territorial and federal states banning the sale of tobacco to minors.

The legislation, however, was largely ineffective, and World War I quickly put an end to the critique of young men's cigarette smoking. In the trenches cigarettes were easier to smoke than pipes, and tobacco companies, the military, governments, and newspapers organized a constant supply of cigarettes to the troops—an official recognition of the importance of tobacco in offering immediate relief from physical and psychological stress. Certain companies did extraordinarily well from the war: Imperial's Players and Woodbine brands in Britain and, more spectacularly, R. J. Reynolds's Camel in the United States. Introduced only in 1913, Camel had reached sales of 20 billion cigarettes by 1920, following a government supply order and a successful marketing campaign.

The war, therefore, transformed smoking habits. As early as 1920, more than 50 percent of the tobacco consumed in Britain was in the form of cigarettes. A less-urban U.S. population lagged behind, but a similar story in World War II saw cigarettes achieve more than 50 percent of all tobacco sales in 1941. Several other industrial countries matched this trend.

The first half of the 20th century was the golden age of the cigarette. In 1950 around half of the population of industrialized countries smoked, though that figure hides the fact that in countries such as the United Kingdom up to 80 percent of adult men were regular smokers. Smoking was an acceptable form of social behaviour in all areas of life—at work, in the home, in bars, and at the cinema—and advertisers were keen to show the full range of leisure activities made complete only through the addition of a cigarette. Smoking cigarettes was popular across all social classes and increasingly among women, once associations of smoking with deviant sexuality began to fade in

the 1920s. This development had less to do with the efforts of advertisers—who, for example, in 1925 introduced the Marlboro brand as a woman's cigarette: "Mild as May"—and more to do with the impact of war and a direct confrontation with societal attitudes by so-called new women. Most important, the cigarette habit was legitimated, celebrated, and glamourized on the Hollywood screen and transported to the rest of the world. Movie stars such as Edward G. Robinson, James Cagney, Spencer Tracy, Gary Cooper, and especially Humphrey Bogart, Lauren Bacall, and Marlene Dietrich raised the image of the cigarette to that of the iconic, ensuring it would never lose its sophisticated and loftily independent connotations.

AMERICAN TOBACCO COMPANY

The history of the American Tobacco Company traces to the post-Civil War period in North Carolina, when a Confederate veteran, Washington Duke, began trading in tobacco. In 1874 he and his sons, Benjamin N. Duke and James Buchanan Duke, built a factory and in 1878 formed the firm of W. Duke, Sons & Co., one of the first tobacco companies to introduce cigarette-manufacturing machines.

Entering the "cigarette war," the Dukes eventually established the American Tobacco Company in 1890, with James as president. Through mergers and purchases, the Duke brothers eventually acquired corporate control of virtually the entire American tobacco industry—some 150 factories in all. In 1911, however, after five years of litigation, a U.S. Court of Appeals judged this tobacco trust in violation of the Sherman Antitrust Act and ordered it dissolved. The main manufacturers to emerge, in addition to American, were R. J. Reynolds, Liggett & Myers, and Lorillard.

In 1916 American introduced its most popular cigarette brand, Lucky Strike, and in 1939 it introduced one of the first king-size cigarettes, Pall Mall (an old name reapplied to a new cigarette). The sales of these two brands made American Tobacco the most successful cigarette manufacturer of the 1940s. The company failed to establish equally strong brands of filter cigarettes in the 1950s, however, and by the 1970s it had slipped to a minor position among U.S. tobacco makers. With further diversification and dilution in the later decades of the 20th century, the company—which had been renamed American Brands in 1969—took on a different identity, and by the end of the century it had become known as Fortune Brands, formally departing from the tobacco industry.

BRITISH AMERICAN TOBACCO PLC

Formerly known as the British-American Tobacco Company Ltd. (1902–76) or B. A. T Industries PLC (1976–98), British American Tobacco PLC is one of the world's largest manufacturers of tobacco products. The company's international headquarters are in London. Its chief American subsidiary, Brown & Williamson Tobacco Corporation, is headquartered in Louisville, Kentucky.

The British-American Tobacco Company originated in 1902 as a joint venture of the U.S.-based American Tobacco Company and the U.K.-based Imperial Tobacco Company, Ltd. The new company was formed to market American Tobacco's products in Great Britain and Imperial Tobacco's products in the United States. Its major stockholder remained the American Tobacco Company until 1911, when a U.S. Court of Appeals dissolved that trust, and British-American Tobacco became independent. The company expanded rapidly as cigarette use grew exponentially during World War I and afterward, marketing cigarettes throughout the world and achieving an especially strong presence in China, where cigarette smoking had become common by the 1920s. In 1927 British-American Tobacco reentered the American market by acquiring the Brown & Williamson Tobacco Corporation, a small tobacco company that grew to become one of the largest cigarette manufacturers in the United States with such brands as Kool and Viceroy.

In 1970 British-American Tobacco acquired majority control of Wiggins Teape Limited, a paper-products manufacturer. Beginning in 1971 it began investing in American department-store chains, eventually buying Marshall Field and Company and Saks Fifth Avenue. In

George Washington Hill

(b. Oct. 22, 1884, Philadelphia—d. Sept. 13, 1946, Matapedia, Que., Can.)

American businessman George Washington Hill was known for his marketing efforts that introduced women to cigarettes. Leaving Williams College before he graduated, Hill in 1904 went to work at the American Tobacco Company, where his father served as vice president. When the company bought the line of Pall Mall cigarettes, the younger Hill was put in charge of sales, and the cigarettes became the most popular among Turkish tobaccos. In 1911, the company was divided into four large competing firms as a result of a major antitrust suit. The senior Hill became president of the new American, and his son became sales manager. Five years later, they introduced the Lucky Strike brand, and Hill made the new cigarette his pet project, designing its marketing and advertising campaign himself, though the campaign's success was largely due to the work of groundbreaking publicist Edward Bernays.

Hill became president of the firm upon his father's death in 1925, and by the following year, Lucky Strike accounted for one-fifth of U.S. cigarette sales. In 1927 he created an industry sensation by gearing advertising toward women for the first time. Female movie stars and singers lauded the brand, and soon Luckys accounted for 38 percent of U.S. cigarette sales. At the beginning of the Great Depression, the company was thriving, and Hill's total salary was more than $2 million. He strongly believed in advertising and invested heavily in radio air time, sponsoring Your Hit Parade and the Jack Benny Show. Hill was an early sponsor for Frank Sinatra, Ethel Smith, and Lawrence Tibbett.

1976 the firm was reorganized as a holding company and renamed B. A. T Industries. It entered the field of financial services with the purchase, in 1989, of the insurer Farmers Group Inc. B. A. T sold its interest in Saks and Marshall Field in 1990, and in 1997 it merged its financial services businesses with the Zurich Group, a Swiss financial-services company.

With its increasing focus on the tobacco business, B. A. T was renamed British American Tobacco PLC in 1998. Its acquisitions have included the American Tobacco Company (1994); Rothmans International (1999), known for its Dunhill and Rothmans brands;

and Canada's largest cigarette company, Imperial Tobacco (2000).

The Antismoking Movement

Within this culture there was little room for opposition to tobacco, except in the privately financed publications of such antismoking cranks as the American industrialist Henry Ford and in the hysterical whims of the German leader Adolf Hitler—although the latter's state-sanctioned attack on the people's habit did lead to some pioneering work on the links between smoking and cancer. In 1950, works by the German-born

American physician Ernst L. Wynder and by the British statisticians Austin Bradford Hill and Sir Richard Doll provided firm evidence linking lung cancer with smoking.

This information came as a considerable shock to smokers, who proved reluctant to give up their habit. Of course, their decisions had already been influenced by physical addiction, advertising, and the denials of the tobacco industry, but, even after the reports by the Royal College of Physicians (1962) and the U.S. surgeon general (1964) clearly stating the deleterious health effects of smoking, quitting rates were not as high as might have been expected. An average of 2 million people gave up smoking every year in the United States in the decade after 1964, but about half that number also began smoking every year, and not all quitters were able to remain nonsmokers. By 1978 the percentage of adults in the United States who smoked had fallen to 33 percent. A significant majority of those who had quit smoking were professional, affluent men, which made smoking a health problem increasingly associated with women and poverty. Whereas the average American smoker went through 22 cigarettes a day in 1954, the number had increased to 30 a day by 1978—a statistic that suggested that the quitting rate was higher among those who smoked less and that the increasing number of smokers who had moved to lighter or filtered brands were smoking more of them.

More recent evidence of the harm done to nonsmokers by environmental tobacco smoke has further helped turn attitudes against smoking. Efforts to curtail the individual's liberty to smoke were at first most pronounced in the United States, as in California's 1995 ban on smoking in most enclosed places of employment, but in 2004 Ireland became the first country to ban smoking in enclosed workplaces, and other countries have since followed suit.

Nevertheless, the strong grip of smoking on the world's popular culture suggests that the practice will persist. While smoking is increasingly frowned upon in a health-conscious age and the smoker has come to feel marginalized and harassed, the very suppression of smoking only increases its power as a symbol of individualism and resistance. For instance, a survey of internationally successful Hollywood films found that motion pictures released in 1995 featured four times as much smoking as those released in 1990, with an increase in the number of positive verbal and visual references made to the habit. These images are being broadcast to the very areas of the world where American-owned tobacco companies are beginning to make inroads selling their products. All this suggests that smoking is likely to remain as entrenched in modern global society as it was in pre-Columbian America. Cigarette use might now be more individualistic and less ceremonial than it was at that time, but this change too is a reflection of the transformation of culture to one that has come to value individualism over tradition. Mark Twain's famous quip regarding his own smoking habit (estimated to have reached more than 20 cigars per day) might be applied to the complex status of smoking in society today:

> To cease smoking is the easiest thing I ever did. I ought to know because I've done it a thousand times.

CONCLUSION

Despite all that is known about the negative consequences of consuming alcohol, smoking tobacco, and taking psychotropic drugs, people worldwide continue to use and abuse these substances. Part of the reason for this is the long history of substance use in societies. It also is a reflection, however, of the complexities of human behaviour, particularly the perception that drugs enable users to cope or to experience life, for a short period of time, in a way that is different. The irony of the common perception that using drugs somehow imparts a unique life experience is that people who use drugs seek out and participate in this "uniqueness," thereby calling this singular perspective into question. Another common reason for drug use, one often invoked by adolescents, is peer pressure, a common entry point into the world of drug abuse that takes advantage of a young person's uncertainty in thinking independently.

The reasons why humans use and abuse substances, however, are far more complex than this. Alcohol in particular has raised difficult questions concerning substance use in societies. Alcohol consumption has formed a part of daily life for people in various societies for thousands of years. Although regulations and ways to control intoxication have been established, consequences such as drunk driving remain serious problems. Thus, alcohol consumption is embraced in moderation and rejected in excess.

The use of other substances continues to be a major area of concern for societies. Young people often experiment with substances such as designer drugs, heroin, anabolic steroids, and cannabis. These experiences, whether a result of peer pressure or socioeconomic factors, can permanently alter the user's course of life, channeling the individual down a path toward drug abuse and addiction before he or she ever has the opportunity to reach his or her academic and professional potential. Because the potential of children and adolescents is so great and because their vulnerability to drug abuse is very high, the loss of these individuals to the world of drug addiction is considered a grave tragedy. It is for these reasons that many societies have invested so deeply in programs oriented toward awareness and prevention of drug abuse.

GLOSSARY

addiction A craving or need for a substance, wherein greater amounts of said substance are necessary for the desired effect.

alkaloid An organic compound with a nitrogen base, occurring in plants and capable of producing psychotropic effects in humans.

amphetamines Colorless, volatile liquids used as central nervous system stimulants.

barbiturates A group of drugs that acts on the central nervous system, working as a depressant or sedative.

benzodiazepines Any of a group of chemical compounds used as anti-anxiety agents, muscle relaxants, sedatives, hypnotics, and sometimes as anticonvulsants.

calumet A sacred pipe used by Native Americans to smoke tobacco during religious and social ceremonies.

cirrhosis An irreversible change wherein normal liver tissue is replaced with fibrous connective tissue, resulting in the degeneration of functioning liver cells.

delirium tremens A condition that racks the body with tremors and even seizures, the result of alcohol withdrawal.

drug abuse The excessive, maladaptive, or addictive use of drugs for non-medical purposes.

fermentation The anaerobic conversion of sugar to carbon dioxide and alcohol by yeast.

habituation Tolerance to the effects of a drug acquired through continued use.

hallucinogen A substance that induces hallucinations.

hypnotics Sleep-inducing substances.

opiates A class of narcotics that are derivatives of opium.

prohibition The legal stoppage of alcohol sales and consumption.

psychotropic Acting on the mind.

serotonin A chemical substance, or neurotransmitter, that occurs naturally in the brain and induces a feeling of well-being; psychotropic drugs enhance or inhibit serotonin levels.

stimulant A drug that increases activity, function, or effectiveness of the mind and body.

temperance Regarding substance use, moderation in or abstinence from the use of alcoholic beverages.

tolerance A gradual decrease in the effect of a certain dose of a drug that is repeatedly taken, to the point where larger doses are needed to achieve the desired effect.

transdermal Capable of being absorbed through the skin.

vasodilator A drug that acts to widen the blood vessels.

withdrawal The syndrome of often painful physical and psychological symptoms that follows discontinuance of an addicting drug.

BIBLIOGRAPHY

Reference works include Marc A. Schuckit, *Drug and Alcohol Abuse: Clinical Guide to Diagnosis and Treatment*, 4th ed. (1995), clearly and economically written; and Jerome H. Jaffe (ed.), *Encyclopedia of Drugs and Alcohol*, 4 vol. (1995), containing more than 500 articles, bibliographic references, and an extensive index.

General discussions about drugs, human behaviour, and social issues include Glen Hanson, Peter J. Venturelli, and Annette E. Fleckenstein, *Drugs and Society*, 10th ed. (2009); and Carl L. Hart, Charles Ksir, and Oakley Stern Ray, *Drugs, Society, and Human Behavior*, 13th ed. (2009).

Glen Evans, Robert O'Brian, and Sidney Cohen, *The Encyclopedia of Drug Abuse*, 2nd ed. (1991); David Courtwright, Herman Joseph, and Don Des Jarlais, *Addicts Who Survived: An Oral History of Narcotic Use in America, 1923–1965* (1989); and Charles E. Faupel, *Shooting Dope: Career Patterns of Hard-Core Heroin Users* (1991), all discuss drug abuse. Broader studies include Charles P. O'Brien and Jerome H. Jaffe (eds.), *Addictive States* (1992); and Malcolm Lader, Griffith Edwards, and D. Colin Drummond (eds.), *The Nature of Alcohol and Drug Related Problems* (1992). David Solomon (ed.), *LSD: The Consciousness-Expanding Drug* (1964), provides the reader with some of the history, rationale, subjective accounts, and mystique that launched the drug movement. Alfred R. Lindesmith, *The Addict and the Law* (1965), offers a broad analysis of the narcotic problem; while United States, Bureau of Justice Statistics, *Drugs, Crime, and the Justice System* (1992), relates the history and laws of drug use. Mark A. R. Kleiman, *Against Excess: Drug Policy for Results* (1992), considers social costs and policy options. Griffith Edwards, John Strang, and Jerome H. Jaffe (eds.), *Drugs, Alcohol, and Tobacco: Making the Science and Policy Connections* (1993), compiles papers on the role of science in forming national drug, alcohol, and tobacco policies. Avram Goldstein, *From Biology to Drug Policy* (1994), discusses the biological actions and the problem of developing policies for different classes of drugs.

More specific works of general interest include Mickey C. Smith, *A Social History of the Minor Tranquilizers* (1991); Gregory R. Bock and Julie Whelan (eds.), *Cocaine—Scientific and Social Dimensions* (1992), discussing this drug's toxicity, history of use, and treatments; Virginia Berridge and Griffith Edwards, *Opium and the People: Opiate Use in Nineteenth-Century England* (1981), a very readable yet thoroughly documented history; Charles F. Levinthal, *Messengers of Paradise: Opiates and the Brain* (1988);

Mark S. Gold, *Marijuana* (1989); and Wayne Hall, Nadia Solowij, and Jim Lemmon, *The Health and Psychological Consequences of Cannabis Use* (1994), a thorough review of the pharmacology, health, behavioral, and psychological effects of cannabis, prepared for the Australian National Task Force on Cannabis.

Technical works covering the same broad scope are *Goodman & Gilman's The Pharmacological Basis of Therapeutics*, 11th ed. by Joel G. Hardman and Lee E. Limbird (2006); Nora D. Valkow and Alan C. Swann (eds.), *Cocaine in the Brain* (1990); John C. M. Brust, *Neurological Aspects of Substance Abuse* (1993); and Andrew Weil and Winifred Rosen, *Chocolate to Morphine: Understanding Mind-Active Drugs* (1983).

Griffith Edwards, *Alcohol: The Ambiguous Molecule* (2000), offers perhaps the best short overview available of alcohol and its consumption and associated problems. Rosalyn Carson-Dewitt (ed.), *Encyclopedia of Drugs, Alcohol, and Addictive Behavior*, 2nd ed., 4 vol. (2001), contains more than 550 articles, bibliographic references, and an extensive index.

Anthropological studies of the drinking practices of early societies are described in Mary Douglas (ed.), *Constructive Drinking: Perspectives on Drink from Anthropology* (1987, reissued 2003); and Dimitra Gefou-Madianou (ed.), *Alcohol, Gender, and Culture* (1992).

The prevalence of drinking or abstaining and the distribution of alcohol problems and alcoholism in specific areas are dealt with in Mark Edward Lender and James Kirby Martin, *Drinking in America*, rev. and expanded ed. (1987); Boris M. Segal, *The Drunken Society: Alcohol Abuse and Alcoholism in the Soviet Union* (1990); Johanna Maula, Maaria Lindblad, and Christoffer Tigerstedt (eds.), *Alcohol in Developing Countries* (1990); and Nina Rehn, *Alcohol in the European Regions: Consumption, Harm and Policies* (2001).

Analyses of classic as well as contemporary attempts to cope with alcohol problems are outlined in Mark H. Moore and Dean R. Gerstein (eds.), *Alcohol and Public Policy: Beyond the Shadow of Prohibition* (1981); Griffith Edwards, John Strang, and Jerome H. Jaffe (eds.), *Drugs, Alcohol, and Tobacco: Making the Science and Policy Connections* (1993); and Griffith Edwards et al., *Alcohol Policy and the Public Good* (1994).

Reference works on alcoholism include overviews by Marc A. Schuckit, *Drug and Alcohol Abuse: Clinical Guide to Diagnosis and Treatment*, 5th ed. (2000), and George E. Vaillant, *The Natural History of Alcoholism, Revisited* (1995, originally published as *The Natural History of Alcoholism*, 1983), both clearly and economically written; Rosalyn Carson-Dewitt (ed.), *Encyclopedia of Drugs, Alcohol, and Addictive Behavior*, 2nd ed., 4 vol.

(2001), containing more than 550 articles, bibliographic references, and an extensive index; and Alan Graham et al. (eds.), *Principles of Addiction Medicine*, 3rd ed. (2003), which provides a comprehensive overview of alcoholism and its treatment.

American Lung Association, *7 Steps to a Smoke-Free Life* (1998), provides a practical approach to helping a smoker quit that anticipates the difficulties and potential setbacks many smokers will face in achieving this goal. Ronald R. Watson and Mark Witten (eds.), *Environmental Tobacco Smoke* (2001), discusses in scientific detail the effects of tobacco smoke on nonsmokers and also the broader issues concerning the reduction of exposure to environmental tobacco smoke.

INDEX